Public Sector Accounting
and Financial Control

The VNR Series in Accounting and Finance

Consulting Editor
John Perrin, Emeritus Professor of the University of Warwick and Price Waterhouse
Fellow in Public Sector Accounting at the University of Exeter

J. M. Cope
Business Taxation: Policy and Practice

J. C. Drury
Management and Cost Accounting (2nd edn)
(Also available: Students' Manual, Teachers' Manual)

C. R. Emmanuel and D. T. Otley
Accounting for Management Control
(Also available: Solution Notes)

D. Henley *et al.*
Public Sector Accounting and Financial Control (3rd edn)

R. C. Laughlin and R. Gray
Financial Accounting: method and meaning
(Also available: Teachers' Guide)

G. A. Lee
Modern Financial Accounting (4th edn)
(Also available: Solutions Manual)

T. A. Lee
Income and Value Measurement (3rd edn)

T. A. Lee
Company Financial Reporting (2nd edn)

T. A. Lee
Cash Flow Accounting

S. P. Lumby
Investment Appraisal and Financing Decisions (3rd edn)
(Also available: Teachers' Guide)

A. G. Puxty and J. C. Dodds
Financial Management: method and meaning
(Also available: Teachers' Guide)

J. M. Samuels and F. M. Wilkes
Management of Company Finance (4th edn)

R. M. S. Wilson and Wai Fong Chua
Managerial Accounting: method and meaning
(Also available: Teachers' Guide)

Public Sector Accounting and Financial Control

Third edition

DOUGLAS HENLEY
Formerly Comptroller and Auditor General
Adviser, Deloitte, Haskins and Sells

CLIVE HOLTHAM
Bull HN Professor of Information Management,
City University Business School

ANDREW LIKIERMAN
Professor of Accounting and Financial Control
at the London Business School

JOHN PERRIN
Emeritus Professor, University of Warwick
Honorary Fellow of the University of Exeter

Published in cooperation with the
Chartered Institute of Public Finance and Accountancy

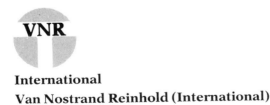

International
Van Nostrand Reinhold (International)

First published in 1983 by
Van Nostrand Reinhold (International)
11 New Fetter Lane, London EC4P 4EE
Reprinted 1983, 1985
Second edition 1986
Third edition 1989

© *1989 D. Henley, C. Holtham, A. Likierman, J. Perrin*

Typeset in Aster 10/11½pt by
Scarborough Typesetting Services, Scarborough
Printed in Great Britain by
T. J. Press (Padstow) Ltd, Padstow, Cornwall

ISBN 0 278 00103 3

British Library Cataloguing in Publication Data

Public sector accounting and financial
    control. – 3rd ed.
    1. Great Britain. Public bodies. Accounting
    I. Henley, Sir, Douglas.   II. Chartered
    Institute of Public Finance and Accountancy
    657'.835'00941

    ISBN 0–278–00103–3

Contents

Preface

Since the second edition of this book was published in 1986 the rapid pace of development and change in public sector finance, financial control and accounting has continued, indeed accelerated. In the field of central government the financial management initiative has matured and there has been progress in developing improved performance measurement, reporting and individual accountability. Important changes have been made in the content of the public expenditure planning total and in the reporting of expenditure programmes, with the White Paper being superseded by more extensive presentations by the Treasury and the spending departments. The phased privatization of nationalized industries has continued, and regional water authorities also are now intended for privatization. In local government the plans to replace domestic rates by community charges, and new capital controls and possible changes in capital accounting pose new problems and challenges for financial managers. In the National Health Service the previous initiative to involve hospital doctors more closely in financial management has made limited progress and has been overtaken by a more selective yet at the same time wider-based approach called resource management. The impact of the government's full review is currently being assessed. In public sector audits there has been continued advance in the importance, scope and techniques of assessing and reporting on value-for-money performance and accountability.

The main aim of this book remains the same as in previous editions – to help to improve financial management, control and accounting throughout the public sector by financial practitioners and those who are studying to join them. A new edition has become essential to ensure accurate and up-to-date treatment of a subject area of such widespread importance.

All the text in this third edition has been completely reviewed and much of it rewritten. In addition three main improvements to the content and format have been made. First, there are two entirely new chapters, on financial reporting and management accounting respectively. These seek to identify distinctive features, principles and approaches of the public sector in these subject areas, as background to the discussion in later chapters of the significant differences between its constituent parts.

Second, updated source and readings references have been consolidated into a single bibliography at the back of the book, with brief suggestions for recommended reading at the end of each chapter. Third, questions for use in discussions, essays and examinations have been assembled together, also at the back of the book. These changes should ease the reading and understanding of what is not only a complex subject, but also one of the highest importance to the future management and performance of public sector activities and operations.

DOUGLAS HENLEY, CLIVE HOLTHAM,
ANDREW LIKIERMAN, JOHN PERRIN

Foreword

Noel Hepworth, OBE, IPFA, DPA
Director, Chartered Institute of Public Finance and Accountancy

Accountancy in the public sector is about financial management. Those accountants who define their role either implicitly or explicitly in traditional terms as a keeper or inspector of accounts are not able to provide the style of accountancy expertise which public sector financial management now requires. Therefore accountants, if they are to be successful, while they need an accounting technical background, also require a thorough understanding of the political and economic climate in which the public sector in general, and their part in particular, has to operate. But they also need to recognize that politics is as much about relationships between institutions as between political parties.

The public sector, though, is not a uniform organization. Parts of it are very similar to and are subject to the same influences as commercial organizations, yet because they are part of the public sector, the final sanction of bankruptcy does not exist. Other parts operate as commercial organizations but in practice are in their own field monopolies and are consequently subject to constraints other than those of the market place to prevent exploitation of the consumer or to promote value for money. Other parts of the public sector could in no way be described as running commercial services, hence trading and profit and loss accounts are entirely inappropriate ideas, but the problems remain of how to contain costs, measure performance and promote value for money.

Value for money is of underlying concern throughout the whole of the public sector. It surfaces in the need for consistent planning, for clarity in the statement of institutional or policy objectives, for the adequate recording of events and for review of achieved performance against objectives. Value for money is an expression of the economy, the efficiency and the effectiveness with which the institutions of the public sector operate.

The different parties involved in the management of public sector institutions have different interests. Perhaps the most important difference of interest is between the politician and the professional manager or administrator. The politician has a relatively short time horizon, often no more distant than the date of the next election; the professional manager is concerned with the long-run success of his service or activity but he has to discharge his responsibilities under whichever political party controls the government or local authority. The difference is most marked over attitudes towards capital investment where consistency of decision and long lead times may be required but are not always forthcoming, for example investment in nuclear power generation. Again, political success in terms of potential electoral gain may be regarded from the professional manager's point of view as a failure. An example of this is a decision to manipulate the prices of the products of the nationalized industries for reasons which are unrelated to the interests of those industries, to optimal resource use, or even in the longer term to the interests of their customers. Divergence of interest may sometimes emerge between different parts of the public sector – for example, between the Treasury and other central government departments, between both and the nationalized industries, between central and local government, between the Department of Health and the regional health authorities. These differences of interest may lead to a concentration by one party on a definition of success which the other may not subscribe to. The Treasury may define success as causing spending departments and local authorities to keep within defined public expenditure plans, and the nationalized industries to keep within their external financing limits. Their paramount concern is the management of the economy and the control of total public spending. But central government also has a concern about the efficiency with which the public sector operates, and cash limits and external financing limits can be used in a crude generalized way to impose a resource squeeze upon the affected organization in an attempt to force out greater efficiency. In a sense this does create the opportunity for a coincidence of interest with the manager of the industry or local authority service. He has a direct interest in maximizing value for money in order to enable him to provide the most efficient and effective service in response to demand, but in practice this coincidence of interest may not emerge and in the face of constant pressure on public sector resources the relationship between central government and the other institutions of the public sector has tended to be one of greater or less friction.

A complicating factor in all of these relationships is inflation. The economist is intellectually used to the problems which inflation brings. But the accountant has only latterly sought to find ways of showing the impact in accounting terms of inflation upon the performance of any organization. The accounting standard which had been devised to allow for the effects of inflation had as its objective the informing of shareholders of the effects of inflation upon the operation of their business and the consequences for themselves as shareholders. This is clearly an inappropriate standard to apply to the non-commercial public sector where capital expenditure is met either from the proceeds of borrowing on public credit or from public revenues, as in central government and the health service.

Yet what is clear is that the accountant in the public sector must recognize that inflation has important effects. These can distort the management of the undertaking unless properly recognized, can make day-to-day budgetary control and cash flow control difficult, can distort pricing policies whether or not attempts are made to recover full costs, can change the relative value of assets employed, and can lead to an unplanned switch of economic resources into the public sector where private sector pricing responds to inflation and public sector pricing does not.

The nationalized industries adopted current cost accounting using the principles set out in the relevant accounting standard. The trading undertakings, run directly as part of central government, prepared their accounts using the same principles. The accounts of local authority direct labour organizations follow this pattern as well.

But outside these parts of the public sector the implications of price movement have not been fully recognized. For example with local authorities, annual budgets are usually fixed on a November price base, with central reserves or contingencies being set aside to finance inflation as it occurs. The service manager's weekly or monthly statement of costs incurred includes inflation and throughout the financial year the actual price level is moving away from the November date. The service manager's problem is then how to identify the element of cost associated with the underlying level of service and the element caused by price change.

The role of the accountant in the public sector should be to organize accounting systems so that the redistributive effects of inflation upon the equity interests of the different parties are properly recognized. Management's responsibility (probably the political management's) is then to make decisions about how and when the different equity interests should in fact be redistributed or restored to their original position.

For example, basing council rents upon historic costs gives a benefit to the tenant in an unplanned way because the extent of the benefit depends entirely upon the incidence of inflation. The use of current cost accounting would identify that benefit (at least to a degree) and a political managerial decision could then be made about what was the proper benefit for the tenant to get.

Current cost accounting as at present conceived may not be the ideal system for controlling the distribution of equity but it is a workable system capable of adaptation and evolution. The problem of managing the public sector and of maintaining the efficiency of public sector operations has become more difficult with inflation. The accountant needs to recognize first that that has occurred and consequently what ought to be done to respond to the circumstances created by inflation.

Finance permeates most organizations because it is the measure of resource use and of priorities, but to provide a sensible message to management, finance needs to be related to work done or performance. The traditional attitude towards budget preparation and the provision of information to management has been a concern with cash. Obviously this is important because of the significance of cash flow management. In the private sector the developing position of the company treasurer (a post which exists also in some nationalized industries) recognizes this. But the accountant's role, particularly in the public sector, goes beyond that. The emphasis of central government controls upon the institutions of the public sector is certainly upon cash and the accountant needs to have the expertise to understand how far in the interests of his organization the rules governing the cash controls can be developed and defined. The accountant, though, needs to strive to establish a workable relationship between cash and organization performance because only the two combined give any real understanding of the efficiency with which the organization is operating. And that relationship needs to be established on a systematic basis, not limited to the result of *ad hoc* enquiries about which management may occasionally think.

In the trading part of the public sector, target rates of return can be established and performance compared with the target. But elsewhere the problem is more difficult to solve. In theory output measures should be developed as indicators of performance, but in practice such measures are difficult, indeed frequently impossible, to devise. The main source of information available to the accountant and manager is therefore about inputs – the number of employees, their pay levels, expenditure on textbooks and class materials, the number of hospital beds maintained; or at best 'intermediate outputs' – miles of motorway constructed, usage of vehicles, occupancy of hospital beds and so on. The financial manager in these circumstances needs a comparative yardstick to evaluate performance. That yardstick may be the performance of the same organization in a previous period or the performance of another organization.

Local authorities are particularly good at publishing comparative information at the most detailed level. Within the health service comparative information is also available, but not easily accessible to the public. The nationalized industries have developed a wide range of performance measures individually but there is no way of systematically comparing the discharge of similar functions between industries. To make comparative information more widely available for analysis would be particularly helpful to the public sector accountant in providing management with better performance indicators.

While the public sector accountant has the responsibility of developing systematic arrangements to assist management in comparing and improving the performance of the service or institution, the public sector auditor has, among other duties, the complementary role of examining whether management actually performs that task efficiently. In this way, the responsibility of the public sector auditor, apart from the auditor of the nationalized industries which are subject to the same type of audit as private companies, goes beyond the responsibility of auditors to companies in the private sector. Like them, the public sector auditor has to satisfy himself that the accounts have been prepared in accordance with statutory and constitutional requirements and regulations, and that proper accounting practices have been observed in their compilation. But in addition to this he has other responsibilities, including those which in the local authority context take the form of satisfying himself that the accounts 'do not disclose any significant loss arising from waste, extravagance, inefficient financial administration, poor value for money, mistake or other cause'. That is a fairly wide, not to say daunting, remit.

The Chartered Institute of Public Finance and Accountancy has recognized these special responsibilities in its training arrangements for accountants in the public sector. It not only aims to provide basic technical skills, but emphasizes within its training scheme the need to develop financial management and audit skills, including analytical skills, within the context of the special requirements of the public sector including a knowledge of public sector finance, economics and institutional relationships.

This book is written for this style of accountant and auditor, and for others engaged in financial management in the public sector. The authors have examined the financial control mechanisms that affect the different institutions within the public sector at various levels, including those of policy formulation, policy control and intra public sector institutional relationships.

Critics of the public sector tend to adopt a simplistic approach to the management of its institutions. They frequently fail to recognize the political element in management and to detach their own political judgements in making criticisms of the non-political managers in the public sector. The skill of the successful professional manager in the public sector is to be able to cooperate fully with the political policy maker but to retain that degree of independence which enables him to work just as closely with the present political policy maker's opponent should that prove necessary in the future, and to retain the confidence of both. But to do that the manager has to have a thorough understanding of the environment in which he operates as well the appropriate techniques. This is an authoritative up-to-date book, now in its third edition, which fills a significant gap and will help him gain that understanding.

Chapter 1

Introduction

Financial management and control issues in the public sector have become the focus of increasing attention in recent years. Cuts in public expenditure have been one cause. These have put pressure on public authorities to maintain services with less money (in real terms) and to do so they have had to improve their financial analysis so that action can be taken to improve efficiency and value for money. Another cause has been the call for improved measures of performance, as part of pressure for stronger accountability. This has brought accounting practices in public services under scrutiny. A third cause has been pressure within the accountancy profession to standardize accounting practices and to examine whether public sector practices should not be brought more into line with those in the private sector. Finally, on the heels of government interest in cutting expenditure and trying to improve performance and accountability in the public services, all the professional accountancy institutes have become more interested in public sector practice. No doubt this is because they feel that their members have marketable skills to help improve accounting and performance information.

At the same time, many accountants in the public services have become more conscious of, and more concerned about, the differences of methodology and of philsophy which have separated their work from that of the other branches of the accountancy profession. This may have been the result of interests widened by the various (aborted) attempts to integrate the profession. It may also stem from cross-fertilization of thinking resulting from the increased mobility of accountants from different backgrounds. There were certainly moves into new branches of public service employment following the reorganization in the 1970s and 1980s of local authorities, the National Health Service and water authorities. The moves to encourage the public sector to behave more like the private sector and privatization in the 1980s also helped to break down a number of barriers. But these pressures have become more insistent and more political in recent years, as those who believe that the public sector is chronically inefficient have moved to the centre of the political stage. Such people have maintained with increasing vehemence that the only way to remedy the position is to transfer the provision of services where at all possible to the private sector, and that what remains in the public sector should follow private sector financial and management practices.

In general the public sector has not succeeded in mobilizing support for its own ways of doing things, and the political attacks at national level have been reinforced by calls at the local elected level for improved efficiency. All this has undoubtedly led to a lower morale in many public sector bodies, even though there are considerable misgivings about whether much of what is done in the private sector is in practice transferable. Accountants have not been immune to this fall in morale, though their status within the public sector may well have risen because of the increased importance attached to financial skills.

As a result of all these pressures and influences, there has been a growing self-consciousness among accountants in the public sector about following practices which are markedly different from those in the private sector or which do not receive the understanding and approval of fellow accountants and financial managers. There has also been a good deal of questioning, not only in the public sector but throughout the accounting profession, about whether or not some public sector accounting practices are anyway conceptually sound. The attempts in recent years to increase the degree of cooperation between separate professional institutes in the quest for improvement and greater standardization of accounting and financial practices have served to intensify this self-questioning. A more visible sign of the need for action in the public sector was the establishment, early in 1982, of an ASC standing subcommittee – the Public Sector Liaison Group – to explore how far the scope of present accounting standards, or other new standards or guidelines, might appropriately be extended within the public sector.

The issues

Some of the financial and accounting issues which have been the subject of public debate, for example external reporting and monitoring, are common to several parts of the public sector, and these are dealt with in this book. Some of these are conceptual issues, some practical. Some are related to external reporting and monitoring, others to internal financial control. But two general questions arise.

The first concerns how specific accounting and control problems should be tackled in a public sector context. Such problems arise because of the distinctive constitutional, economic and financial features of public sector bodies. These are bound to affect the way in which their operations are accounted for and controlled. Areas of special concern include, for example, the accounting treatment of capital equipment and the need to provide non-financial indicators to supplement financial data because of the non-profit basis of most parts of the public sector.

The second question, following naturally from the first, is how far should public sector practice relate to practice in the private sector and in what respects, if any, should it diverge? This question has been asked about most aspects of financial reporting, including the form of financial statements and the treatment of individual items in the accounts, such as capital asset valuation and depreciation. The question is also asked about internal financial and economic issues, such as the use of investment appraisal techniques and monitoring.

That such issues cannot be taken in isolation applies to almost all the main aspects of this book. For example, questions about the form of external financial statements cannot be separated from the nature and objectives of particular public sector operations and the fact that there are a variety of users for financial statements in the public sector, with different kinds of needs. Similarly, the relationship between auditing practices in the public and private sectors cannot be examined without looking at the different ways in which accountability is exercised for public sector institutions compared to the purposes and forms of accountability of private concerns.

A number of other issues span the main chapters. In the area of financial reporting, for example, there is the question of how far there should be uniformity, and how much flexibility ought to be allowed between similar types of institutions. Another recurrent theme is the issue of how accounting rules should be developed, while on the use of external financial information the nature and rights of different user groups are not always clear. As for internal financial control, the pressure on resources has in most cases given rise to a call for improved systems for monitoring, not only internally but also for external disclosure and performance review. Finally, on a more personal level, the role and status of accountants within their organizations and in relation to the accountancy profession as a whole continues to be a matter of concern to many public sector accountants.

Public sector diversity

The public sector is both extremely diverse and, despite privatizations, extremely large. Even ignoring the large sums expended on transfer payments (such as pensions, welfare benefits and subsidies), the total expenditure of the public sector on employing people, goods and services in carrying out both trading and public service activities is enormous – about 40% of the gross domestic product. Figure 1.1 gives an idea of the relative size of net public sector expenditure analysed in four ways. It can be seen that local authority expenditure amounts to more than a quarter of all public expenditure, and expenditure on health rather more than 10%. The nationalized industries, by contrast, make little overall demand on the public purse because, although the amounts they spend are large,

Table 1.1 Public expenditure by department, 1978–79 to 1991–92[1] (£ billion)

	1978–79 Outturn	1982–83 Outturn	1983–84 Outturn	1984–85 Outturn	1985–86 Outturn	1986–87 Outturn	1987–88 Outturn	1988–89 Estimated outturn	1989–90 Plans	1990–91 Plans	1991–92 Plans
Ministry of Defence	7.5	14.4	15.5	17.2	18.0	18.2	18.9	19.3	20.1	21.2	22.1
FCO – Diplomatic wing	0.3	0.5	0.5	0.6	0.6	0.6	0.7	0.8	0.8	0.8	0.8
FCO – Overseas Development Administration	0.8	1.0	1.2	1.2	1.2	1.3	1.3	1.5	1.5	1.6	1.7
European Communities	0.8	0.6	0.8	1.0	0.8	1.1	1.7	1.0	2.0	1.9	1.6
Ministry of Agriculture, Fisheries and Food	0.8	1.8	2.0	2.0	2.4	1.8	2.0	1.9	1.9	2.2	2.4
Department of Trade and Industry	1.8	1.9	1.5	1.6	1.5	2.1	0.7	1.7	1.4	1.3	1.2
Export Credits Guarantee Department	0.4	0.3	0.3	0.5	0.3	0.3	0.2	0.1	0.2	0.1	0.1
Department of Energy	0.6	0.9	1.1	2.6	0.7	-0.2	0.2	0.2	-0.2	-0.5	0.6
Department of Employment	1.1	2.4	2.9	3.1	3.4	3.9	3.9	4.1	4.0	4.0	4.0
Department of Transport	2.6	4.3	4.3	4.6	4.6	4.7	4.6	4.8	5.4	5.5	5.7
DOE – Housing	3.6	2.7	3.2	3.3	3.0	2.8	2.7	2.1	1.7	2.0	2.4
DOE – Other environmental services	2.3	3.6	3.8	4.0	3.9	4.0	3.6	4.4	4.5	4.6	4.7
Home Office	1.9	3.8	4.1	4.7	4.7	5.1	5.7	6.3	6.9	7.2	7.4
Legal departments	0.2	0.4	0.4	0.5	0.6	0.7	0.8	1.0	1.1	1.2	1.2
Department of Education and Science	7.7	12.7	13.4	13.9	14.4	15.7	17.1	18.4	19.6	20.2	20.8
Office of Arts and Libraries	0.3	0.6	0.6	0.7	0.7	0.8	0.9	1.0	1.0	1.0	1.1
Department of Health	7.4	13.9	14.7	15.8	16.6	17.9	19.7	21.7	23.2	24.4	25.4
Department of Social Security	16.4	32.5	35.2	38.1	41.5	44.4	46.2	47.6	51.0	55.3	58.7
Scotland	3.9	6.5	6.8	7.1	7.2	7.7	8.1	8.7	9.0	9.1	9.7
Wales	1.6	2.5	2.7	2.7	2.8	3.1	3.3	3.6	3.8	3.9	4.0
Northern Ireland	2.2	3.6	3.8	4.1	4.4	4.6	4.9	5.2	5.5	5.7	5.9
Chancellor's departments	1.4	2.6	2.5	2.6	2.8	3.2	3.4	3.7	4.1	4.3	4.5
Other departments	0.4	0.6	0.1	0.2	0.2	0.2	0.3	0.4	0.3	0.3	0.3
Reserve									3.5	7.0	10.5
Privatization proceeds		-0.5	-1.1	-2.2	-2.7	-4.5	-5.2	-6.0	-5.0	-5.0	-5.0
Adjustment								0.3			
Planning total	**65.7**	**113.6**	**120.4**	**129.9**	**133.8**	**139.3**	**145.7**	**153.6**	**167.1**	**179.4**	**191.6**
General government gross debt interest	7.4	13.9	14.5	16.1	17.7	17.6	17.5	17.7	17.0	16.0	15.5
Other national accounts adjustments	1.8	5.2	5.5	4.7	6.7	7.5	8.2	9.6	9.5	9.5	9.0
General government expenditure	75.0	132.6	140.4	150.6	158.2	164.4	171.5	180.9	193.7	205.0	216.0
General government expenditure (excluding privatization proceeds)	75.0	133.1	141.6	152.8	160.9	168.9	176.7	186.9	198.7	210.0	221.0

[1] The departmental figures for 1989–90, 1990–91 and 1991–92 make no allowance for allocations from the Reserve.

Who plans it
Public expenditure[1]
by department

Who spends it
Public expenditure[1]
by spending
authorities

Where it goes
Public expenditure[1]
by function[2]

What it is spent on
Public expenditure[1] by
economic categories

Who plans it	Who spends it	Where it goes	What it is spent on
19.2 Ministry of Defence	42.6 Local authorities	19.2 Defence	36.9 Purchases of assets, goods and services
20.7 DHSS-Health & personal social services		21.8 Health	6.0 Transfers to the corporate sector
48.5 DHSS-Social security	114.2 Central government	50.0 Social security	56.9 Transfers to the personal sector
18.0 Department of Education & Science		21.9 Education & Science	(running costs receipts − 2.9) 13.7 Departmental running costs
17.1 Scottish Office, Welsh Office & Northern Ireland		6.2 Transport	
		8.3 Law & Order	44.7 Other public service pay
34.9 Other	1.5 Public corporations	30.8 Other	2.9 Payments overseas

1. Departmental spending, i.e. excluding the Reserve and privatization proceeds.
2. This differs from the analysis by department mainly because Scottish, Welsh and Northern Ireland expenditure is distributed between functions.

Fig. 1.1 Public expenditure 1988–89 (£ billion).

they are trading entities and as such recoup their costs in whole or part from their customers. Table 1.1 puts the figures for public expenditure as a whole in the context of changes in the period 1978–79 to 1991–92.

While the scale of the public sector is essentially a matter of political choice, the financing of whatever size is chosen through a variety of combinations of taxes, rates, charges and prices is a matter of both politics and economics. In this book the financing of the public sector as a whole is taken as given. The concern is rather with the financial management and control of public sector activities, and with the accounting, financial control and audit practices whose underlying aims are to provide satisfactory accountability and promote the best service and value for money.

The private sector has managed to achieve a higher degree of standardization of financial, accounting and audit practices than has so far been achieved in the public sector. This is not surprising. There are some differences in accounting practices between, for example, industrial firms, retail firms and banks, but their common basic objectives relate to profitability, and managers, shareholders and employees of all three types of private sector organization have broadly the same information needs. They relate in particular to information on current profits and the stability and trend of profits (for guidance on valuation and risk) and, for lenders, further details on assets, liabilities and capital structures.

In contrast, the public sector has a considerable diversity of activities and aims. While nationalized industries operate commercially as trading entities, government departments, local authorities and health authorities do not exist to produce goods or services for sale, do not have shareholders, and are funded by compulsory levies – rates and taxes – or by borrowing on public credit. It is not therefore surprising that the results are presented in a different way. Another factor in explaining the diversity even within the public services sector is the factor of history. As an example, whereas local government has a long history of relatively autonomous development of its own distinctive accounting practices, the history of the National Health Service is much briefer and its accounting methods have been more closely influenced by the direct and explicit monitoring and control requirements of central government.

For the future therefore it is still questionable how far and how fast it will be desirable and feasible to effect greater standardization of financial, accounting and reporting practices between the private and public sectors, and between different types of non-trading public sector bodies. Agreement on change between a number of interest groups would be needed. Many of these interest groups have their own reasons to oppose change and that change would then have to be reflected in extensive amendments to government regulations and perhaps legislation. For anyone seeking to understand the pros and cons of change, a clear understanding of the differences between public sector bodies and their financial practices is essential. This book sets out many of those differences in some detail.

The authors' approach

The diversity in financial, accounting and control practices in the various parts of the public sector is reflected in the use of authors who are experts in their own areas. Each author of this book takes responsibility for the coverage and views expressed in his own chapters. The authors claim no consensus on the detail of any standardized model of public sector accounting and finance in the future. They are deeply grateful to numerous contacts – too numerous to mention individually – within the several branches of the public sector, who have given much time to the reading of drafts and the framing of advice.

Chapter 2

Financial reporting in the public sector

Financial reporting in the public sector is a key element in the accountability of public sector bodies. This chapter deals with those elements of external reporting which cover financial matters, the rules for which vary greatly between different parts of the public sector. The objectives of public sector financial reports are first analysed, then the rules and potential users are categorized. After discussing what rights to financial information might mean in practice, the chapter goes on to provide an analysis of the differences between financial reports in the public and private sectors and a discussion of some current issues in financial reporting. The chapter concludes with details of what might be expected from a well presented financial report.

Introduction

In the reporting of their activities, as in all other public sector accounting and control matters, the public sector cannot be treated as a single entity. It is true that there are **some** common factors in the financial reports of United Kingdom public sector bodies which mean that it is also possible to identify differences from private sector financial reports. But within the public sector there are a variety of organizational and functional arrangements which give rise to a similar variety of reporting arrangements. So while there will be at least some exceptions to almost every generalization about financial reporting, this chapter is intended to give an overview of the financial aspects of published annual reports, not only the formal financial statements, but also those aspects of the reports which deal with performance in financial terms. It therefore excludes those elements which are of a purely descriptive or policy nature, though the boundaries are often difficult to draw in practice.

The degree to which trading is involved is the key element in whether the financial reports follow private sector practice. At one end of the spectrum come those trading concerns which are very similar to private sector organizations. Nationalized industries, such as British Coal, come into this category. At the other end come those bodies where there is almost no trading element such as health authorities and most central government departments. In between come a host of different types where there is a combination of trading and non-trading activity – local authorities, central government agencies, etc.

But even trading organizations in the public sector cannot be compared in a straightforward way to those in the private sector. The very fact that they are in the public sector at all normally means that they are subject to non-commercial constraints and have objectives which are likely to conflict with purely commercial considerations. If they are monopolies they will be subject to political and other limitations on the exercise of their monopoly power. For example, nationalized water authorities would not be expected to increase charges to a level which exploited their position.

Even if trading organizations are not monopolies, they are likely to have restrictions on seeking to increase their revenues regardless of the wider social and economic implications. Thus there has been great moral pressure not only on central and local government but also on some nationalized industries to 'Buy British'. British Airways, when nationalized, was under pressure for many years to buy British planes and undertake certain non-commercial obligations such as flying some uneconomic routes for reasons of national prestige. (Moves to greater European harmonization will diminish these particular pressures at an official level, but unofficial pressures will certainly remain.)

In his 1978 report *Financial Accounting in Non-business Organisations* Professor Robert Anthony divided United States non-profit organizations into two types:

(a) 'Those whose financial resources are obtained entirely, or almost entirely, from revenues from the sale of goods and services';
(b) 'Those who obtain a significant amount of financial resources from sources other than the sale of goods and services'.

This distinction has also been made for the United Kingdom, but the emphasis on privatization and revenue generation in the past few years has meant that the variety of UK 'types' has greatly increased and there is a spectrum of many different kinds of organizations, ranging from wholly trading to wholly non-trading.

The objectives and functions of public sector financial reports

Despite the diversity of public sector organizations, there are some similarities between the broad objectives and functions of their financial statements, though all do not apply in all cases.

(a) Compliance and stewardship:
   — To provide authorities and users with the assurance that there has been compliance with legal and other mandatory requirements in the organization's use of resources.
(b) Accountability and retrospective reporting:
   — To monitor performance and evaluate management, providing a basis for looking at trends over time, achievement against published objectives and comparison with other similar organizations (if any);
   — To enable outsiders to have cost information on goods or services provided, and to enable them to assess efficiency and effectiveness in the use of resources.
(c) Planning and authorization information:
   — To provide the basis for planning future policy and activities;
   — To provide supporting information for further funds to be authorized.
(d) Viability:
   — To help readers judge whether the organization can continue to provide goods or services in the future.
(e) Public relations:
   — To give the organization the opportunity to put forward a statement of its achievements to influential users, employees and the public.
(f) Source of facts and figures:
   — To provide information for the wide variety of interest groups who want to find out about the organization.

What is published varies greatly in the relative emphasis given to each of these objectives and functions but throughout the public sector the importance of public relations is steadily increasing. Indeed some published documents are effectively **only** exercises in public relations and the financial information plays a relatively minor role or is relegated to an additional, purely technical, document. On the other hand some public bodies are required to publish only accounts and do not publish any more information to expand on them. The position of some major central government documents, moreover, is different to that of other sectors, as Chapter 4 makes clear. These have a planning focus and some are used to support requests for public funds.

What are the rules for financial reporting?

There are four different types of rules for financial reporting by public sector organizations.

The law

Financial statements are governed by a legal framework, though the relevant legislation varies considerably from one part of the public sector to another. As examples, for local authorities in England and Wales, the 1980 Local Government Planning and Land Act gave powers to the Secretary of State to regulate the publication of information. For nationalized industries and bodies such as government trading funds, the relevant sections of the 1985 Companies Act are normally applied, with any necessary amendment or extension by any specific legislation by which a body has been set up or is governed.

Accounting standards

The SSAPs (Statements of Standard Accounting Practice) developed by the Accounting Standards Committee are framed in terms of private sector organizations. Technically the position is that they apply to 'all financial statements whose purpose is to give a true and fair view', a technical term not used in much of the public sector. The distinction in practice is less clear. Some SSAPs have obvious applications to public sector organizations, others do not. So SSAP 3, which deals with earnings per share, is clearly not relevant to organizations without share capital, while SSAP 2 (Disclosure of Accounting Policies) could potentially relate to every organization with financial statements. There are also grey areas where the position is less clear, notably where a public sector body is involved in trading, or where only part of an SSAP might be applicable.

The Accounting Standards Committee has also been involved in the providing of a seal of approval for specific rules by 'franking' SORPs (Statements of Recommended Practice) which are developed by bodies representing parts of the public sector. SORPs are of particular importance to the public sector since the franking process involves not only a strong moral commitment to follow recommended practice by the relevant professional body, but also comes within the scope of the work of external auditors. Local authorities and universities have both discussed SORPs and in 1987 a local authority code of practice became a franked SORP.

Accounting practice

This provides a framework for decisions about how items should be treated by those compiling the accounts. The basic structure of financial reports and the treatment of items which go into them have been developed over many years as part of accounting practice. For much of the public sector the framework is derived from accepted practice by professional accountants, though central government relies little on accepted practice and is bound much more by rules (see below).

Specific rules

In many cases there are rules laid down about how organizations in one part of the public sector, or indeed individual organizations within it, should lay out their financial statements. Within government, the sponsoring department for a public body will issue any directions or discuss codes of practice, though the Treasury will be highly influential behind the scenes. Thus while the nationalized industries have received directions on their accounts from the sponsoring departments, the Treasury determines many of the key aspects of each direction. Parliamentary committees may also be influential in asking for certain kinds of information to be included in published reports, though they can do no more than recommend.

It is also worth remembering that the organizational links of some public bodies are reflected in their accounts. Education and the police, for example, cannot be seen in isolation from local authority accounts, or health authorities from those of central government.

Users of financial reports

When looking at many public sector financial statements it is not always clear who the intended readers are. Sometimes this may be a reflection of the multiplicity of audiences for these statements. At other times, those who compile the statements are evidently not clear themselves about their potential readership. This could include the following groups.

Elected members

Financial reports are very important in informing elected members, either as individuals or collectively, about the way in which the organization has fulfilled its functions. A distinction, however, needs to be made between Members of Parliament and elected members of local authorities. The reports provide both sets of elected members with information for assessing policy, judging efficiency and effectiveness, and providing the assurance that spending is within budget and has been on approved activities. But while Members of Parliament have no responsibility for the information (which they receive from the government), local authority members are themselves responsible for the information which is produced, though in practice there is little participation in the process of compilation.

Members of Parliament use examination of the reports of some organizations, such as nationalized industries, as a point of entry for monitoring their activities. Other bodies will be under Parliamentary scrutiny only if there is a scandal. But while individual Members may well take an interest, the vast majority of the financial reports of public sector bodies are not considered directly in Parliament.

The public as voters and/or taxpayers

Those who pay for the services provided, whether or not they are also consumers, will want to know how money is being spent on different types of activity. They will also want to evaluate performance, ensure that there is value for money in what is provided and that the interests of consumers are being served.

This group will also want information on the relationship between budget and actual spending and whether such spending was on approved activities. Where the performance of elected members is being judged, the statements may even be used to decide whether there are grounds for change.

The media will have an important role in informing the public on developments and interpreting the complexities of financial information for them. Although reporting is patchy and often sensationalized, at its best the media can play an important role in public perception of the relative importance of issues.

The customers or clients

Those who are the customers/clients (or equivalent) of the service provided by the public sector organization may well wish to know how the service is organized and its prospects for the future. Financial matters may also be of interest – students, for example, may want to know more about the distribution of resources within a university or tenants about the position of the housing budget. However, the financial reports are less likely to be used by individuals than by pressure groups and representative organizations (such as community health councils in the Health Service) looking after the interests of groups of consumers or clients. Such organizations are likely to have the task of interpreting complex financial information to those who are less financially aware.

The management

Top management will of course have much more detailed and current information than whatever is provided through the external financial reports, but the middle and junior levels are likely to find the published reports useful in putting their own efforts in perspective. For the management as a whole, publication of information will provide the focus for the need to agree on how policies are explained and presented.

Customers and suppliers

Those buying from, or selling to, the public body will be interested in the organization's plans and position. Customers will be specifically interested in the future security of their supplies, suppliers in the financial strength of one of their customers.

Employees

Individuals who are not members of the management group or (more commonly) their representatives and trade unions, will be interested in the prospects for security of employment and the organization's ability to pay increased wages. In some cases the financial statements will even give clues as to the opening bid in wage negotiations for the coming year.

Government

A number of government bodies are likely to be interested in the financial reports of other public sector bodies. Each of the major parts of the public sector will have a 'sponsor' department with specific responsibilities – the Department of the Environment for local authorities, the Department of Health for health authorities, etc. Individual public sector organizations also have sponsor departments and each major government department will have a larger number of bodies reporting to it. A few taken at random are:

(a) The British Council reports to the Foreign and Commonwealth Office.
(b) The BBC reports to the Home Office.
(c) English Heritage reports to the Department of the Environment.

The sponsor departments will almost always be aware of, or be given, the financial results before publication but will not necessarily know about all other parts of the report. Government departments other than the sponsor may well be interested in aspects of the work of a public sector body. Thus a good deal of the work of the British Council is of considerable interest to the Department of Education and Science, and because of its responsibility for tourism, the relevant section of the Department of Employment will be interested in English Heritage.

In addition to these groups, a further five groups have interests in certain circumstances.

Competitors

Organizations in competitive markets will want to know as much as possible about their public sector competitors. For example, Her Majesty's Stationery Office is in competition with other suppliers of similar goods. For obvious reasons public sector bodies in this position will want to disclose as little as possible about their competitive position other than what is required by relevant statutory and professional reporting requirements.

Lenders

The financial position of those organizations which borrow money from non-government sources will be of great interest to those that have lent them money, assuming the loan is not guaranteed by the government itself. The information they require includes updated information on plans and prospects as well as commitments for the long and short term, though in practice the historic basis of the accounts can give only very limited information of this kind.

Donors or sponsors

A number of institutions which rely on funding by donors, such as universities for research, use their annual financial reports to inform benefactors of progress and to acknowledge publicly the support which they have been given.

Investors or business partners

Where ventures have been set up in association with partners in the private sector, the partners or investors will obviously be interested in the financial position of the organization as a whole.

Other pressure groups

In some cases – environmental groups in relation to the activities of some government departments, for example – the financial reports will provide important information, such as the relative priorities attached to different aspects of their work.

These groups have some similarity with the potential users of private sector accounts. The groups were identified in *The Corporate Report* (ASC, 1976) as equity investors, loan creditors, employees, analyst–advisers, business contacts (including suppliers, creditors, customers, competitors and rivals), the government and the public. Yet while there is an overlap between the user groups, the coverage is different, as well as the relative importance of each group, not only between public and private sectors, but also, as already emphasized, between different parts of the public sector.

Rights to financial information

The user groups listed above would claim a variety of rights to the financial information in which they are interested. What is the basis of the rights which they claim? There are three kinds of assertions which are made to justify requirements for disclosure by public bodies.

First, there are statements implying user rights, without spelling out the basis of those rights. Such statements often reflect the influence of private sector reporting. The most influential examples have come from the United States, including the 1973 report from the American Institute of Certified Public Accountants known as the Trueblood Report. The report stated that it was 'fundamental and pervasive' that 'the basic objective of financial statements is to provide information useful for making economic decisions.'

Next there are statements of needs implying rights. Such statements refer to user needs as justifying claims by users to have information. In the United Kingdom, *The Corporate Report* declared that statements 'should seek to satisfy, as far as possible, the information needs of users' and the Trueblood Report claimed that in the United States, 'financial statements of not-for-profit organizations should provide information which serves users' needs.' It is unclear from either report how needs are to be defined and reconciled with each other. The late Professor Stamp (1980) concluded in a study for the Canadian Institute of Chartered Accountants that:

There is no doubt that users' needs are different. Research is necessary to establish not only how wide the differences are but to monitor changes in user needs.

So it may be that some needs are difficult to define and potentially irreconcilable. If members of the public ask how much is being spent on the Secret Service, are they seeking to destabilize society or exercising democratic rights? Do the same considerations apply to nuclear power, rubbish collection, landing rights?

Finally there are statements conferring user rights. *The Corporate Report* stated that:

Users of corporate reports we define as having a reasonable right to information concerning the reporting entity. We consider that such rights arise from the public accountability of the entity whether or not supported by legally enforceable powers to demand information.

It would be difficult to disagree with such sentiments, but here again there are questions about what is meant by 'reasonable' and how the conflicts between the claims of different users can be reconciled with each other. An indication of how it is likely to be done in practice came from Macve (1981) in a study primarily concerned with the private sector when he concluded that:

Recognition of the variety of user needs and of conflicts between different interests and different rights leads to the view that reaching agreement on the form and content of financial statements is as much a political process, a search for compromise between different parties, as it is a search for the methods which are technically best.

Differences from the private sector

The differences between user groups for public and private sector accounts has already been mentioned and this section can only be a brief analysis of the differences between public and private sector financial reporting. This is because while certain aspects of reporting – notably accountability and the stewardship of public funds – have common features across the public sector, the subject in detail is a complex and many-faceted one where it is difficult to make many generalizations without having to qualify them. Yet again this diversity of practice reflects significant differences between parts of the public sector.

The differences are in purpose, scope and method of performance measurement, as well as other factors, including the nature of audit (see Chapter 9). Thus it is true that there is no 'bottom line' profit measure for most, but not all, of the public sector, which helps to explain the great variety of performance measures used, including non-financial measures to reflect social as well as economic considerations.

The fact that most public sector organizations are not subject to competition accounts in part for the greater degree of disclosure which is possible. This extends to the disclosure of plans, often in great detail as, for example, in the government's Supply Estimates. Another key factor influencing the difference between public and private sector accounts is the fact that the vast majority of public sector organizations cannot 'go broke'. Except in very special circumstances, the government would step

Table 2.1 Performance against budget and an explanation of variance (West Midlands Police)

Revenue Expenditure	Actual expenditure 1986/7	Revised estimate 1986/7	Actual expenditure 1985/6
	(£m)	(£m)	(£m)
NET EXPEND. BEFORE GRANT	154.6	156.6	142.1
Less Home Office Grants	78.0	79.1	70.6
NET EXPEND. AFTER HO GRANT	76.6	77.5	71.5
Less WMPA Rate Support Grant	37.4	36.9	nil
Less WMCC Funding	nil	nil	71.5
NET WMPA-FUNDED EXPEND.	39.2	40.6	nil
FUNDED BY:			
WMPA Rate Precept	46.0	45.6	nil
Contribution to Balances	6.8cr	5.0cr	nil
	39.2	40.6	nil

The reduction of £2.0m between the revised estimate and actual expenditure in 1986/7 reflects the following variations:

	£m
Additional Emergency Overtime	0.7
Saving on Pension Costs	0.7cr
Additional Interest on Working Balances	0.9cr
Saving on Capital Financing Charges	0.5cr
Changes in Accounting Policy	
— Treatment of Stocks	0.9cr
— Capitalization of Vehicles	0.3
VARIATION IN TOTAL NET EXPENDITURE	2.0cr

Capital Expenditure	Actual expenditure 1986/7	Revised estimate 1986/7	Actual expenditure 1985/6
	(£m)	(£m)	(£m)
Vehicles	1.82	1.86	1.31
Equipment and Computers	1.01	2.12	0.56
New Police Buildings	0.61	1.11	0.80
Improvements to Police Buildings	0.51	0.88	0.84
TOTAL CAPITAL EXPENDITURE	3.95	5.97	3.51

Source: *Annual Report and Accounts 1986–87.*

in to support the public sector, something which is clearly crucial for lenders and suppliers.

The emphasis on plans reflects the need, where relevant, for elected members of public sector bodies to be able to have the information to vote on the spending priorities for the coming year. This aspect of the difference from the private sector is a manifestation of an even more significant factor than the lack of competition in influencing the financial statements – one which is common to all public sector bodies – ultimate accountability to an elected body. Responsibility of this kind is quite different to the position of private sector organizations' responsibility to their shareholders. (Those tempted to think about whether elected bodies are rather like public sector shareholders should think whether the public, or their representatives, can sell their 'shares' in a public body.) The importance of public accountability also means that the scope of the audit is normally wider in the public than in the private sector.

The importance of assessing plans has a further implication for the difference between private and public sector organizations in the way in which performance is measured. While the focus in the private sector is on trends and on comparisons with other, similar, organizations, the emphasis in the public sector is much more on achievement of objectives and on performance against budget, as the illustration in Table 2.1 from the report of the West Midlands Police illustrates. Not that published statements are always completely helpful to readers in allowing them to make these comparisons. Often readers have to compare statements from different years to do so.

As the basis of their accounting, public sector organizations are split between those which use cash accounting and those which use accrual accounts. Thus the West Glamorgan Health Authority has produced a 'Source and Application of Funds' as the main financial statement (Table 2.2) while British Rail not only produces conventional historic cost accounts, but supplementary current cost accounts as well (Table 2.3). Practice varies greatly within each of the categories. For example some organizations have an income and expenditure statement, others a profit and loss account, but only in a few cases is it possible, or indeed relevant, to have a balance sheet.

Despite the differences in the nature of the organizations, much of the terminology used in accounts is very similar between public and private sector organizations. The similarity is misleading in some cases, however, and can give rise to confusion. For example, the term 'loan' is used to cover the long-term government financing of nationalized industries which in practice is their permanent capital. In the private sector much of the permanent capital is provided by equity capital, with loans having precise repayment requirements, although refinancing is common. Care therefore needs to be taken before it can be assumed that the meaning is transferable from private to public sector or vice versa.

Finally, it is worth considering whether public sector financial reports

Table 2.2 Source and application of funds as the main financial statement (West Glamorgan Health Authority)

> This statement identifies the Authority's total resources for the year and how they were spent on day-to-day expenditure (Revenue), major schemes and expensive equipment (Capital), and Medical, Dental, Optical and Pharmacy services in the Community (Family Practitioner Services). It also shows the movement of balances in outstanding invoices, unpaid bills, stocks and cash between the beginning and end of the financial year.

31st March 1985	Source of Funds	31st March 1986
£000		£000
	REVENUE	
68,373	Money Received from the Government	75,610
283	Money Received from the Public	172
	CAPITAL	
4,991	Money Received from the Government	8,457
30	Sale of Property	14
	FAMILY PRACTITIONER SERVICE	
27,044	Money Received from the Government	—
100,721	**Sub total**	84,253
	MOVEMENT IN BALANCES	
(103)	Stocks	192
16	Outstanding Bills	(491)
726	Unpaid Invoices	384
(137)	Cash Book	30
101,223	**TOTAL**	84,368

31st March 1985	Application of Funds	31st March 1986
£000		£000
56,504	Hospital Services	63,014
7,007	Community Services	7,581
1,859	Ambulance Services	1,995
788	Other Services	924
2,439	Administration Services	2,436
71	Community Health Councils	70
5,258	Capital Developments	5,348
7,423	General Practitioners	—
14,690	Chemists	—
3,988	Dentists	—
1,196	Opticians	—
101,223	**TOTAL**	84,368

Source: *Annual Report and Accounts 1985–86.*

Table 2.3 Current cost accounting as a supplementary statement (British Rail: Group Current Cost Profit and Loss Account)

Year to 31 March 1987		Year to 31 March 1988
£m		£m
3,183.5	**Turnover**	3,384.2
73.7	**Historical cost operating surplus before interest**	113.0
(94.2)	Current cost operating adjustments	(93.9)
(20.5)	**Current cost operating surplus/*(loss)***	19.1
71.3	Interest payable and similar charges	65.7
(91.8)	**Current cost loss on ordinary activities**	(46.6)
(86.3)	Extraordinary surplus/*(loss)*	239.2
(178.1)	**Group current cost surplus/*(loss)* for the year**	192.6
	Appropriation of surplus/*(loss)* for the year	
104.5	Transfer to Reserves	177.7
(282.6)	Surplus/*(deficit)* after transfer to Reserves	14.9
(178.1)		192.6

Source: *Annual Report 1988.*

are in some way intrinsically worse than those of the private sector. The fact that this accusation is often levied against them may be due to a number of possible factors – the cash basis of some accounts; the reports being tarred with the image of allegedly poorly-run organizations; the restraining influence of government and other public authorities; perhaps even the frustration of readers accustomed to a private sector format. Certainly, producing public sector accounts is more complex than producing them for private sector organizations. This makes accounts different rather than 'better' or 'worse'. Those who believe that private sector accounts are superior need to bear two factors in mind. First, that there are no immutable accounting or other financial reporting rules which apply irrespective of the nature and purposes of the organization whose activities and results are being displayed or the objectives of presentation. Second, that private sector accounts are far more open to manipulation and that cash accounts, despite their crudeness, have a degree of transparency that accrual accounts cannot give, and that many private sector financial reports do not seek to offer.

Issues in financial reporting

Little information is available for almost any part of the public sector on how far any user groups actually do use the accounts. The position appears to vary very considerably from one sector to another. Pressure groups are highly active in some areas (road transport) but virtually dormant in others (psychotherapy). Electors and voters are generally ill-informed as individuals and rely on their representatives to interpret the information on their behalf. Their expectations are often unfulfilled. Despite the importance of financial matters, few elected members in either central or local government have financial training; some are indifferent to detailed financial matters. In comparison with members of Congress in the United States, Members of Parliament have pathetically small allowances for expert assistance if they require help.

So readers of financial reports have not been in a strong position to insist on improvements. Individuals have been dismissed as unrepresentative and representative bodies have not been strong in pressing their case. Nevertheless facts on who uses the information and therefore how the financial reports can be made more useful are hard to come by, making it more difficult to offer precise suggestions for improvement.

A factor which militates against greater accessibility is that, despite the requirement to produce financial reports, there is no direct incentive to make them better. While it is recognized that financial reports **should** be readable and intelligible, improved reader understanding is sometimes felt by those who compile them to be a disadvantage. Giving what are often considered to be ill-informed readers the necessary ammunition to criticize the organization could therefore be seen as a hostage to fortune. This view is reinforced by the importance to many in the public sector of maintaining an element of ambiguity in how the performance of organizations is assessed. Such ambiguity provides a welcome freedom to blur outcomes so that elected members and officials feel less

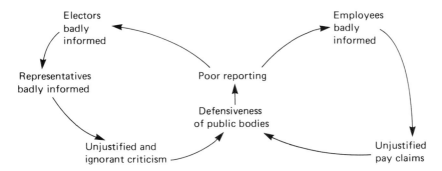

Fig. 2.1 Two vicious circles arising from poor reporting.

General Net Cost of all Services (£ per head of population)

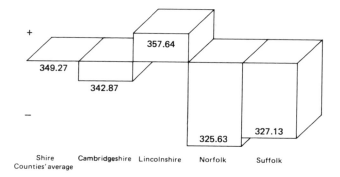

General Rate Precept for 1982–83(p)

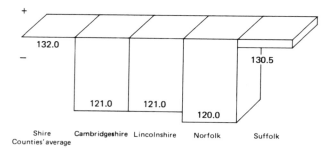

General Proportion of Net Expenditure met from Government Grant (%)

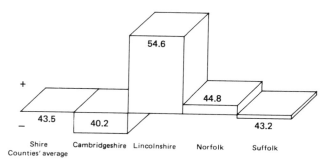

Introduction

The performance of Cambridgeshire may be compared in many different ways, none of them perfect. The method chosen here is to compare statistics for Cambridgeshire with those of three neighbouring authorities that are broadly similar to Cambridgeshire and with an average for the 39 English Shire Counties (which includes Cambridgeshire and the three neighbouring counties).

The statistics shown represent the more important indicators recommended by the Code of Practice on Local Authority Annual Reports. It should be noted that whereas figures in the other sections of this publication mainly relate to the financial year 1983–84, the statistics in this section are based on information for the year ended 31st March 1983 (1982–83) unless otherwise indicated.

The statistics by themselves cannot explain variations in local policies, practices and circumstances, which are an inherent feature of local services. Nor can they fully measure comparative levels of efficiency or service provision. However they can provide a starting point for more detailed enquiries.

Comparisons with other Local Authorities

Some statistics are expressed in terms of 'per head' which means that the total figure for Cambridgeshire has been divided by the June 1982 population (598,600). Similarly, for the 'per 1000 population' statistic the total has been divided by 598.6.

	Cambridge-shire	Lincoln-shire	Norfolk	Suffolk	Shire Counties' Average
Population (as at June 1982)	**598,600**	551,800	704,900	611,200	736,487
Area (Hectares)	**340,892**	591,481	536,774	379,663	312,476
Population Density (per Hectare)	**1.76**	0.93	1.31	1.61	2.36

Fig. 2.2(a) Example of comparative information (Cambridgeshire County Council).

Source: *Report and Accounts 1983–84.*

Education Net Cost (£ per head of population)

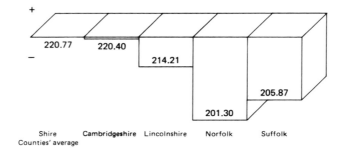

+

220.77   220.40

–

214.21

205.87

201.30

Shire   Cambridgeshire Lincolnshire   Norfolk   Suffolk
Counties' average

Education Proportion of Children aged under 5 years in Education (%)

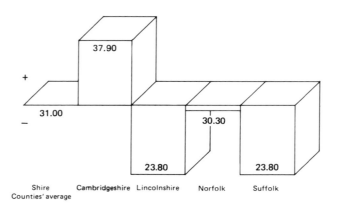

37.90

+

31.00

–

30.30

23.80

23.80

Shire   Cambridgeshire Lincolnshire   Norfolk   Suffolk
Counties' average

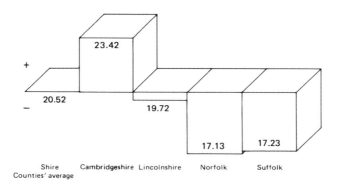

Education Net Cost of Non-Advanced Further Education (£ per head of population)

Education

The Education Service is by far the largest of all Shire Counties' services. The number of schools required is related to the population size, its distribution and the size of each particular County.

	Cambridge-shire	Lincoln-shire	Norfolk	Suffolk
Number of Schools	**357**	432	513	381
Number of Pupils	**98,702**	90,791	108,837	96,912

Fig. 2.2(b) Example of comparative information (Cambridgeshire County Council).

Source: *Report and Accounts 1983–84.*

vulnerable to criticisms. Yet the dangers in such a strategy include two potentially dangerous vicious circles, shown in Fig. 2.1.

Many of the issues in reporting in the private sector apply equally to the public sector. Creative accounting – slanting figures to show an organization in a favourable light – has been a feature of both in the past few years. But a number of areas have been of particular interest. For example, the question of whether capital assets should be valued and depreciated has been raised in the context of central government, health authorities and local government in recent years on the grounds that the value of what is invested each year, the value of capital tied up and the rate of using up that capital should all be known. Among the arguments deployed against changes from current practice are that the division between capital and current expenditure is too difficult to draw, that the valuation process is too complex and that the purpose of valuation is unclear unless the assets have alternative uses. This is a complex area and one which is discussed in other chapters for different parts of the public sector.

A more general issue which has been the cause of considerable concern in the past few years is the basis on which rules for financial reporting are set. It is well known that the private sector's problems in this area are bad enough, with difficulties in agreeing standards, and non-compliance with some of those which are agreed. Yet with a higher degree of control over the form of accounts, enforcing compliance in the public sector is probably easier than in the private sector. But the standard-setting process itself is much less straightforward. There is a lack of clarity about whether some standards should apply to public sector financial bodies and ambiguity about the role of the government in setting standards. The nature of the ambiguity is nicely illustrated by the fact that there is government representation on the Accounting Standards Committee with observer, rather than member, status.

A different aspect of rule-making is the issue of whether there should be greater standardization of financial reports. It is understandable that readers should have a reasonable expectation that they will find similar information in the financial reports of different bodies in the same sector, and indeed be able to make comparisons on the basis of such information. It is also reasonable that the way the information is compiled and presented should not be at the mercy of the management of each organization. On the other hand there are variations in the circumstances of different bodies in the same sector and there is room for doubt about the best way of presenting information because many rules are by no means well established. So it could be argued that it would be wrong to stifle all initiatives for clearer, though less uniform, accounting.

One of the ways in which variations are possible is in the cost of producing the annual financial reports. The issue here is whether or not the cost of producing a more expensive document is worthwhile. In some cases the public relations aspects of the financial reports are so important that the management regard the cost of more expensive statements as completely justified, not only as a sign of professionalism but also important in influencing those who deal with the organization. Others regard highly glossy presentation as a waste of public money, and considering the limited readership of some of the glossiest, it is difficult to see how the expense can be justified. The decision is in essence one of politics, not accounting.

Finally the question of whether, and if so, how far, public sector bodies should follow private sector practice in reporting, is often a matter of controversy which goes beyond the purely accounting issues which have already been outlined in the previous section.

What is a well-presented financial report?

The annual Public Sector Accounts Award sponsored by the Chartered Institute of Public Finance and Accountancy (CIPFA) has given rise to a number of suggestions on good presentation. The list below is not comprehensive but may help to provide a basis for those seeking to compile financial reports of a high standard or those wanting to assess an existing report.

Basis of compilation

As a minimum, reports should be:

(a) Relevant to the identified needs of users;
(b) Not blatantly biased or simply a defence of the record of the management;
(c) Timely, that is, produced soon after the end of the financial year;
(d) In conformity with the relevant accounting rules;
(e) Cost effective in presenting the information.

Usefulness

It should be possible to:

(a) Identify the current activity level of the organization, recent changes in activity and the prospects for the future;
(b) Identify income from all sources, including a split between income received from grants and those from trading and other sources;
(c) Understand the split between expenditure on the organization's main activities;
(d) See, in appropriate cases, whether the organization is maintaining its assets;

POLICE & FIRE COMMITTEE

million due to interest rates being lower than anticipated.

SERVICE DELIVERY

1985/86		1986/87
41,155	Number of Calls Received	40,541
19,242	Fires Attended	22,365
744	Road Accidents Attended	824
89	Fatalities at Fire	87
	Premises Visited by the Fire	
22,647	Protection Unit	21,316
5,334	False alarms/malicious calls	5,368

	1985/86	1986/87
Net Annual Expenditure Per Head of Population	£16.43	£17.54

WHAT THE SERVICES COST

1985/86 Actual £000		1986/87 Budget £000	1986/87 Actual £000
33,255	Employees	35,146	35,618
4,483	Property, Supplies, Transport	4,696	4,629
3,271	Loan Charges	3,363	3,004
157	Other Expenditure	169	165
41,166		43,374	43,416
2,928	General Income	2,806	2,868
	Net Expenditure met from Rates and Rate		
38,238	Support Grant	40,568	40,548

MANPOWER NUMBERS

1985/86 Actual		1986/87 Budget	1986/87 Actual
2,891	Fire Service Personnel	2,896	2,893
286	Civilians	296	292
3,177		3,192	3,185

FIRE

RESPONSIBILITIES

The basic responsibilities of the Brigade remain the protection of life and property from fire and other emergencies.

The Technical Support Team, formed in response to the growth of chemical incidents, provides specialist assistance in dealing with, and advising on, hazardous substances within and outwith the Region, and is now recognized nationally for its high level of expertise.

The brigade also gives advice and enforces statutory legislation on matters of fire prevention.

DURING THE YEAR

The brigade control computerized mobilizing system dealt with 40,541 calls in 1986, despatching appliances and crews to a wide range of incidents.

In Glasgow, Springburn Fire Station was replaced by a modern building and the new Polmadie Fire Station replaced the former stations at Queen's Park and South.

A major refurbishment of Parkhead Fire Station was completed. Work was also completed on new stations at Muirkirk and Carluke, the latter now having become fully operational.

Appliance replacement continued as planned.

Seventy-one firemen were recruited during the period and a total of 854 members of the Brigade attended courses at the Brigade Training School.

During 1986, fire prevention officers inspected or gave advice on 21,316 sets of premises. In addition, 3,737 sets of plans were inspected for architects and building control authorities.

BUDGET PERFORMANCE

The net variance on this account was insignificant.

Employee costs were overspent by £0.5 million due to an increase in pension costs where 68 officers retired against an estimate of 45. Loan Charges were underspent by £0.4

Fig. 2.3 A service encapsulated (Strathclyde Regional Council).

Source: *Annual Report and Financial Statement 1986–87.*

(e) Establish variances from budget or target;
(f) Understand links between financial and other objectives;
(g) Establish trends;
(h) Make comparisons with other comparable bodies or services;
(i) Establish indebtedness;
(j) Establish, in appropriate cases, whether the organization is solvent.

It should be possible to do all these from information which is at an appropriate level of detail to meet user needs.

Accessibility

A common complaint among those who compile public sector financial reports is that they are not read. While minimal response and low sales might seem to justify such comments, it is often difficult for compilers to understand that few people even know that their reports exist or, if the documents are distributed automatically, that readers need help in understanding them. Potential readers of a report should be helped in this way after being made aware of its existence.

Pricing is also an issue in accessibility. If documents are too highly priced for potential readers, they can hardly be said to be very accessible.

So as a minimum, financial reports should be understandable, available and affordable by those interested and willing to make a reasonable effort to understand them. A number of steps can be taken to help the process. For example, the report should:

(a) Minimize jargon and acronyms, but not be patronizing;
(b) Have a logical structure and layout;
(c) Have a summary of key points;
(d) Not have an overwhelming amount of detail (regular pruning helps);
(e) Not be unduly distorted by public relations considerations;
(f) Be clear about the nature, cost and progress of major projects;
(g) Be clear about the impact of changing price levels.

Presentation is a particularly important aspect of accessibility. Despite the significant advances in the presentation of many financial reports in the past few years, there is still a great deal of room for improvement. The considerations to be taken into account will vary greatly between reports, but among those worth bearing in mind are the need for:

(a) Good balance between figures, text and photos/charts;
(b) Clear textual explanation of figures.

Figures 2.2a,b and 2.3 show examples of how information can be attractively presented. They are taken from the annual reports of Cambridgeshire County Council and Strathclyde Regional Council – two organizations which have won CIPFA awards in recent years.

Summary

This chapter has illustrated the varied nature of public sector financial reports covering financial matters. It has shown how the multiplicity of objectives of such reports reflects the variety of different kinds of bodies and different kinds of users. Nor can private sector practice simply be transferred to a public sector context – the nature of accountability is different and affects not only the formal differences of structure and rules but also the way the reports are used. Improvements in financial reporting are nonetheless widely acknowledged to be possible in both content and presentation.

Further reading

There are many different kinds of sources on aspects of public sector financial reporting. At a conceptual level, there is little work specifically on the public sector in the UK. Much of the discussion either emphasizes the private sector, for example *The Corporate Report* (ASC, 1976), or comes from other countries, as with the Australian Accounting Research Foundation's *Financial Reporting in the Public Sector* (1985). Each part of the public sector has some literature on the practical aspects of financial reporting and details of the latest developments are available from the relevant professional organizations and their journals. Good practice in presentation is exemplified in the results of the annual CIPFA Public Sector Accounts Award which are written up in *Public Finance and Accountancy*.

Chapter 3

Management accounting

Management accounting in nationalized industries and other public trading enterprises supplying goods or services for sale is very similar to the theory and practice of the private sector, as set out in many established textbooks which most readers of this book will doubtless have previously studied. Therefore, this chapter will concentrate on the distinctive features of management accounting, and related issues of financial management and control, in public service organizations which include central and local government, universities and polytechnics, and the National Health Service (NHS). Given that the co-author responsible for this chapter specializes in NHS financial issues, many of the examples of problems and practice cited in this chapter are drawn from the NHS – and readers interested in the NHS may usefully re-read this chapter again after they have read Chapter 8.

The chapter is divided among four main sections or themes: public services financial management and control to cash limits, cost and performance criteria and concepts, capital investment and project evaluation, and budgetary planning and control. In public services, where financial resources typically are cash-limited but the demand for service outputs often seems limitless, management by budgetary control against planned workload targets may be the most important single tool of successful management accounting and financial control.

Public services financial management

Public services exist primarily to provide service for the community, whether to individuals, families or the wider community. Additional to their service role, however, most public service organizations can trade, including seeking a profit or contribution on that trade, and/or they can make charges for some or all of their services. But it is of the essence for them that the making of profit is not a primary objective, and indeed in general most public services are funded from taxation or from rates or community charges which are independent of the amount of service consumed by individual payers. They do not have share capital, make profits or pay dividends. They may end up with annual surpluses (i.e. excesses of income over expenditure), but this is not usually a planned objective and any surpluses will normally be carried forward or in some way reinvested within the service – except that in the case of services funded **directly** by central government unspent balances/surpluses at the end of each financial year lapse and revert to the Treasury. Indeed in most public services there is a culture of belief in there being an important unmet need for their service, so that it would typically be seen as a sign of management failure to end the year with a revenue surplus, certainly if this reverted back to central or local government.

One virtue of the profit motive and of the need for reasonable profit in order for the private sector enterprise to survive, is the focusing of attention on a single, dominant objective. In the public sector, and taking the NHS as an example, it may appear that there is a single objective, the improvement of the nation's health. But how do you measure this in a single number, like net profit? Life expectancy perhaps? But that is only an estimate and the final outturn may be influenced more by education, prosperity and good housing and diet, the control of pollution, restraint in smoking and drinking, and the reduction of accidents at work and on the roads, than by the positive contribution of the NHS. And as people live longer, they need ever-increasing amounts of treatment or at least caring attention: people aged over 75 cost the NHS eight times as much per head on average, as do people of working age between 16 and 65. Almost by definition, health care (and services such as education, personal social services, road improvements, environmental upgrading, and leisure and welfare for the handicapped and disadvantaged) offer almost limitless potential for public benefit. So, as resources are not unlimited, there has to be a process of sharing or rationing among multiple objectives. In the case of the NHS the multiple, competing objectives include preventive, curative and caring medicine; acute, community and family-practitioner services; and particular target care groups such as maternity, children, the elderly and so on. We will return to this example in the context of programme budgeting, but it serves to illustrate the complexity of objective setting, and therefore of resource allocation and performance evaluation, in the public services.

Traditionally in public services, objectives and priorities, resource allocation, and the work ethos and values of the workplace culture have been determined by the leaders of the senior profession(s) in the particular public service – hospital consultant doctors, university professors, senior social workers, chief planning officers, etc. Thus the emphasis has been on professional service and values, and on professional leadership, rather than on managerial skills in the context of giving priority to issues of efficiency, productivity and the setting up of rigorous control systems. The government seeks to change this where it can, notably in the civil service, and in the NHS where the implementation of the Griffiths Report (DHSS, 1983) has resulted in the appointment of chief executives titled 'General Managers' in place of the former multidisciplinary management teams in which senior hospital doctors (and nurses) could exert great influence. However, it yet remains to be seen how far the culture of the general manager, and the strengthening of financial controls and management information systems, will succeed in permanently bringing doctors and other professionals into line with corporate management objectives. Here, and indeed also perhaps in universities, polytechnics and even local authorities, the term 'corporate management objectives' should perhaps be read as a euphemism for defining that set of objectives, policies, priorities and supporting management information and control systems as will enable the institution to score a high approval rating with central government and thus maximize future funding allocations and grant income.

Management to cash limits

The funding of most public services controlled by central government is by way of annual cash-spend allocations, commonly known as 'cash limits'. These have evolved since 1973 from the public expenditure planning process described in Chapter 2. Arguably the most important task of financial management in cash-limited services is to assist the other managers of the services to meet their operational objectives and cope with funding new developments and unexpected contingencies, yet still complete each year within the totals of the cash limits. Certain 'demand led' services such as social security payments for pensions and benefits, and some service costs of that part of the NHS providing family practitioner services, are not subject to cash limits – even though their costs of administration do come under cash limits, like also the external financing limits (EFLs) of nationalized industries and other public corporations such as water authorities.

Finance officers in each service usually should have some foresight of their likely cash limit (or, resource allocation) in time to be well advanced in their own internal budgeting before the new financial year begins. And then commences the annual cycle of expenditure control to cash limits, as illustrated in Fig. 3.1. The cycle begins with often extremely large cash limits (e.g. up to £100m or more for a large district health authority), and the art of financial management requires that this entitlement to draw cash at intervals through the year will result in successful balancing to the total cash limit by the end of the year. And while internal management budgeting and financial reporting will often be done on an income and expenditure accounting basis, arguably the predominant financial control system has to be cash flow accounting to comply with the cash limits.

Close monitoring and control of cash flow is critical at all times, but it becomes doubly critical for fine-tuning to balance to the cash limits target close to year-end. Respectable ways of slowing down spending

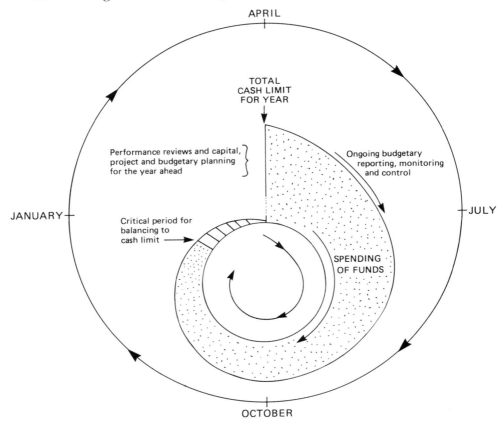

Fig. 3.1 Annual cycle of control to cash limits.

towards year-end include temporary freezes on filling non-urgent staff vacancies, delaying the start-up and staffing of planned new service developments, tightening stock control and delaying reordering of consumables, or sometimes transferring small amounts of capital funds to balance revenue expenditure. (It should be noted that this latter process is termed 'virement' and usually operates only under fairly strict rules.) A less respectable way of slowing spending (defined in cash terms) is simply to delay paying invoices from suppliers of goods and services at ever-longer intervals before year-end. Most of these slowdowns can be put into reverse if the following year's cash limit turns out to be larger than otherwise needed, but this is nowadays seldom the case, and the most pressing problems arise when two or three or more years in succession have cash limits inadequate to fulfil planned service pro-grammes, as in the NHS until recently. Most of the ways of slowing down cash spend cannot be repeated for more than a year or two, after which the only recourse may be to make cuts in services, as recently experienced in the NHS. Given that fixed costs are typically 60–80% of total costs, mainly for staff pay, spending cuts in public services tend first to affect postponable variable costs or costs of consumables, sometimes leading to a disproportionate reduction in the volume of service delivery.

Other sources of funds

Perhaps the second most important task of financial management in public services is to help find and administer supplementary sources of funding (including capital as well as revenue). Most UK public services historically have been government owned and supervised, and have been funded directly (e.g. the NHS) or indirectly (e.g. the universities) from public funds. This is in contrast to the much more pluralistic American scene, where services such as hospitals are frequently privately-run charities with little close governmental supervision. Thus the standard American text by Anthony and Young (1984) is about financial management in 'non-profit organizations' more widely, not just about the public sector. 'Non-profit' status does not require that an organization should not trade and seek to **earn** a profit/margin on that trading in order to build up reserves and to modernize and expand services, but rather that it does not **distribute** any profit to owners (although, it should be noted, a hospital can be founded as non-profit by local doctors who then use the hospital premises to earn themselves profitable fees in their personal capacities). Thus, most of the financial and accounting methods explained in Anthony and Young are almost the same as found in standard for-profit industrial textbooks – although their numerous case studies are distinctively based on public bodies and charities.

   Now it appears that the British government would like to go some way in the American direction, with public services becoming more commercial both in outlook and in sources of income. First it is thought this could encourage greater **efficiency** through a change of attitudes and increased competition (although this might not always result in greater **effectiveness**). Secondly, and perhaps even more importantly, this could aid the control and reduction of public expenditure through the substitution of other sources of funding for at least some public services. Against these two arguments, it is thought some civil servants and ministers are reluctant to accept the reduction in central direction and policy control which would almost certainly have to accompany any major transfer of fundraising from the public purse to locally driven, more commercial programmes. To trade and compete effectively with each other and perhaps also with the private sector, most public services would need much greater discretion or autonomy in selecting their programmes and priorities in services, in pricing those services to be marketed commercially, in raising capital reasonably freely by borrowing, and in entering more freely into legally binding contracts. They would also need freedom to determine pay by local negotiation.

Nevertheless, it does seem likely that commercial activity by the public services will increase. More local leisure and educational services may be asked to make a profit. Universities already seek to make profits from science parks and active recruitment of students from overseas. Health authorities have been assigned new tasks, under the lable of 'income generation', to increase the proportion of funds they raise from taking private patients and promoting advertising income and using their space to earn rental from shopping malls and businesses providing healthful leisure activities, etc. Finding capital for new initiatives may become an increasingly important task for senior financial officers in public services, while all their staff will need to work on improved costing systems and the application of cost analysis, and market and contract information, in search of optimal pricing and revenue situations.

Cost and performance criteria

In the nationalized industries (NIs) and in other public trading organizations the concepts, criteria and systems of cost and performance measurement and evaluation are closely similar to the practice of the private sector, as detailed by authors such as Wilson and Chua (1988), Drury (1988), and Emmanuel and Otley (1985). In essence these are geared to the measurement of profit or 'profit contribution' assessed at several levels: overall, by segment or division, by site or unit, and by product or service produced and marketed.

In the public services there is no single, tangible, easily quantifiable operational objective to take the place of 'operating profit', and so more complex concepts and measures of objectives and of performance review are needed. These include considerations of 'economy', 'efficiency', 'effectiveness' and 'value for money', all of which are summarized later in this section of the chapter. However, the measures of cost which are used in public services decision-making, control and performance review are not different in concept or definition from those normally used in business management accounting – even if the feasibility of producing certain types of cost information may be different. Very few public services are organized on a 'factory production line' basis. The costing situation sometimes approximates to process costing, sometimes to batch costing, and sometimes to the costing of customized contract units of output (e.g. every NHS hospital in-patient has a unique treatment need which is customized so far as resources permit). Thus data collection for the monitoring and cost control of public services can be complex and expensive.

Cost concepts and measures

At the risk of some over-simplification, cost concepts and measures can be subdivided between those especially relevant for planning and decision-making, and those continuously relevant for routine output costing, budgeting and formal performance review systems. As regards the first subdivision, the cost concepts under this heading are broadly as relevant in the public sector as in the private sector, and in the public services as in trading organizations.

Opportunity cost – the notion that the true cost of any use of (financial or other) resources is the forgone benefit from using those resources to generate the best alternative output or service – is basic to planning and decision-making in every type of enterprise, as in our private lives. Marginal cost – the concept derived from economics regarding the trade-off of cost and benefit at the margin (i.e. the extra unit of resource input required to generate an additional unit of output) – seems equally valid throughout the public sector. Related to this, and again equally valid, is the more conventional accountancy concern to distinguish accurately between fixed and variable costs, and their effect upon incremental or differential changes in the volume of output or service provided. And linked to this is contribution analysis, with its emphasis upon interrelating changes in variable costs and in the revenue generated. In the context of public services the practical application of the contribution analysis approach will often take the form of studying how cost savings can be made in existing services in order to free a contribution of funds to meet other unavoidable costs or assist the launch of approved new service developments.

Turning to the second subdivision, cost concepts and measures for use in routine costing, budgeting and performance measurement (and here the word 'routine' refers to regular, repeated and prompt monitoring of financial data at daily, weekly, monthly or other appropriate time intervals), comparability between public services and trading organizations, public or private, is much weaker. Whereas most trading enterprises produce or distribute a largely standardized product or service, such as a car or a bag of sugar, a high proportion of public services are labour-intensive with the input/output requirements very much tailored to the individual needs of beneficiaries (e.g. social service cases, hospital patients and PhD research students). It follows that commercial accounting techniques such as 'standard costing' have a much more limited range of application in the public sector, at least as regards setting target costs for the **final** outputs of public services. However, standard costing may become increasingly important for measuring and controlling **intermediate** outputs of public services, such as school meals, road resurfacing or X-ray tests in hospitals.

Most public sector organizations other than nationalized industries and some other public corporations maintain both their financial accounts and their cost accounts on a 'cash accounting' or 'income and expenditure' basis. Both of these systems disclose capital expenditure outlays, but neither includes charges for depreciation or alternative estimates of the annualized cost or value (e.g. replacement cost) of capital assets 'consumed' (i.e. worn out or made obsolescent). Such accounts provide incomplete and potentially misleading information for assessing performance in economy, efficiency and effectiveness (and value for money).

Much of the cost accounting in public services is essentially no more than reporting, sometimes with analysis into unit costs (typically of inputs rather than outputs), of categories of cash expenditure set against line-item budgets. However, sometimes this is modified to 'income and expenditure' accounting, bringing in changes in debtors, creditors and stocks so that cost accounts can reflect **consumption** of inputs and not just **cash expenditure** on inputs. Systems consciously structured around the concept of responsibility accounting, with its aim of identifying cost and budget accountability at every level, clearly discriminating between costs which are 'controllable' and 'not controllable' at each level, have so far not been widely used in public services, with the exception of the more progressive local authorities. But this approach is bound to expand throughout the public services. For example, the latest budgetary systems under development in the NHS involve tracing cost through from inputs to outputs, using intermediate (process) cost and budget centres with cost transfer/recharges in the form of standard costs with separate components for variable costs (mainly consumables) and fixed costs (mainly salaries).

Cost and management accounts typically are linked to financial accounts partly through sharing a common database of ledger information, and partly through an apparent instinctive feeling of the accountancy profession that cost and financial accounts should reconcile. Thus in many public services where depreciation accounting or other capital charges in lieu are not permitted in the financial accounts, then similarly, annualized capital charges are omitted from the cost and budget reports. Much work and systems development remains to be done in many public authorities before the cost information (and indeed the workload and output information) is of the desired quality for taking close judgements on performance in economy, efficiency, effectiveness and value for money.

Economy (inputs)

'Economy' defines the minimal cost of 'inputs' to an activity, whether achieved by purchasing cheaply or by closely restricting the consumption of resources. Whilst economy as a concept in isolation may be considered virtuous, it tells us nothing about the overall merit of expenditure or management: for example, the use of cheap lubricants in the propeller shaft of a frigate could result in the loss of a ship at sea or high salvage costs. Or, the use of cheap drugs following surgery could result in the death of a patient, or at least the need to repeat an operation where – aside from distress to the patient – the repeated costs of staff time may far exceed any original savings from economical purchasing. Thus 'economy', on its own, is a very limited concept for providing guidance to good management.

Efficiency (outputs/inputs)

'Efficiency' defines the relationship achieved between the outputs of a service or activity (such as the number of students taught and examined) and the volume or value of inputs consumed (e.g. teaching time, books, materials, space and heating, etc.) in generating those outputs. Thus efficiency is essentially a ratio relationship which can be improved by increasing the outputs relative to the inputs. Efficiency is similar to the concept of productivity, except that the latter is often used in the narrow sense of comparing output just to the volume or value of labour inputs, whereas a proper concept of efficiency will include the value of materials, support costs **and capital** within the inputs. Efficiency measures are often used as surrogates, or substitutes, in estimating the 'value for money' from particular public services.

Effectiveness (outcomes)

'Effectiveness' relates to the degree of success or failure attained in meeting objectives. It relates to the 'outcomes' achieved. Thus, to continue a previous example, a performance measure based on the number of students examined would not be very useful if all the students failed. So, we could amend the previous efficiency ratio to compare examination **passes** against the volume or value of teaching resources consumed. But merely passing examinations may not be good enough, so to cope with this we can assign weighting factors to the different grades of exam results. Have we now measured effectiveness, or success in achieving desired outcomes or objectives? The answer to this of course depends on what the objectives are. Are they to pass exams with good grades? Are they to provide a balanced education? Are they to prepare people for employment? Or some combination of all these?

Politicians, professionals and managers may set objectives for particular public services, and they will have their own, sometimes differing views on the desired outcomes and the criteria by which to measure success or failure. There are two points here: first, setting **objectives** and specifying **criteria** for measuring effectiveness and the quality of outcomes is both difficult and subjective. Secondly, the actual *measurement* of effectiveness and outcomes is often difficult, either because of the subjectivity or because it takes years to determine the full results or consequences of a public service initiative in areas such as education, social policy, health care and the environment.

Take one further example. Hospital consultant doctors have been discharging patients more quickly after operations and other treatments than in former years. Partly this is because of improved drugs and medical technology, but almost certainly it is also because of the doctors' awareness of the pressure on beds, admissions and waiting lists. However, some patients sent home too early relapse and have to be readmitted to hospital for further care and treatment, but probably without having to stay in hospital for as long a period as in the first episode of treatment. Under the present system of statistics-collection and efficiency assessment, the hospital would be credited with two separate admissions (i.e. higher productivity) and a shorter average length of stay (again higher productivity or efficiency), even though the actual events have resulted from a deterioration of service to the patient involving a low level of effectiveness and, temporarily at least, a reduced quality of outcome.

Value for money (VFM)

Increasing the 'value for money' (VFM) from public expenditure has been on the political and civil service agenda for many years under a variety of labels and with changes of emphasis between governments. The important priority given to VFM rose during the 1980s, and specific initiatives for particular branches of the public sector are discussed in the relevant chapters throughout this book, including the Rayner scrutinies, the financial management initiative (FMI) in central government, and the movement to general management and formalized performance reviews in the NHS. And in many parts of the public sector both internal and external audit are asked to devote up to 40 or even 50% of work time on VFM topics, as distinct from compliance and systems auditing. Success in improving VFM may require a change of attitudes or cultural behaviour among senior staff in many public services, where the traditional approach was to emphasize the quality of professional service, within available funding. The preceding subsections on the '3 Es', economy, efficiency and effectiveness, illustrate the risks of over-reliance on simple performance measures when the dominant objectives of public services such as education and health care should be the optimization of long-run benefit both to the individual and to the community.

The FMI has evolved mainly since 1979 but is based also on experience from earlier experiments in governmental planning and performance measurement. The FMI is specific to the management of central government but also has influenced the improvement of information and control systems in a wide range of public services accountable to central government. FMI involves the clear specification of objectives for organizations and managers, the clear definition of responsibilities in pursuit of the objectives, and the development of supportive information and training systems. In practice FMI is evolving not as a single 'uniform' system, but rather as an approach to good management tailor-made to the needs and problems of particular organizations and programmes. Some of the latter have been written about in informative articles in *Public Finance and Accountancy*, and a selection of these has been published in a booklet (CIPFA, 1988) which also includes a foreword by Professor Peter Jackson, providing historical context and a most useful set of source references. The essence of FMI is the search for improved VFM and the achievement of the '3 Es' discussed previously.

Investment and project evaluation

Capital

It is a characteristic of many public sector organizations that they are very capital intensive, at least if we define this as the ratio of **accumulated total value** of capital stock relative to annual revenue spending. It was one of the arguments for the original nationalization of industries such as coal, steel and electricity that fragmented private ownership in those days was unable to raise the large amounts of capital needed to modernize. Enormous sums of capital (especially if valued at replacement cost) are involved also in other public services including motorways and other roads, dams and pipelines, sewers, prisons, universities and schools, hospitals, and city and county halls. The bulk of these public assets have very long lives, typically 30–100 years or more. They do require often-expensive maintenance in order to fulfil their life potentials, but measurement of this, and of the expiry of useful economic life and the optimal timing of capital replacement, is largely subjective.

Not all public service work is capital intensive. Much civil service and other public administration can be conducted in general-purpose office accommodation leased or rented from the private sector with the capital costs borne by the private developer but annualized into the rent payments and thus fundable from public sector revenue allocations. Rents and many other costs being higher in London and other city centres, there is continuing pressure to relocate government offices to lower-cost areas on economy grounds, aside from regional policy. But administrative and some other public service activities not thought of as capital intensive do nevertheless cause substantial investment requirements in vehicles and increasingly in computers and related office systems. Here public sector funding practice can often depart from commercial accounting practice. In conventional accounting all assets with a useful life exceeding one year are classified as 'fixed assets', and investment in these is properly treated as capital expenditure. However, it is often the case in public services that while the initial supply of furnishings, equipment and computers, etc., to a new installation is funded out of capital grant, later renewals or replacements must be met out of revenue funds.

Universities and local authorities are allowed to set aside portions of revenue, comparable in amount to depreciation charges, to invest in 're-newal funds' in anticipation of future replacement needs, especially for vehicles, mechanical plant and office equipment where service lives and/or technical obsolescence are reasonably predictable. In contrast, the NHS is not allowed to have formal renewal funds, and indeed it is not allowed to save, or put aside, any current funding in the form of invest-ments to meet future needs.

Investment appraisal

Investment appraisal, also sometimes termed capital appraisal, project appraisal or option appraisal, appears to vary considerably in relative importance and in the way in which it is applied across the various branches of the public sector. Clearly the importance is greatest in nationalized industries and in other public corporations, trading funds and direct labour organizations (DLOs) required by government to earn all or most of their revenue from trading activities. Indeed, the actual mechanics of investment appraisal in these organizations should be closely comparable with the private sector, since they are enjoined to behave in a commercial manner, either largely ignoring social cost benefits or else dealing with these by separate analysis, and preferably with any consequential funding of social responsibilities provided by way of separately identifiable grants or subsidies (e.g. for the continuance of specific types of loss-making public transport services, or for the encouragement of alternative employment in localities where public enterprises have been shut down). Good practice for the private sector in respect of investment appraisal and decision analysis is detailed in standard texts such as Drury (1988), Lumby (1988), Puxty and Dodds (1988), Samuels and Wilkes (1986) and Van Horne (1986).

It is not the purpose of this book, nor is there space, to attempt to explain or to illustrate the details of discounted cash flow (DCF) analysis in investment appraisal. But it may be in order to add a word of warning for readers who have not studied standard texts such as the above. Basic models in DCF often ignore the implications of inflation, so that students – or indeed even practising accountants – may be misled into using current market rates of interest to discount future cash flows estimated in today's market prices. The problem is that current market rates of interest reflect estimated future inflation, but today's market prices of cash-flow trading inputs and outputs do not do this. As Lumby shows (1988, Chapter 6), one can discount using either (1) today's market interest rate applied to estimated future inflation, or (2) the 'real' rate of interest (i.e. market rates discounted for inflation) applied to constant or present-day valuations of net cash flows (ignoring future inflation but taking account of relative market price movements, and of expected technological and efficiency changes). In perfect markets both methods should yield identical results – in theory. However, markets are not perfect and human beings estimating the future will often make errors. The alternative favoured by many economists, and certainly those at the Treasury who influence the guidelines for public sector capital investment, has been (2) (see Treasury, 1982).

Moreover, whereas an approximation of the 'real' (i.e. true or long-term average) rate of interest can be generated by discounting the current market rate of interest (for a given level of risk) by the current rate of inflation, this short-run estimate of the 'real' rate of interest can be badly distorted by current market sentiment. Government and academic researchers have studied the long-term 'real rate of return' of British industry and commerce during this century. Allowing for the distortions from two world wars, the statistical information systems that developed changed their measurement criteria and became increasingly sophisticated. When the debate over how to treat taxation which changed in composition and rates during the period, is also considered, it seems a reasonable approximation that the real (i.e. inflation adjusted) rate of return in British industry and commerce was of the order of 8% per annum. Successive governments broadly agreed that public sector investment should not be made at the expense of investment in industry with export potential. Therefore a test discount rate (TDR) of 8% (1967) rising to 10% (1969) was imposed as the discount rate to be used in nationalized industries and in other public corporations where investment decisions were to be made on a commercial basis. See Perrin (1984) for detail and reference sources.

By the 1970s the recommended approach to analysis became more sophisticated, or certainly more realistic. Whereas the original concept of the TDR was that of a discount rate to be applied to each individual project, except for some essential/replacement projects, it was realized that many projects in the public sector have to be undertaken, even in public trading organizations, for safety or environmental reasons. The emphasis therefore shifted (White Paper, 1978) to annual reviews of total investment programmes, based on inflation-adjusted required rates of return (RRR). Also it was realized by the 1970s that the real return to British private industry had fallen below the 8% figure earlier mentioned under pressure of domestic and international competition.

The new RRR (often even now still referred to as the TDR) was set at 5% (both as the target overall earnings rate and as the discount rate for composite investment programmes) for trading activities in the public sector. Initially, the non-trading sector was told to add a further 2%, i.e. to 7%, when using a discount rate on cost-saving investments, in order to compensate for likely 'appraisal optimism'. Later guidance (Treasury, 1982) authorized the 5% RRR/TDR to be used generally in all types of public sector organizations.

Cost-benefit and cost-effectiveness analysis

Investment appraisal is a method of financial analysis developed mainly in the for-profit private sector. When carried out properly it attempts to take account of risk and uncertainty, but the analysis is usually restricted to quantifiable market costs and revenues. For the public sector, in contrast, the attempt has been made (more by economists than by accountants) to develop wider-ranging systems of evaluation which will take account also of social costs and benefits. The main techniques here are cost-benefit analysis (CBA) and cost-effectiveness analysis (CEA). Both approaches are widely discussed in many economics texts, and also in Glynn (1987) and Jones and Pendlebury (1988). For some branches of the public sector specialized texts on appraisal, CBA and CEA have been written – for example, Drummond's book (1980) on the NHS.

In principle CBA seeks to identify, measure and value all the significant costs, and likewise all the significant benefits, arising to society from a particular project. Normally projects subjected to a thorough CBA study need to be fairly large and costly – such as a new airport, new motorway, major innovations in the provision of education or health care, etc. – in order to justify the heavy expense of thorough and expert study. Of the three stages, identification of the significant costs and benefits should generally be the easiest, yet where there is a high level of innovation, especially involving new science and technology, experience teaches that important aspects can be overlooked or underestimated for their long-term significance. Nuclear power and nuclear waste disposal provide extreme examples. Taking these examples further, note that the relevant costs and benefits to society extend beyond issues of efficiency, profitability, local employment and staff safety, to encompass issues of wider concern to the entire community, including not only the macroeconomic need for cheap power but also critically the public health of present and future generations.

In practice it is extremely difficult to bring into account all relevant social costs and benefits to be fairly weighted in the CBA analysis. For example, many of the programmes of care and welfare for priority groups such as the handicapped, the elderly or young children ideally need the integrated contribution of skills, facilities and other resources from both local authorities and the NHS. But these two types of public services are funded so differently and have such different frameworks of political accountability that it becomes very difficult for them to cooperate efficiently in many cases, for example at the stage of major project and investment planning for community care services when good CBA evaluations should embrace both sides of the cooperation boundary with equal weight and detail.

The second stage, measurement, involves the quantification of the physical volumes or other characteristics of the identified cost and benefit factors, e.g. freight ton miles on a motorway, deaths arising in motorway accidents related to deaths avoided on other types of transport, deaths and congenital consequences from nucelar radiation, mobility of the elderly and their differing abilities to look after themselves in community hostels compared to traditional long-stay hospitals. Here the measurements are often no more than estimates or forecasts of likely but problematic future events or innovations interdependent with other assumptions contained within the CBA study. Sometimes formalized risk analysis may be feasible, with probabilities and weights calculated, although if this is used just to produce a 'one best solution' dependent on the experts' hunches and biases, there is wide room for human error and the reaching of misleading conclusions. Therefore it is widely encouraged to introduced sensitivity analysis and produce a CBA report which reflects a range of assumptions and possible outturns, so that skilled managerial and political readers of the reports can obtain a better 'feel' for realistic future probabilities.

The third stage of CBA, applying monetary value to costs and benefits, involves judgemental problems and risks of biases similar to the two preceding stages. In the example of motorways, increased ton miles of freight moved, decreased lorry travel times, the net loss or gain in numbers of road deaths and injuries, and the environmental value of removing more lorries from town and village streets, cannot directly be aggregated to a single net cost or benefit unless the physical measurements are first allocated fair monetary values. Here again it is wise to recognize that experts cannot be certain and may not be free of professional bias, so it can be useful to apply further sensitivity analysis. Then, where feasible and likely to yield useful information, discounted cash flow (DCF) analysis can be applied to identify a range of possible/probable net present values (NPV) or equivalent annual cost (EAC) estimates. Each CBA report should fully document the assumptions, measurement and valuation criteria, and the sensitivity analysis methods used, in order to assist readers to evaluate the technical quality and the practical credibility of the CBA study and its findings.

Turning to cost-effectivenss analysis (CEA), this approach can be used where the scale of the project does not merit a full-blown CBA, where the prospective social benefits are too vague to attempt to quantify, or where the benefits would be unchanged and the decision will turn mainly on the comparative cost effectiveness of alternative solutions. For example, if a university campus or a large hospital is going to install new central heating boilers because the old boilers are too expensive on fuel, too expensive to maintain, or are emitting an unacceptable level of pollution, and if moreover it is confirmed that new boilers using alternative fuels all have similar levels of pollution control, then the project decision normally will turn on comparative cost efficiency or effectiveness, taking account of capital outlays and life expectancy, fuel costs now and as forecast for future years, and predicted maintenance costs. Thus the problem appears to have been reduced to the same elements found in commercial industrial investment appraisal or capital budgeting decisions (Drury, 1988). Perhaps the one main difference is that in a good CEA study a more thorough search for the less tangible costs and benefits will have been made, and even though some of these may be unquantifiable or seemingly of only marginal importance, the attempt will be made in a good CEA report to describe and evaluate them for the assistance of decision-makers.

This section has discussed public sector capital in the context of project evaluation for new commitments. This is most important for obtaining best value from public money. But there is also the problem of how to adapt cost and management accounting to monitor the consumption and maintenance of public capital after it has been invested (Perrin, 1984). This problem, in essence the question of whether or not depreciation accounting (or asset lease charges or some other measure of capital consumption) should be adopted widely in the public services, has been controversial and unresolved for more than a decade. There is the related question of whether, how and to what degree the financial accounts of public services should report the impact of inflation on asset values, depreciation and other costs. These questions have vexed the nationalized industries, water authorities and other public corporations also, and a major study, the 'Byatt Report' (Treasury, 1986), has strongly commended the use of a modified form of current cost accounting as the basis for valuation and depreciation of public sector assets.

Planning, budgeting and control

Planning comprises looking ahead and attempting to forecast the future (in technological, market, economic or political terms and contexts), searching out and evaluating alternatives (i.e. options) for future action, deciding objectives and priorities, and then proceeding to work out resource needs and sources, and how to allocate and control resources, to achieve the targeted objectives and priorities over a particular period of time. Planning is one of the basic elements of the management process. Thus 'planning' is not uniquely or even primarily a financial or accountancy function, and this applies also to the definition and process

of 'management control'. In both cases the main role of the accountant or
finance officer is to act as a 'facilitating agent', providing the relevant
management information and reports upon which management should
act in order to plan, control and improve performance.

Planning can be short term, medium term (i.e. one to five years ahead),
or long term (up to ten years ahead, as with complex initiatives such as
the total planning of major hospitals, new universities or new weapon
systems). The more senior the level of management, the higher the
proportion of planning time and responsibility which is focused on the
longer term and on projects with relatively high capital investment
relative to annual revenue funding. The greatest amount of long-term
planning should thus occur at the top of the management hierarchy.
Nationally, this should mean at ministerial level with the senior civil
servants, but there is some evidence that this has not always happened
(see Heclo and Wildavsky, 1981), perhaps because political criteria and
decision timescales do not extend so far into the future as may be
required for optimal management.

Budgeting is the process of measuring and converting plans for the use
of 'real' (i.e. physical) resources into financial values. It is the classic
problem of how to add together quantities of apples and oranges into a
meaningful economic measurement – the only practical way for everyday
use is to express their economic values in terms of monetary costs and
revenues. Through this process of budgeting, the finance function
provides the essential link between management planning and management control.

Basics of budgeting

The basic principles and mechanics of budgeting are the same for the
family, the private sector for-profit firm, and the public sector. These
principles and mechanics, including the behavioural dimension which is
receiving ever-growing recognition for its importance, are discussed at
length in standard texts such as Drury (1988), Emmanuel and Otley
(1985), and Wilson and Chua (1988). However, it is interesting to note
that the concept of budgeting developed in the public sector, presumably
because governments were the first extremely large organizations (aside
from the Roman Catholic Church, which was possibly the western
world's first 'multinational' organization), and also because governments
effectively decide their total revenue once a year when decisions on
taxation are taken, so that the spending of money has to be 'rationed out'
to stay within the expected inflow of tax revenues.

In contrast, in the private sector the biggest budgets – for labour and on
goods for conversion or resale – need to be 'flexible' to respond quickly to
success or failure in obtaining new orders and sales. However, even in the
private sector there are many budgets which are 'fixed' (i.e. predeter-

mined in total amount for the budget year) in the same way as the budgets for most activities in cash-limited public services. Fixed budgets are often used in private firms for cost centres such as head-office expense, research and development, personnel and training, advertising and promotion, and other activities where there is no direct, short-term linkage between expenditure and the generation of new income.

The evidence that budgeting is basically a public sector concept arises from the origin of the word 'budget'. 'Budget' derives from the Old French word, 'bougette', a kind of leather bag, in which during the Middle Ages the Chancellor of the Exchequer took his tax proposal papers into Parliament. The tradition still continues in the annual display before television cameras of the Chancellor's dispatch case on Budget Day.

Line-item budgeting

Traditional budgeting in public services, designed to aid the allocation of funds and the monitoring and control of expenditure against allocations and uses approved by Parliament, is termed 'line-item budgeting', or sometimes 'subjective budgeting' which is perhaps a more apt description. This kind of budgeting simply provides one line of information for each kind (or 'subject') of income and of expenditure. On the expenditure side of the budget, payroll costs, typically 60 to 80% of total costs in public services, are the main items. Other items will typically include costs such as categories of consumables (e.g. stationery, drugs, provisions) and other running expenses (e.g. telephone, rent, travel expenses, etc.). At its most basic, this line-item budgeting provides a single, overall budget for a government department or other organization as a whole – that is, as a single organizational entity.

As organizations have grown bigger and managerially more complex, line-item budgets have been subdivided between the different managerial parts of the organization. This subdivision can be done on the basis either of the operational sub-units (e.g. schools, libraries, hospitals), or of the particular professions or functions where organizational leadership and control are centred. Thus, for example, the NHS used 'functional budgeting' from 1974 until after the full implementation of the Griffiths Report (1983), with all budgets allocated vertically down through the particular professional (i.e. 'functional') officer (e.g. district nursing officer) to be held accountable.

The essence of line-item or subjective budgeting is that primary concern, and control, is on the **kinds** of pay, goods and services on which public money is spent. This does not provide information or motivation greatly helpful to managerial efficiency and performance accountability at the local level. That is because this type of budgeting is simply a system for allocating, or rationing, particular kinds of **inputs**. These input allocations are not related in any way to the intended outputs, let alone outcomes, of the particular public service – nor are they necessarily closely related to the internal management structure of the local public service unit. To illustrate this, we can take an example from universities and polytechnics. Until recent years telephone costs (and often stationery costs and many other support service costs) were budgeted as an overall cost for the entire organization, with a central administrator (typically the bursar or registrar) notionally accountable for the level and control of expenditure. If telephone costs looked like going significantly over budget, admonishing letters would be sent out to staff in academic departments. Often these had little effect. So it was realized that the only effective way to control telephone costs was to make each department accountable for its own costs, in a budgetary control context where staff could see that if money was spent on telephones there was the opportunity cost that less money could be spent on stationery, photocopying, library orders, computer support, conference attendance, etc. Of course, in order to introduce departmental user budgets for telephones it was first necessary to invest capital in telephone logging equipment or to require departments to have 'direct lines' for all external telephoning.

Input v. output budgeting

Fixed budgets (i.e. firm allocations of money as a maximum limit to spending on specific categories of resources over a given period of time) are characteristic of the public services. This is perfectly natural, given the historical desire of governments and administrators at all levels to control and limit spending within politically determined parameters. But such budgets only deal with resource inputs consumed, and they tell us nothing about the level (or quality) of the outputs of services provided. In contrast, a factory or other trading business can use 'flexible budgets' which separate out fixed and variable costs and show differing allowable levels of total cost for different levels of output. It is then up to good marketing and sales management to maximize profit contribution from sales, while production management strives to meet or improve upon the flexible budgets of production and other supply costs at the sales volume achieved. Thus, industrial and commercial budgeting broadly reflects both inputs and outputs, though it is the marketable outputs which drive the financial system as a whole. In contrast, the problem for public services typically is that an increase in demand for services in excess of forecasts produces no extra revenue but if met will often force an increase of spending on variable costs. Taking the NHS as an example, a winter 'flu epidemic will raise expenditure on drugs, staff overtime and support costs, but will bring in no extra NHS grant revenue.

There has been criticism, especially from economists, regarding the failure of public sector resource allocation and budgeting to relate

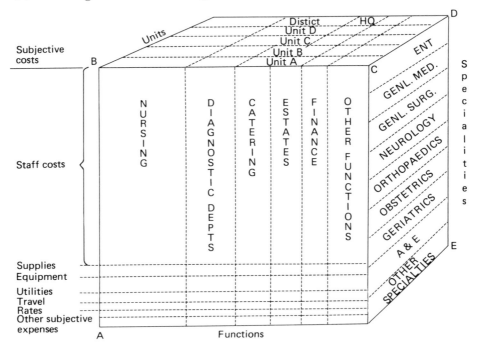

Fig. 3.2 Budgets subdivided by subjective costs, functional management, management units and specialties (or clinicians).

expenditure to outputs intended or achieved. Some useful suggestions have been made (Culyer, 1973) and indeed many public bodies in recent years have greatly improved both their planning and budget documentation, and their financial reporting of outturn, so as to reclassify their line-item/subjective/functional expenditure by categories of output. But of course even 'outputs' is only a half-way position in the measurement of performance. Our objective is good outcomes: good education, permanently cured patients, roads which will give a good surface longer before needing repaving, and sewers which will not collapse under the weight of lorries and release plagues of rats. However, it may take years to establish the results of many public-service programmes before outcomes such as the foregoing can be properly evaluated, even assuming they are capable of objective measurement for evaluation. Thus, although conceptually desirable, it seems unlikely that the use of target outcomes (e.g. a given proportion of former students qualifying in recognized professions, or of heart surgery patients who live for at least a further ten years) will become a practical feature of public sector financial planning and control reporting systems within the foreseeable future.

The problems of moving from line-item or input budgeting to a form of output budgeting more useful for management planning and control can be illustrated by the experience of the NHS, summarized in Fig. 3.2. From 1948 to 1974 the main financial information system in the NHS was subjective (i.e. line-item) costing and budgeting. This is shown in the figure by the subdivisions along line AB, but for simplification only a few token cost headings are listed. The annual expenditure reports required from the NHS authorities extended to some fifty pages of line-item cost detail.

Following the 1974 reorganization of the NHS the principle of 'functional' (or profession-led) management structure and resource accountability was introduced. This is represented in the figure by the plane ABC. That is, the subjective cost headings were retained but these had to be subdivided and reallocated to budgets controlled by the heads of the functions, such as Nursing and individual diagnostic departments such as Pathology or Radiology. Hospital doctors in general held no budgets, even though they were the main driving forces dictating the workload of patient admissions and treatments, and the resource demands on expensive drugs and other support services.

However, doctors and others were critical of delay and remoteness in decision-taking and resource accountability in the NHS, and so it resulted that one of the features of the 1982 reorganization was that new, subordinate 'units' (e.g. individual hospitals) of management were established as separate budget centres within the health authorities. Thus, in the figure, plane BCD illustrates how the subjective cost and budget categories, already subdivided between functions, were then re-subdivided between the units of management. The further management reforms which followed the Griffiths Inquiry (1983), including the appointment of new 'general managers' (i.e. chief executives) at every organizational level from unit upwards, served to strengthen the importance of budgetary planning and control centred on the units. However, although we have briefly described three stages in the evolution of NHS accounting and budgeting, ending up with budgetary accountability much closer to the 'sharp end' of patient services, the systems described are still basically line-item input budgets, and not output budgets.

The doctors who provide the outputs from NHS hospitals are the 'clinical consultants' who work together in teams based on their medical or surgical specialities. Their patients are individuals, each with separate problems and needs, and yet, averaging over large numbers of patients in each individual speciality, there should be some consistency in their resource requirements, costs and budget funding needs. This potential development is illustrated in the figure by plane CDE. But 'easier said than done'. The data for input budgeting are easily available from payroll records and invoice files which have to be kept anyway for cash expenditure control. But recording, costing and tracing the cost of every X-ray, drug prescription, pathology test, physiotherapy session, etc., for every patient, so that this gets accurately charged to the costs/budgets of the relevant specialty supervising treatment, is not easy. It is expensive of staff time, and research and development work over some fifteen years has confirmed that the information cannot be processed quickly enough to meet budgetary control monthly-reporting requirements without extensive, and again expensive, computing support. The nagging question is, will the benefit from more sensitive management and budgetary control information justify the cost of providing that information and the advisory staff needed to interpret it and influence professional staff to take action? Or would it be better to forget about the sophisticated computers and support staff, and instead spend the money directly on the public services the organization exists to provide?

As will be seen more clearly from Chapter 8 on the NHS, our National Health Service is an extremely complex multi-product/service organization. It is also an example – perhaps the ultimate example – of a public service organization driven by 'the professionals' as distinct from 'the managers', although the present government has set out to change that culture and indeed even to introduce the notion of the primacy of the consumer.

Programme budgeting

An extension to the idea of output budgeting, where units of output can be fairly small or specialized (such as an accounting graduate, a mile of road repaved, or a hernia cured) is to try to plan and budget services for a complete 'client group' or other logical combination of service activities or objectives. Thus in the NHS the attempt has been made to plan services and resource allocation (budget) needs for the elderly, the mentally handicapped, and other priority groups. One hospital specialty, 'geriatrics', is exclusively concerned with the health care of the elderly. But elderly people are treated also by most of the other hospital specialities, and by family doctors, dentists and opticians. And they are cared for in the community by district nurses and other specialized carers. Thus, a 'programme' of care for the elderly has to bring together activity, commitment and funding from a variety of sources. Ideally, one would include services not just from the NHS, but also related services provided by local government and social security, and indeed by voluntary organizations and other charities. All this becomes very complex. It may provide a very useful exercise for global planning by academics, civil servants, economists and other planning specialists. It may help also in assisting judgement and decisions at the margin on priorities for resource allocation between competing uses in spending public money.

Formalized systems of programme budgeting have been tried. The best known of these is PPBS (i.e. Planning, Programming and Budgeting System), which evolved in the USA and achieved some success and fame in its application within the US Department of Defense in the 1960s and 70s. High priority and a great deal of time and money were invested in this PPBS exercise, but when attempts were made to introduce similar programme budgeting initiatives in other public authorities with less money and commitment available, the results were not encouraging in the USA, or in the UK where the approach was tried in a few local authorities. Jones and Pendlebury (1988) provide a comprehensive discussion of PPBS and of programme budgeting more generally.

Probably the fundamental weakness of PPBS and programme budgeting is that the approach inherently conflicts with the natural logic of hierarchical management accountability and control systems. That is, good accountability and control for use of resources is difficult to achieve if responsibility is shared, diffused or 'splintered' (in management jargon) among several managers or budgetholders. A basic principle of conventional management budgeting is that budget allocations, reports and accountability must conform precisely to the organizational responsibility structure (i.e. as illustrated in organization charts – provided these are accurate and up to date, which frequently they are not). And so to the extent that programme budgeting has any future, it may be that it would be more useful if it were retitled programme resource allocation planning (PRAP) to emphasize that this is primarily a **planning** exercise.

Zero-base budgeting

An alternative approach is called 'zero-base budgeting' (ZBB). In its most pure or extreme form ZBB operates by putting it to every senior budgetholder each year that there is no prima facie reason why his budget (and his job, staff and activities) should continue to be funded, unless he can demonstrate the importance, value and cost efficiency of each of his activities and uses of resources. ZBB is the direct opposite of traditional public sector budgeting (often called 'incremental budgeting'), in which the customary assumption is that existing activities will be continued with automatic uplift for allowed inflation rates, and with any real debate about the budgets being focused on the 'increment' – that is, what new money can be made available and what is the most useful improvement or development to which it should be applied. If this incremental approach is the only dimension to a budgetary review, then the opportunity to search for obsolete activities, and for efficiency and productivity improvements, will have been missed.

Implementation of ZBB can involve the commitment of a great deal of top management time (and the expense of support staff or management consultants) that arguably could be better spent on getting on with other current tasks of good managment. The ZBB process involves identifying organizational decision units and decision packages: these relate to modules of activity and resources which are relatively self-contained and could be continued or 'switched off' independent of other parts of the work programme. Next, these decision packages or modules require to be ranked for relative social and political importance, and for efficiency and value for money (VFM). The budgetholder and support staff then have to present and argue their case in front of a panel of other senior staff, peers or assessors. All this consumes a great deal of expert and top managment time so **annual** ZBB budget reviews may not be worth the expense – or the opportunity cost – while the amount of savings or change achieved would presumably diminish quickly from year to year as the initial insights and benefits were implemented, and as the participants became accustomed to the gamesmanship of managerial survival under the ZBB system. However, this does not mean that the broad concept behind ZBB is invalid or that public authorities would not benefit from applying this approach to all activities or units on a cycle of, say, every five to ten years.

ZBB is but one particular and formalized approach to discover and correct the waste of resources. For years it has been widely recognized that managers attempt to pad their budgets with marginal income to cope with inefficiency and/or with unpredictable contingencies – this is known as 'budgetary slack'. Eminent writing on these problems has come from Hofstede in his *Game of Budget Control* (1968) and in his classic article specific to not-for-profit organizations (1981). Quite aside from the natural desire of all managers/budgetholders, whether working in the private sector or in the public sector, to minimize their personal stress by holding some budgetary slack in reserve, there is the further problem, more specific to the public sector, that many budgetholders see themselves first and foremost as professional leaders of services, with the quality and quantity of service provided being more important than budget watching.

Summary

Nationalized industries and other public trading organizations usually follow 'best commercial practice' in their financial accounting, and also use cost and management accounting methods very similar to those of the private sector as described in standard textbooks. But for public services including central administration, social services, local government, education and the National Health Service, industrial-style cost and management accounting is not so easy to apply – the service outputs are much more diverse and tailored to individual needs rather than to a standard product. This chapter therefore has concentrated on the distinctive management accounting, and related financial management and control issues, of public services. Most public services are funded by cash-limited resource allocations, and so the dominant element of financial control has to be cash control.

Increasingly, however, there has been pressure on public services to prove that they are achieving economy, efficiency and effectiveness (or value for money) in their use of real resources. This has involved the development of better management accounting and control systems, and performance measurement and review systems. Central government has developed the FMI, local government has improved its budgetary control, and the NHS has experimented with new costing and budgetary systems which will be explained in detail in Chapter 8. However, although sometimes more difficult to apply in practice in public services than in industry, the same basic principles and concepts of good costing for decision-making and control apply in both sectors: opportunity cost, marginal cost, and fixed/variable cost and contribution analysis.

Many public services are 'capital led'. If society invests in a motorway, school, university or hospital, there is inevitable pressure to use, staff and maintain that facility. It is thus clearly of high importance that realistic and thorough investment appraisal should take place before capital investment decisions are taken. Where there is no measurable financial return (or saving) from an investment, then techniques of option appraisal, cost benefit analysis, and/or cost effectiveness analysis, must be used. The use of depreciation accounting, and how to reflect the effects of inflation, remain controversial and unresolved issues in management and financial accounting for the public services.

Given that most public services are cash limited and therefore have fixed budget allocations for each year's workload, regardless of the 'demand' made by the public on services after the start of the financial year, it follows that the dominant financial control system in most public service organizations is budgetary control, typically based on 'fixed' as distinct from 'flexible' budgets. Various specialized techniques such as programme budgeting and zero-base budgeting have been tried in the public sector, but they have not proved highly successful. A fundamental problem is that most public services have multiple outputs and objectives, unlike the profit-maximization role of private business, so that it becomes much harder to take decisions on funding allocations between competing services. In the end, many decisions have to be based on a trade-off between political and professional priorities.

Further reading

Management accounting in the public sector uses most of the techniques explained in standard textbooks, but with distinctive sociopolitical and behavioural constraints – see *Issues in Public Sector Accounting* (Hopwood and Tomkins, 1984). Current technical coverage is provided in *Public Finance and Accountancy*. Academic articles of relevance appear occasionally in *Accounting, Organizations and Society, Financial Accountability and Management, Public Administration*, and *Public Money and Management*.

Chapter 4

Central government

The planning and control of public expenditure is an essential element in the government's financial and social policy. This chapter explains how public expenditure is planned, controlled and monitored by central government and how that relates to the role of Parliament. It describes the system of central government accounts and the development of financial management within government departments.

The meaning of public expenditure

In the United Kingdom the public sector comprises central and local government and the public corporations, including the nationalized industries. Broadly speaking, public expenditure is the total of central and local government spending, plus financial transfers from the former to the public corporations. Central and local government expenditure together form 'general government expenditure', which is a definition also widely used in Europe. The 'public expenditure planning total', which is discussed below in the description of the public expenditure survey system, excludes government debt interest because it is not so immediately under control as other government spending, but includes all the external finance which public corporations need to obtain. A large part of local authority expenditure is financed by grants from central government – in effect from the taxpayer – so these amounts are netted out when calculating general government expenditure. But they are included in the funds for which central government has to apply to Parliament through the 'Supply' procedure explained below.

As Fig. 1.1 showed, public expenditure can be examined in various additional ways, for example:

(a) By department (ministry) – Department of Health, Ministry of Defence, Department of Trade and Industry, and so on;
(b) By function – health, social security, employment, housing, transport;
(c) By economic category – direct calls by government on labour and other resources, transfer payments to individuals or companies.

The departmental and functional categories may largely coincide, for example in defence, where all the functional responsibilities fall to one ministry. In other cases several departments may be involved in the provision of a functional service, for example law and order, where not only does the Scottish department share responsibility with the Home Office but there is a major local authority component as well. For nearly thirty years it has been accepted policy to consider the total demand of public expenditure programmes in relation to the nation's taxable capacity, including taxes locally imposed, and in relation to national resources.

The public expenditure survey system

There have been major changes in the way in which public expenditure is planned, controlled and presented in the last decade or so and changes are still in progress. Their significance is best appreciated in the light of a brief review of the public expenditure survey system.

The system originated with the report in 1961 of the Committee chaired by Sir Edwin Plowden: *The Planning and Control of Public Expenditure.* The central recommendations were that 'regular surveys should be made of public expenditure as a whole, over a period of years ahead, and in relation to prospective resources; decisions involving substantial future expenditure should be taken in the light of these surveys.' This system has formed the basis of successive governments' approaches ever since, though the techniques have been progressively developed and policy on the scope and purposes of public expenditure has changed markedly from time to time.

The main features of the system were as follows:

(a) A factual forward costing of 'existing policies' governing expenditure was made annually by a committee of senior officials – the Public Expenditure Survey Committee – with proposals for further spending by departments separately identified;

(b) This was done at 'constant prices', which led to severe problems of estimating and budgetary control;

(c) Although the estimates – for up to four years ahead – covered the whole of public expenditure, important parts of it, notably local authorities' current expenditure, were not subject to direct control by central government.

The survey completed, ministers had to take decisions. The Chancellor of the Exchequer put forward his own proposals for levels of public expenditure in relation to his judgement of their validity and of the prospects for the economy. The way in which this judgement was made, and the methodology used, varied over the years. The following alternative methods have been used in the past:

(a) The expected growth rate of the national output (gross domestic product) was compared with the estimated growth of public expenditure, generally with the object of avoiding the latter exceeding the former;

(b) An assessment was made of the demands of 'prior claims' on the national output – the resources required for productive investment and the balance of payments – and a view was taken of the desirable division of the remainder, itself the bulk of the total, between public expenditure and private consumption. This work centred on the 'medium-term economic assessment' and was related to the use of resources in the economy rather than to financial objectives;

(c) Linked to (b), attention was concentrated on the implications for personal and company taxation of public expenditure plans, to see if prospective tax levels appeared acceptable or not.

When ministers had taken decisions about the totals of public spending in the next years ahead and its distribution among the departmental programmes, the annual Public Expenditure White Paper was prepared and presented to Parliament. This was done every year from the late 1960s, until the major changes in the presentation of public expenditure described below were made in the late 1980s.

The survey system had the great merits of bringing together, for Ministerial consideration, the whole of the spending plans which had to be financed by publicly imposed rates, taxes or charges, or by public borrowing and doing so, not just for a year ahead, but for several years. Thus future costs could in principle be foreseen and taken into account. In practice, the successive costings even of unchanged policies showed large increases from one survey to the next, and additional spending decisions continued to be taken throughout the year, on a scale which could not be met from the contingency reserve established for that purpose. It was therefore necessary both to reform the technique of expenditure planning and control and to strengthen the system of ministerial decision-taking based upon it.

The cash limits system

The major problem of technique in public expenditure control to emerge in the mid-1970s was the absence of an effective cash budgeting system. Some programmes were necessarily planned and controlled in cash terms, for example the large social security schemes and other types of transfer payments. Local authorities' spending was determined by their own cash budgets for the year ahead. The allocations to individual health authorities, from within the total health programme, were also made in cash terms. In addition, cash controls were superimposed on some other types of government expenditure when exceptionally high cost inflation made this essential, for example building and construction in 1973. But the greater part of central government spending was not subject to cash, as distinct from volume or 'real term', limits: pay and price rises were provided for as they occurred. The Parliamentary procedures did ostensibly provide for full cash control: departments were not allowed to overspend their original Estimates without submitting a Supplementary Estimate. But in practice Parliament had no option but to grant the extra funds, so that the formal control was illusory.

Control in resource or real terms had some advantages. It enabled departments to staff, build, equip and supply the projects and services that had been authorized without risking shortfalls and disruption due to their cash provision falling short of actual inflation. But if all wage and price increases were 'for free' so far as departmental managers were concerned, there was little incentive to keep cash costs within bounds and the discipline of firm cash allocations was absent. More seriously, the government had no means of knowing, within wide margins, how much money would actually be spent at a time when financial policy was moving strongly towards monetary controls.

The working out of the cash limit system in 1974/75 was designed to remedy these problems and it remains a crucial element in the current system of control. It has the following essential features:

(a) Cash limits are set for as many central government programmes as possible for the next financial year;
(b) They are set in terms of current prices, with an allowance for inflation;
(c) The cash limits are regarded as firm, not to be increased save in highly exceptional circumstances, and then only with Treasury permission;
(d) Consideration is given to extending cash limit control to as many further programmes and services as possible. The main exclusions are services which are 'demand-determined', such as social security benefits, where the sums paid out follow automatically from the numbers of qualified recipients and the levels at which benefits are set from time to time by policy decisions.

Cash limits could not be applied to the current expenditure of individual local authorities without extensive machinery for approving the plans of over 450 authorities. It was therefore originally decided to apply a cash limit to the rate support grant (block grant) made available by central government. (The present system of control of local authority expenditure is explained in Chapter 6.) Cash limits were clearly not appropriate to the expenditure of the nationalized industries and other public corporations, but their borrowing is controlled by external financing limits (see Chapter 7).

At the same time as the cash limit system was being worked out in 1974/75, a new central financial information system was developed by the Treasury, in consultation with the spending departments, to provide early and accurate information about current central government spending in relation to both the vote provision and the Public Expenditure White Paper figures. The course of actual expenditure was analysed on a monthly basis. This analysis was compared with the expected 'profiles' of expenditure for the year as a whole, since the rate of spending might not be uniform either throughout the year or by different types of service. Any necessary corrective action could thus be considered in good time. It was clearly essential that for cash limits to be monitored and enforced, an effective financial reporting system of this kind should be in operation.

Cash limits are essentially the same as the cash budgetary arrangements in force in many other countries. But they are closely related to the broader public expenditure survey system, some of whose limitations they were designed to remedy; and they were not imposed where they could not have been enforced. The main developments in the cash limit system have included:

(a) Extension of cash limits to some services not originally covered – for example, certain forms of assistance to industry where as a policy decision an overall limit was imposed to override the 'demand-determined' criterion;

(b) Cash limits covering Supply expenditure have been aligned with Votes in the Parliamentary Estimates, thus facilitating the reconciliation between the Parliamentary and governmental control systems.

In 1982/83, a major change was made by the government in the basis of the public expenditure survey itself and its relation to cash limits. Previous to this date the cash limits had been grafted on to the volume system of planning public expenditure; no change had been made in the constant price or real terms basis of the survey. From 1983 the survey itself was conducted in cash terms. The previous year's cash figures for the various services were the starting point. Any increases, also in cash terms, for inflation or policy changes had to be justified.

The present system of expenditure control

Building on the foundations and methods summarized above the present system for managing public expenditure shows distinctive features which derive from the government's economic, financial and social policies and objectives. The survey system itself has spanned many governments with widely differing views of the role of the state and the priorities to be accorded to different spending programmes. In recent years, for example, funds for certain types of government assistance to industry and for publicly provided housing have been severely reduced, while spending on industrial training and law and order services has been substantially increased. But the methodology of control can be applied in the interests of efficient management to any level of total spending and to any variations, large or small, in its composition or objectives.

It is of interest that the decision to introduce cash limits was taken by the Labour government of 1974–79. The aims of tighter spending control and improved financial discipline were given priority over the guaranteed achievement of departmental projects in resource terms. It is highly improbable that any government, whatever its view of the state's role in the provision of services, would revert to the former system of planning and control in resource or real terms. It would be possible to apply the present system of cash budgeting with more flexibility if full delivery of certain projects or programmes within a given time scale was held to take priority over the maintenance of spending allocations in money terms. But a slippery slope, leading in some circumstances to a nasty looking precipice, awaits ministers who weaken methods of public expenditure control instead of applying them efficiently in the furtherance of their chosen policies.

It is useful to have the present (1988) government's objectives for the economy in mind in setting out the current approach to control. They are to reduce inflation, and to promote improvement of the industrial and commercial performance of the economy. The chosen means, in so far as they impact on public expenditure, are to restrain its rate of growth below the growth of the economy as a whole so that taxes can be reduced and public sector borrowing minimized. It is believed that the public sector, generally speaking, uses resources inefficiently. In applying these beliefs it has been found necessary in recent years to increase substantially the amounts spent on social security, partly because of persistent high unemployment, and to increase moderately in real terms spending on defence, education and industrial training. An attack has therefore been necessary on other programmes, and on the government's own calls on manpower.

The same machinery for planning and control could be used to serve quite different objectives. A previous Conservative government (1970–1974) spent large sums in the attempt to stimulate employment and exports. A future government might take a different view of the effect of taxation on incentives and the growth of national income, and thus alter the guidelines for the planning of public expenditure. It is possible that the primacy accorded to monetary objectives could lose favour. But the public expenditure management system as it has evolved – and as it will no doubt continue to do so – can be applied to widely differing political requirements.

The public expenditure cycle

In the spring of each year ministers give general guidance about the way the survey is to be conducted, including the kind of information they will require in taking their decisions and any changes in their priorities. Thus in 1988 the survey reviewed plans for 'years 1 and 2', i.e. 1989–90 and 1990–1, and formulated plans for the first time for 'year 3', i.e. 1991–92. The cash figures for the first two years will be those in the previous Public Expenditure White Paper, as modified by any subsequent decisions. For the third year they will, on current policies, be those in year 2 increased by a specific percentage, related to but not necessarily identical with forecast inflation rates. This procedure cuts out the earlier sometimes protracted argument about the estimated future costs of 'existing policies'. It also carries the implication that if inflation turns out to be higher than expected, the additional costs will have to be met from within the allotted cash provision.

Existing policies nevertheless exist, and their periodic review is an essential component of any coherent policy for public expenditure. Major reviews have recently included the social security and education systems. But such major studies cannot sensibly be run as part of the public expenditure survey itself, into whose machinery the financial effects of the new policy decisions will eventually be fed.

Any new bids resulting from new policy initiatives, and the latest estimates for demand-led programmes, e.g. social security benefits, will be examined between the Treasury and spending departments as part of the survey process. When costings are complete, by early summer, the Chief Secretary puts to the Cabinet an assessment of the position and his own proposals for the planning totals for the next three years. Ministers then decide what total spending can be afforded in the light of the prospects for revenue and expenditure shown in the medium-term financial strategy, published earlier as part of the Budget. Whatever future policies on monetary control or other approaches to economic stability may be, it is unlikely that public expenditure decisions would be taken without consideration of their effects on the economy as a whole.

Further ministerial decisions are necessary during the summer or early autumn to agree:

(a) The level of local authority current expenditure on which the government will base their support grants for local authorities for the coming year;
(b) The departmental spending programmes;
(c) The external financing limits for the nationalized industries.

All these decisions are required for the preparation of the Autumn Statement. Those at (b) in particular can involve strong argument between Treasury and spending ministers. The ministerial decisions on the totals for expenditure are invariably followed by extra bids from spending departments. If bilateral discussions between the Chief Secretary to the Treasury and spending ministers cannot settle departmental allocations, it is the practice for the issues to be discussed in the 'Star Chamber', a small group of senior ministers without large departmental programmes of their own, in an effort to reach acceptable solutions, sometimes with a modest further allocation of funds from the Treasury. The last resort, avoided if possible, is reference to the full Cabinet.

In addition to the agreed expenditure figures for the three years ahead, the Autumn Statement gives the estimated outturn for the current year and includes the Treasury's economic forecast for the next calendar year. The publication of the Public Expenditure White Paper usually follows in January or February. In May 1988, the government responded to suggestions from the Public Accounts Committee and the Treasury and Civil Service Committee for a new structure of expenditure documents, with the following proposals (Cm 375):

(a) The Autumn Statement would include as much as practicable of the key material from Chapter 1 of the White Paper;
(b) Volume II of the White Paper, which gives the individual departments' plans, would be split into separate volumes, to be published before Budget day, in conjunction with the Parliamentary Supply Estimates which they would help to clarify;
(c) The remaining material in Volume I – the so called 'additional analyses' – which depends on detailed information about departmental sub-programmes and the English, Scottish and Welsh components, takes more time to produce and could be made available in various ways in the spring.

Figure 4.1 shows the transition to the proposed new forms of publication. These proposals recognize the need for a further improvement in the content and style of information relating to public expenditure following advances already made in recent years, and for the integration of the main elements in the complete picture: the Autumn Statement, the White Paper, cash limits, and the Supply Estimates.

The government has also redefined the public expenditure planning total (see Cm 441, July 1988). Up till now this total has included local authority spending on all public expenditure programmes, the policies for which are determined by the responsible government departments – education, law and order, roads and so on. But central government has not directly controlled this component of the total expenditure. The planning total will now include only the grants, current and capital, general or specific, which central government provides to local authorities, and the 'credit approvals' which are to be issued authorizing local authorities to incur expenditure financed by borrowing. The public

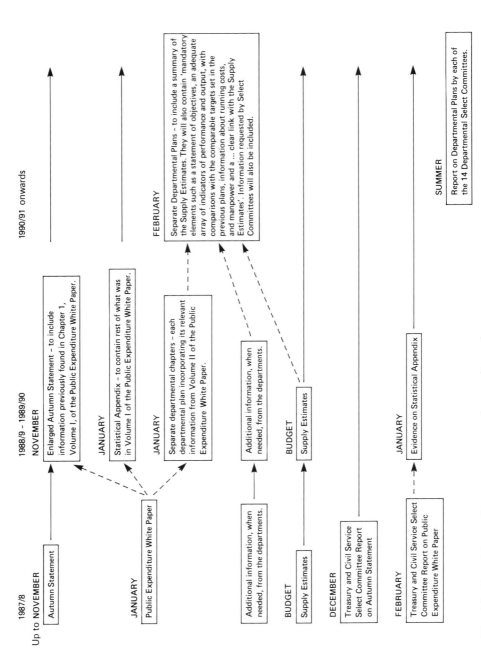

Fig. 4.1 Transition to the new structure of expenditure documents.

expenditure planning total will then comprise only those components over which the government exercises direct control. They will be:

(a) Central government's own expenditure;
(b) Grants to local authorities;
(c) Credit approvals to local authorities;
(d) The external finance of the public corporations;
(e) Payments to local authorities from the yield of non-domestic rates;
(f) Privatization proceeds, as a credit to the total;
(g) The reserve.

The significance of these changes is discussed in the section on local authorities below. They should be kept in mind, together with the arrangements for superseding the Public Expenditure White Paper, in reading the following summary of its current contents.

The Public Expenditure White Paper

Introduction

The introduction to the January 1988 White Paper (Cm 288–1), concentrates on the main public expenditure totals, relates them to the government's objectives for the economy and for the management of the public sector, and illustrates the movement in general government expenditure both in real terms and as a percentage of gross domestic product over the periods 1978–79 to 1990–91. This brief historical snapshot is greatly extended in the chapters on historical trends, which go back in some comparisons to 1963 and in others to 1890. The introduction also shows how expenditure plans for individual years have varied since a particular year first featured in a White Paper. The different ways of looking at expenditure are well illustrated in Fig. 1.1 in Chapter 1.

Department plans

The total figures for each department follow, with comparative outturns for two past years (see Table 1.1, Chapter 1). The departmental and functional divisions tie in closely; but in line with the current emphasis on departmental responsibility, and to ease assimilation with the Vote structure explained below, the former now takes precedence. The figures for departmental plans will in future include only the grants made to local authorities in respect of their parts of the functional programmes, and not, as hitherto, an estimate of their actual spending on those programmes. Specific grants will be included in the responsible departments' allocations, e.g. for law and order in those of the Home Office and the Secretary of State for Scotland. The general grant – revenue support grant – will be shown as part of the Department of the Environment's programme.

A brief explanation of the scale and content of each department's allocation now includes a statement of the programme's broad objectives. Illustrating this:

Defence: 'The Government's aims for defence are to ensure the security of the nation and maintain its freedom, in particular by maintaining the effectiveness of the NATO alliance.'

Transport: 'The department seeks to increase efficiency and reduce the unit cost of transport (for example by maintaining and improving the arterial road system), to protect and improve safety, to conserve the environment and to advance United Kingdom interests abroad.'

DOE-Housing: 'The aim of Government policy is to give people a better choice of housing by encouraging the spread of home ownership for those who want it and providing a wider variety of housing for rent, and in so doing to focus public spending more effectively.'

These statements are extremely broad, but:

(a) They are a start, and a start of comparatively recent origin;
(b) Other governments would no doubt, in similarly short compass, give an indication of different policy objectives;
(c) They are substantially expanded in Volume II of the White Paper, and in many cases form a broad foundation for a sophisticated framework of performance indicators for use in internal monitoring and external accountability.

Public expenditure by spending authority

Local authorities

Central government is responsible for spending over 70% of the public expenditure total. Local authorities are responsible for spending most of the remainder.

Local authorities are elected bodies accountable to their own electorates, not to Parliament, for their policies and administration. But Parliament determines their powers and responsibilities as the sovereign legislature. That role is currently exercised mainly in the following ways:

(a) Services provided by local authorities are authorized by statute, e.g. education and housing Acts, which lay down, in considerable detail, what is to be or may be provided and how services are to be administered;
(b) Legislation also provides for the way in which local authority expenditure is to be financed, including arrangements for central

government contributions by way of block grants or specific grants, and the financial relations between central and local government generally;

(c) Parliament holds accountable to itself the government departments responsible for national policy on locally provided services, e.g. education, housing, personal social services, roads and transport, and, in the case of the Department of the Environment, policy on relations generally between the central and local authorities. This accountability is usually pursued through the select committees which may examine ministers and officials on the exercise of their responsibilities under the governing statutes.

In this constitutional situation, expenditure by local authorities is treated for many purposes as part of public expenditure as a whole. Cm 441 states: 'In the UK the Government formulates policies which may be implemented by either central or local government', and: 'It is total public spending which is the main expenditure aggregate and of importance in the macro economic context.' The definition of 'general government expenditure' will continue to reflect this analysis, and figures for it will continue to be given in public presentations and policy statements. But the new definition of the public expenditure planning total includes only the expenditure which is under the direct control of the government, including the grants to local authorities.

Among other objectives this change is designed to clarify responsibilities. But it is not intended to weaken control over public expenditure as a whole. Quoting again from Cm 441: . . . if the Government felt that this expenditure was growing too rapidly. . . . (they) would need to consider whether to take action to moderate the growth of spending within the planning total, whether its own spending or grants to local authorities.' The intention clearly is to bring pressure to bear on local authorities by their own electorates if increases in 'their' spending, with a squeeze on subventions from central government, forces them to raise the community charge to a politically difficult degree.

While these objectives are clear, it is not in fact usually possible to distinguish in policy terms between those parts of an expenditure programme for which central and local government are respectively responsible. In some areas – education is the outstanding current illustration – central government is centralizing policy, and thus heavily influencing expenditure, even in areas formerly left to local decision. And as the figures in Cm 441 make clear, 'local authority self-financed expenditure' is a comparatively small proportion of the total programme.

Nationalized industries and other public corporations

The nationalized industries and several other public corporations, for example the Scottish and Welsh Development Agencies, have the following distinguishing characteristics:

(a) They are established by Act of Parliament which lays down their constitution, powers, responsibilities and relations with the government;

(b) Subject to (d) below, their boards are not directly answerable to Parliament, but are subject to the control of their sponsoring ministers as provided for in legislation, those ministers in turn being accountable to Parliament for the discharge of their statutory duties in respect of the industries;

(c) As a corollary of this constitutional position the industries are fully backed by the Exchequer and have no independent credit standing of their own;

(d) Their annual reports and accounts are required to be laid before Parliament, which brings them formally within the purview of the Public Accounts Committee. But by Parliamentary agreement they are investigated by the Select Committee which shadows the government department sponsoring the industry. Note that this right to question boards and to report on their operations depends on convention and not on the statutes establishing the industries;

(e) Though by agreement with other select committees the Public Accounts Committee has in general not examined the industries, the Committee has shown an increasing interest in the sponsor departments' actions in relation to their industries and has issued reports in this area.

The nationalized industries and some of the other public corporations are trading bodies which operate in the market like private corporations. Others, for example the Royal Mint, trade with the private sector but have obligations also to the government. Yet others are not essentially trading bodies at all but discharge a variety of public responsibilities, for example the Bank of England, the BBC, the General Practice Finance Corporation. The main elements in the public expenditure total deriving from this sector is the external financing of the nationalized industries and some other corporations, that is the total of the finance they need which is not provided from their own operations, whether by way of grant, subsidy or loan, and whether met by the government or from private sources. By controlling these external financing limits the government influences commercial policies and management. Other 'contributions to the expenditure planning totals' are enumerated in Chapter Four of the White Paper, and the industries are dealt with in full in Chapter 7.

Further information in the White Paper

Volume I of the White Paper gives much further information in the 'additional analyses' and otherwise, covering, *inter alia*, the following:

(a) A more detailed functional breakdown of the departmental programmes;

(b) Linkages between expenditure by departments, spending authorities and economic categories;
(c) Capital spending;
(d) Public sector manpower and departmental running costs (staff costs plus other administrative expenditure);
(e) Spending on science and technology;
(f) Debt interest;
(g) Privatization proceeeds.

In future this will be split between the Autumn Statement, the supplementary January statement and the departmental plans.

Volume II gives still more detailed descriptions of the departmental and other programmes, with discussion of objectives and performance indicators. It is this part which will be split into separate departmental publications, for which the spending departments, rather than the Treasury, will take prime responsibility.

The role of Parliament

It is the government which formulates plans for public expenditure and manages their execution. It is Parliament which exercises formal control over the spending of public funds, as over the raising of public revenue. This section summarizes how this is done and relates the Parliamentary process to the governmental planning and control systems.

Parliament exercises constitutional control over the annual expenditure of government departments and certain closely related bodies, for example the research councils and national museums, by what is known as 'Supply' procedure. Every department prepares its Estimates for expenditure in the coming financial year and is required to agree them with the Treasury. The Treasury submits the approved Estimates to the House of Commons, thus meeting the long-established constitutional practice by which the Crown (the government) demands money from Parliament. In recent years the main Estimates have been presented on Budget day. Three 'Estimate Days' are allotted in the House of Commons timetable each session for debating the Estimates, usually on the basis of reports from the relevant select committees (see below). Statutory authority for the supply of funds to meet the expenditure set out in the Estimates, or Votes, is given in the Consolidated Fund (Appropriation) Act, passed before the summer recess.

The Supply procedure also has to meet further requirements. Government departments need authority to start spending money from the first day of the financial year, whereas the Appropriation Act will not be passed until some months later. Parliament is therefore asked to provide it by a system of 'Votes on Account', usually presented in December and amounting to about 45% of the amount authorized to date in the current

Table 4.1 Summary of 1988–89 Supply Estimates by class (£ billion)

Class	Department	1986–87 Outturn	1987–88[1] Original provision	1987–88[1] Total provision	1987–88[1] Forecast outturn	1988–89 Provision
I	Defence	18.2	18.8	19.7	18.6	19.2
II	Foreign and Commonwealth Office[2]	1.9	1.9	2.0	1.9	2.1
III	European Communities[3]	0.5				
IV	Ministry of Agriculture, Fisheries and Food[4]	0.7	1.0	1.1	0.9	1.2
V	Trade and Industry[5]	2.6	1.4	1.9	1.9	1.5
VI	Energy	1.7	1.2	1.4	1.4	0.8
VII	Employment	3.1	3.6	3.6	3.4	3.7
VIII	Transport	2.6	2.7	2.8	2.8	2.6
IX	DOE – Housing	2.0	2.1	2.1	2.0	2.1
X	DOE – Other environmental services	10.1	11.0	11.1	11.0	11.4
XI	Home Office and legal departments[6]	4.7	5.1	5.2	5.2	5.6
XII	Education and Science	3.2	3.7	3.7	3.7	4.0
XIII	Arts and Libraries	0.3	0.3	0.3	0.3	0.4
XIV	DHSS – Health and personal social services	13.1	13.8	14.3	14.2	14.6
XV	DHSS – Social security	23.7	24.1	24.8	24.3	24.8
XVI	Scotland	5.5	5.8	5.8	5.6	6.1
XVII	Wales	2.4	2.6	2.7	2.7	2.8
XVIII	Northern Ireland	1.3	1.5	1.5	1.4	1.3
XIX	Chancellor's departments	2.2	2.3	2.4	2.3	2.4
XX	Other departments[7]	1.4	1.7	1.7	1.7	1.6
	Total	**101.4**	**104.5**	**108.2**	**105.3**	**108.3**

(1) The original provision in 1987–88 relates to the Estimates published on Budget day and included in last year's *Summary and Guide*. Total provision includes Supplementary Estimates.
(2) Including Overseas Development Administration.
(3) No funds were sought for payments to the European Communities in 1987–88 main Estimates, nor are any sought in 1988–89 main Estimates.
(4) Including Intervention Board for Agricultural Produce and Forestry Commission.
(5) Including Export Credits Guarantee Department.
(6) This group comprises the Home Office, Lord Chancellor's Department, Northern Ireland Court Service, the Crown Prosecution Service, the Serious Fraud Office, the Crown Office, Procurator Fiscal Service and Lord Advocate's Department.
(7) Including Property Services Agency, Civil Superannuation and the Treasury Solicitor's Department.

Source: *Summary and Guide to the Supply Estimates* (Cm 328, 1988–89).

financial year. Statutory authority for these advances is given in a winter Consolidated Fund Act. Second, departments are permitted to present Revised Estimates before the Appropriation Act is passed, but this normally occurs only where reduced financial provision is sought, or to take account of transfers of departmental functions. Third, the government may need to ask Parliament for additional money during the year, necessitating the presentation of Supplementary Estimates at various times, and authorization in a Consolidated Fund Act. Fourth, it is sometimes essential, in ministers' judgement, for urgent additional expenditure to be incurred in advance of provision by Parliament. The Contingencies Fund, established by Parliament, exists for this purpose, but money advanced from it under strict criteria applied by the Treasury must be repaid when the sums have been subsequently voted.

In 1988–89 the separate Estimates or Votes totalled 176, grouped into 20 classes closely aligned with the functional programmes set out in the Public Expenditure White Paper. Table 4.1, reproduced from the government's *Summary and Guide to the Supply Estimates*, shows this classification and the amounts provided in 1988–89. It will be seen that the classification aligns completely with the departmental presentation in the Public Expenditure White Paper, though the figures differ for reasons explained below.

Each Vote contains the following main information about the services for which it provides.

(a) An introductory note describes the expenditure, indicates whether the Vote is treated as a cash limit (see below), and compares the provision sought with the provision and/or likely outturn in the previous year;

(b) Part I gives a brief formal description of the services to be financed (known as the 'ambit' of the Vote), the net sum required, the department which will account for the Vote, and the amount allocated in the Vote on Account. The ambit is important because it describes and limits the purposes for which the expenditure can legally be incurred;

(c) Part II analyses the provision by functional public expenditure programme and subdivides it into subheads. The provision sought is compared with actual expenditure in the last completed year and total provision in the current year (actuals will not be known at this stage), and for the Vote as a whole the forecast outturn for the current year is also shown. Expenditure must be accounted for by subheads: savings on one subhead may be applied, with Treasury sanction, to meet excesses on another – a process known as 'virement'. Part II also shows those receipts which may be 'appropriated in aid' of the Vote, i.e. used to meet some of the gross expenditure. Any receipts above the amounts so specified must be surrendered to the Exchequer (Consolidated Fund) as 'extra receipts';

(d) Part III shows particulars of receipts which are expected to be received but will be paid into the Consolidated Fund and not 'appropriated in aid';

(e) Additional information about the expenditure on the Vote is sometimes given in appended tables, e.g. details of long-term projects and works services.

The Estimates are entirely on a cash basis, as is the public expenditure system. The sums authorized to be spent are those which 'come in course of payment' during the year, i.e where the liability to pay has matured and the instrument of payment has been issued. Any money not so spent must be surrendered to the Exchequer: no carry forward into the next financial year is permitted.

While the Appropriation Act gives annual authority for expenditure which conforms to the ambit and structure of the votes, Parliament expects government to seek specific statutory powers for continuing services. For example, the extensive system of social security benefits and the various forms of agricultural and industrial assistance are authorized by special legislation, which governs the preparation of the relevant annual Estimates.

Moreover, the fact that money has been made available in the Estimates and the Appropriation Act does not necessarily give departments the right to spend within those limits: they must also seek Treasury approval for individual projects not covered by their own delegated powers, though in the case of major departments such delegations will be large. Any new policy proposals which involve expenditure – and there are few which do not – must be discussed with the Treasury before ministerial approval is sought. The Treasury's views on such proposals will take full account of their likely cost, current and future, in relation to the forward planning and control of public expenditure as a whole.

The Supply Estimates, public expenditure plans and cash limits

The Supply Estimates cover expenditure only by central government. Public expenditure plans include spending by local authorities and the external finance of public corporations. Some funds provided to government through the Supply Estimates are transfers within the public sector, notably the large grants to local government, and are therefore netted out in calculating the public expenditure totals. Some funds spent by central government come from sources other than the annual Parliamentary Votes. The most important are contributory national insurance benefits, such as pensions, which are met from the National Insurance Fund, and 'Consolidated Fund services', such as payments to the European Communities and the salaries of judges and the Comptroller and Auditor General, which it would not be appropriate to submit to annual Parliamentary authorization. Cash limits are aligned with the Estimates, each of which is, or is not, subject to cash limit control. Some non-voted expenditure, including certain capital expenditure by local authorities, is subject to cash limits although not voted in the Estimates. There are a number of other differences between the coverage of the three main control systems.

All this needs detailed numerical reconciliation, but with the substantial progress which has been made in aligning the interlocking systems the main features can be fairly simply illustrated and their rationale understood. This is done in the Treasury's *Summary and Guide to the Supply Estimates* (Cm 328, 1988–89), from which the chart in Fig. 4.2 is taken. It should, however, be noted that the layout and information in the Supply Estimates may well change, and should be monitored from year to year.

Cash limits are the closest form of budgetary control which can realistically be imposed. Where they are imposed the intention is to avoid if at all possible any increase in spending during the year, so that unexpected demands or increases in cost are expected to be absorbed or offset. Where, however, expenditure is 'demand-led', so that once policy is decided there is no option but to provide the necessary funds, it would be pointless to declare a cash limit because it could not be enforced. Of the total of Supply Estimates 61% were cash-limited in 1988/89. The principle is well illustrated by two of the largest services. The defence budget, at just over £19 billion, was wholly cash limited; social security (DHSS), at nearly £25 billion, was cash limited only to the extent of £1.6 billion.

A final point needs to be added to the discussion of the Parliamentary aspects of expenditure control. All public expenditure must be authorized by statute. But neither the Public Expenditure White Paper, the Chancellor's Autumn Statement nor the cash limits receive formal Parliamentary authority. They are presented for Parliament's information as executive acts by the government. Parliament gives the necessary authority:

(a) By legislating to provide for defined services, e.g. assistance to industry and agriculture, provision of housing, health and education, or the establishment of permanent funds;
(b) By providing funds each year through the Supply procedure for most of central government spending, including the block grant and other financial support to local government;
(c) By authorizing certain permanent charges directly on the Consolidated Fund.

Select committees

The traditional, somewhat complex arrangements whereby Parliament, assisted by the Comptroller and Auditor General, (see Chapter 9) controls departmental spending and its allocation to particular services are constitutionally important but have little substantive impact on the government's plans. The enormous growth in the size and range of governmental expenditure since the main features of these procedures

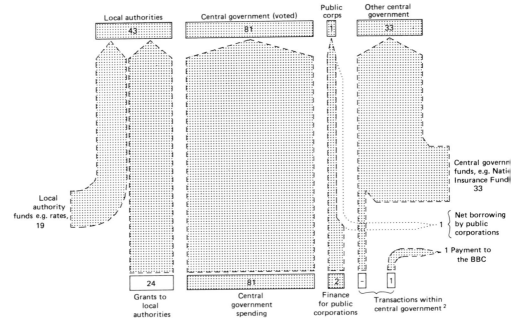

Fig. 4.2 Relationship between public spending plans and the Supply Estimates for 1988–89 (£ billion).

Source: *Summary and Guide to the Supply Estimates* (Cm 328, 1988–89).

were instituted in the nineteenth century has made it impossible for the House of Commons to make any effective examination of it or exercise any appreciable influence on its composition or development. Increasing attention has therefore been given in recent years to the activities of Select Committees of the House in this role. The numbers and terms of reference of these committees, normally consisting of 11–15 members reflecting the party composition of the House of Commons, has varied, but the present system includes:

(a) The Public Accounts Committee, originally established in 1861, with a continuous but developing interest in the examination of departmental and other accounts laid before Parliament, and the related conduct of financial management (see Chapter 9);

(b) A number of departmentally related committees, charged with 'shadowing' the policies and operations of the main government departments and scrutinizing their Estimates, e.g. defence, trade and industry, transport, energy, health and social services;

(c) As a special example of group (b), the central Treasury and Civil Service Committee which oversees the operations of the Treasury in

---

Supply Estimates (£108 billion)

The chart shows, in round figures, the relationship between the planning total and Supply Estimates. Taking the different flows, in turn:

(a) **Local authorities** expenditure is planned to be £43 billion. Some £19 billion is financed from rates, rents, loans, etc, and some £24 billion by grants from central government. All local authorities expenditure is counted in the planning total (but now see page 63), whereas the Estimates only include the grants from central government (mainly Rate Support Grant in Class X).

(b) **Central government (voted)**: both the planning total and Supply Estimates include direct expenditure (£81 billion) by central government departments on such items as defence, the National Health Service, running costs and that part of social security which is not financed from the National Insurance Fund. When voted the funds are drawn from the Consolidated Fund.

(c) **Public corporations**: the planning total includes the external finance of public corporations. Part of this external finance, some £2 billion, comes directly from central government and is included in Estimates.

(d) **Other central government** comprising expenditure not directly provided for in Supply Estimates. The £33 billion in the planning total is financed from other central government non-voted funds such as the National Insurance Fund or directly from the Consolidated Fund (e.g. payments to the European Community).

(1) The figures are taken from Table 2.18 of the 1988 Public Expenditure White Paper. Those for 'other central government' exclude the Reserve (£3.5 billion) and privatization proceeds (−£5.0 billion).

(2) This covers transfers within central government, for example the 'Treasury Supplement' to the National Insurance Fund, less rate rebates and National Health Service contributions (which net out to zero) and a payment (£1.1 billion) to the BBC in respect of licence revenue.

expenditure control and its conduct of economic and monetary policy, as well as the central control and management of the Civil Service;

(d) The Liaison Committee, consisting of the chairmen of select committees, which coordinates their activities.

All these committees select the subjects they will examine within their terms of reference, take written and oral evidence, usually from senior officials but occasionally from ministers, and make public reports. Their recommendations are backed by no formal powers, but are considered on their merits by the government. Some such system is the only way of involving Members of Parliament in a detailed and informed way with the departmental conduct of expenditure and the underlying policies.

Financing of public expenditure

This book is not concerned with the theory or practice of taxation, but mention must be made of the ways in which the government and other public authorities raise revenue or borrow to meet their expenditure. They are as follows:

(a) Central government taxes, imposed or changed under the authority of the annual Finance Act, following the Budget;

(b) Local authority rates, charged on domestic, commercial or industrial property, superseded from 1989 in Scotland and from 1990 in England and Wales by the community charge and the national non-domestic rate;

(c) Charges for goods or services sold by the nationalized industries, the water authorities, other public corporations or bodies, and central and local government. Sizeable trading activities are carried out by central government, for example in the Stationery Office and the Royal Mint, and by local government, for example bus services. Moreover, both central and local government and the National Health Service raise a wide variety of charges for goods or services provided to the public, ranging from council house rents to prescription charges and passport fees;

(d) Sales of surplus assets, for example land or buildings, equipment or stores;

(e) Borrowing on the private capital or money markets, or, in the case of most governmental agencies, from the central government itself.

In addition, the large sums received on privatization of publicly owned undertakings reduce the government's borrowing requirement.

Central government capital expenditure is financed through Votes whatever its economic category, but that part of capital investment by the nationalized industries which cannot be financed from their own internal resources is mostly financed by borrowing. The government may incur deficits on its own spending/revenue balance, and the local authorities also borrow to finance much of their capital spending. The public sector borrowing requirement (PSBR) is the total of these components. It is increased by higher revenue deficits and larger externally financed capital investment programmes. It can be reduced by lower spending, higher taxation, higher nationalized industry prices, and sales of public sector assets, ultimately to the point where borrowing gives way to net repayment of public debt. The size and management of the PSBR have been a major concern of government policy in recent years.

The central government's statutory power to borrow, in the National Loans Act 1968, sets no upper limit to the total which may be borrowed, nor specifies the manner or terms of borrowing. These are matters on which the Treasury and the Bank of England – 'the authorities' – will consult, with final decisions as always in the hands of ministers.

Although Parliament does not at present set any overall limits on government borrowing, it does impose periodic limits on borrowing by each of the nationalized industries and certain public corporations, usually estimated to meet their external capital financing needs for three to four years ahead. All lending to the industries, apart from some short-term bank finance, to other public corporations and the local authorities is centralized through the National Loans Fund in the interests of monetary management.

Accounting for public expenditure

It remains to describe how public expenditure is accounted for, as distinct from controlled. There is no general accounting system for the public sector as a whole: its component parts are too diverse, both constitutionally and operationally, for that. Local government has its own accounting system, fully described in Chapter 6. The nationalized industries and those public corporations that are predominantly commercial in character such as the Scottish and Welsh Development Agencies produce their accounts in full commercial form. They also provide more information in their annual reports than do commercial enterprises in the private sector, to meet the requirements of public and Parliamentary accountability. A summary of central government arrangements follows.

The annual Appropriation Accounts of government departments and closely related bodies follow the form of the Estimates – the Votes and subheads – and show: how much cash has been spent against the amounts provided by Parliament; the composition of shortfalls and, occasionally, excesses; receipts appropriated in aid of the Votes or surrendered to the Exchequer; and supporting information, including

Table 4.2 Royal Palaces, Royal Parks, Historic Buildings, Ancient Monuments and the National Heritage (Department of the Environment 1986–87, Class X, Vote 4)

Service	Grant	Expenditure	Expenditure compared with Grant	
			Less than Granted	More than Granted
	£000	£000	£000	£000
PROGRAMME 8.3				
Section A				
ROYAL PALACES AND ROYAL PARKS				
A1 Royal Palaces – capital expenditure	470	131	339	—
A2 Royal Palaces – operating expenses	1,218	1,304	—	86
A3 Accommodation at Buckingham Palace, Windsor Castle, etc: grant in aid	75	75	—	—
A4 Occupied monuments and certain public buildings – capital expenditure	410	134	276	—
A5 Occupied monuments and certain public buildings – operating expenses	1,373	1,207	166	—
A6 Purchase of souvenirs and publications etc.	950	811	139	—
A7 Royal Parks – capital expenditure	337	381	—	44
A8 Royal Parks – operating expenses	9,303	9,129	174	—
A9 Administration	4,987	4,124	863	—
PROGRAMME 8.4				
Section B				
HISTORIC BUILDINGS, ANCIENT MONUMENTS AND THE NATIONAL HERITAGE				
B1 Historic Buildings and Monuments Commission for England (grant in aid)	62,495	61,495	1,000	—
B2 Board of Trustees of the Armouries (grant in aid)	2,815	2,815	—	—
B3 Redundant Churches Fund	928	819	109	—
B4 The National Heritage Memorial Fund (grant in aid)	1,560	1,500	60	—
B5 Assets accepted in lieu of tax	1,000	1,000	—	—
B6 Royal Commission on Historical Monuments	3,220	3,295	—	75
B7 Temple Bar Trust	265	15	250	—
B8 International Centre for the study of the Preservation and Restoration of Cultural Property, Rome	21	20	1	—
B9 Administration	2,308	2,342	—	34

GROSS TOTAL	£000			
Original (revised sum)	93,570			
Supplementary	165			
	———			
	93,735	90,597	3,377	239

Surplus of Gross Estimate over Expenditure
3,138

	Estimated	Realised
Deduct	£000	£000
Z Appropriations in Aid		
Original (revised sum)	11,734	
Less Supplementary	1,000	
	———	
	10,734	9,689

Deficiency of Appropriations in Aid realized
1,045

NET TOTAL		
Original (revised sum)	81,836	
Supplementary	1,165	
	———	
	83,001	80,908

Surplus
2,093

Actual surplus to be surrendered   £2,093,469.33

Receipts

	Estimated	Realized
Receipts payable to Consolidated Fund		
	£000	£000
Receipts of classes not authorized to be used as Appropriations in Aid	370	1,993
Actual sum payable separately to Consolidated Fund		£1,993,468.42

Details of Receipts

	Estimated	Realized
	£000	£000
(i) Receipts of classes authorized to be used as Appropriations in Aid		
Subhead AZ Admission fees, licences, rents and related receipts, and receipts from sales	10,468	9,440
Subhead BZ Royal Commission on Historical Monuments	35	28
Sale of land at Heveningham Hall	60	—
Miscellaneous	171	221
	266	249
Total	10,734	9,689
(ii) Receipts of other classes		
Pension receipts from the Historic Buildings and Monuments Commission	370	1,993

Source: *Appropriation Accounts, 1986.* HMSO, London. Crown Copyright. Reproduced with the permission of the Controller of Her Majesty's Stationery Office.

statements of losses, special payments and so on. They are audited by the Comptroller and Auditor General and presented to Parliament, where they may form the basis of examination by the Public Accounts Committee. An example from the Department of the Environment is given in Table 4.2.

For many years those departments that carried on commercial or industrial activities were required to produce, in addition to the relevant Vote accounts, trading accounts to exhibit the results of those activities in commercial form. Those which remain in the public sector have now been established as trading funds under the Government Trading Funds Act 1973, and their financing has ceased to depend on the cash vote system under which unspent balances have to be surrendered at the year end to the Exchequer. They are suitably capitalized and expected to be run, subject to overriding government requirements, on commercial lines, and they may be given financial objectives in relation to their earnings. Their accounts are accordingly produced in full commercial form, though they continue, as departmental bodies accountable to

Table 4.3 HMSO Trading Fund: Operating Account for the year ended 31 March 1988

	1987–88		1986–87	
	£000	£000	£000	£000
Turnover	330,306		321,853	
Change in stocks of:				
finished goods	179		(213)	
work in progress	(2,735)		1,368	
Government grants	4,254		3,975	
Other operating income	629		614	
		332,633		327,597
Raw materials and				
consumables	39,420		37,243	
Other external charges	210,319		209,923	
Staff costs	46,718		44,554	
Depreciation	3,742		2,414	
Other operating charges	24,764		25,968	
		324,963		320,102
Operating surplus		7,670		7,495
Interest receivable (net)		315		971
Surplus on ordinary activities		7,985		8,466
Interest payable on long-term				
loans		5,905		6,932
Retained surplus for the				
financial year		2,080		1,534

Source: *HMSO*, London. Crown copyright.

ministers, to be audited by the Comptroller and Auditor General. The following are currently constituted as trading funds:

(a) Her Majesty's Stationery Office;
(b) The Royal Mint;
(c) Crown Suppliers (providing office and other services to government departments).

The HMSO's Operating Account for 1987–88 is reproduced in Table 4.3.

The government maintains the central funds through which money is dispensed for the various services and loans made to nationalized industries and other Exchequer-financed bodies. The Consolidated Fund is the government's main account at the Bank of England, receiving

Table 4.4 National Insurance Fund: Account for the year ended 31 March 1987. Receipts and payments

	£000	£000	1985–86 £000
RECEIPTS			
Contributions	**22,949,571**		
Less Employers' recoveries in respect of SSP	**634,000**		
		22,315,571	20,790,208
Consolidated Fund Supplement		**2,412,000**	2,163,000
Income from investments		**610,328**	540,952
Other receipts		**1,987**	1,778
		25,339,886	23,495,938
Less			
PAYMENTS			
Benefits		**24,005,107**	22,308,825
Transfers to Northern Ireland		**175,000**	60,000
Administration		**738,055**	809,890
Other payments		**7,782**	1,709
		24,925,944	23,180,424
Excess of payments over receipts		—	—
Excess of receipts over payments		**413,942**	315,514
Statement of balances			
Balance at beginning of year		**5,293,024**	4,977,510
Less			
Excess of payments over receipts		—	—
Write-offs		—	—
Add			
Excess of receipts over payments		**413,942**	315,514
Balance at end of year		**5,706,966**	5,293,024

Source: *HMSO*, London.

revenue from taxes and other receipts and providing cash for most government expenditure.

The National Loans Fund, set up by the National Loans Fund Act 1968, handles all government borrowing, payment of debt interest and most domestic lending transactions. Both these are under Treasury control.

The National Insurance Fund, under the control of the Secretary of State for Health, receives the contributions from employees, employers and the self-employed, and a contribution from the government. It pays out the corresponding benefits, about half of which are pensions. Payments from the fund are included in the public expenditure totals, together with the rest of the large social security programme provided through Votes, including the non-contributory benefits such as child benefit.

These three government accounts, though showing the origin and use of very large sums, are simple in structure: see, for example, the National Insurance Fund for 1986/87 given in Table 4.4.

The Redundancy fund, under the Secretary of State for Employment, finances claims from employers for certain payments made to redundant employees. There are a number of other 'White Paper accounts', so-called because they are published in that form, showing the annual outcome, on an appropriate accounting basis, of services financed by statutory funds but managed separately from the departments' own direct expenditure.

There are no accounts, properly described as such or auditable, relating to the spending plans hitherto set out in the Public Expenditure White Paper. But it contained a great deal of statistical information setting the plans in a wide-ranging historical context, provided comparisons between expenditure plans and outturns for a number of years, and analysed features of special interest, such as capital spending, manpower costs and scientific research. This extensive system of financial reporting will continue in the new forms following the supersession of the White Paper.

For day-to-day control the Treasury's financial information system supplies a running check throughout the year on the progress of spending, readily related to the planning figures, the Supply Estimates, and other relevant budgetary provisions.

This set of accounts and financial information has been criticized (a) because much of it is on a cash basis, which is felt to be self-evidently inadequate, and (b) because it shows inputs, in terms of money spent, and not outputs, in terms of what the schools, hospitals, scientific research, defence and other manifold activities of government have achieved. The second criticism is losing much of its force as the development and use of performance indicators and other measures of output have accelerated. The production of more informative and better presented departmental reports, in succession to the somewhat indigestible mass of Part II of the White Paper, will reinforce the improvement.

The criticism of cash – or receipts and payments – as the form of much government accounting often fails to apprehend the relevance of some important considerations and the irrelevance of others. To substitute an obligations basis, whereby expenditure is related to commitments, somehow defined, might achieve a more realistic presentation in some respects at the cost of lack of precision and argument about forward liabilities. Accounts showing how money has been spent in relation to funds voted cannot also show the full costs of services or projects including depreciation of assets and provisions for losses. Most government activities accounted for in cash terms are quite different from trading operations where it is essential for survival to calculate expenditure and fix prices with adequate regard to the full annual costs, capital and current, being incurred. Capital expenditure on a warship or the new British Library should not be incurred without applying appropriate criteria, and it makes the same kind of demand on the construction and engineering industries as capital spending by business. The resulting equipment should be run as efficiently as possible, but it does not result in a stream of saleable products to generate profit, and the criteria for judging it will not be commercial criteria. The total cash spent by public bodies, for whatever purposes, is of importance for the government's monetary policy as it affects the money supply. Spending by a private company has no comparable significance and has to be judged differently by its contribution to profitability over a period of years and by any shorter-term problems of cash flow to which it may give rise.

These arguments, sound in themselves, leave room for manoeuvre in applying commercial concepts to public operations, for example in capital accounting and accommodation and staff costs. For a long time, ready reckoners have been available in the Civil Service to enable officials to calculate quickly, not just the pay bill of extra people, but the full staff costs including superannuation. If the Army provides quarters for its servicemen it is necessary to know the current cost of construction and management in deciding what rents to charge, subsidized or not. It may be operationally acceptable to move part of the Ministry of Social Security out of London at a big saving in accommodation costs, whereas a few hundred people in the Treasury or the Foreign Office may be inhabiting office space in Westminster at extremely high, but unavoidable, opportunity cost. If 'provider markets' develop in the NHS it may be necessary to value hospitals, but it serves no practical purpose to depreciate the latest battle tank or guided missile over an arbitrary period of years.

More sophisticated accounting systems need to be applied to all types of government operations where they can contribute to better decision-making or improved public information. This has been done for a long time where trading activity is involved, and has been emphasized by the establishment of the statutory trading funds. It is an important aspect of better management information in the context of the financial management initiative (see below), and it is increasingly being met by internal management accounts for particular services within departmental responsibility. Examples among many are the annual report of the Home Office's prison service which gives the costs of running the system, and the Ordnance Survey's published commercial accounts, both of which are linked to their management accounting systems. The questions always to be asked are: 'What purposes is the accounting treatment intended to serve?' and 'How will a particular presentation improve decision-taking?', not 'What are the professional accounting rules for this type of expenditure?', because they may or may not, in the public sector, be relevant.

Development of management in the Civil Service

There has been a sustained attempt during the 1980s to change the attitude of the Civil Service towards its responsibilities for the management of those services which the government provides, and the way it is organized to discharge them. The emphasis has been on the importance of the management role; the need to give those in charge of blocks or expenditure at various levels in government the maximum scope for the exercise of their own judgement, with a corresponding degree of personal accountability; and the provision of the necessary financial and other information to support the necessary decisions. It is believed that agreed policies can be carried out in alternative ways and with greater or lesser expenditure for essentially the same results, in contrast to the long accepted conviction by most civil servants that once 'policy' had been decided there was minimal scope for administrative savings in executing it. Policies themselves are not immune from challenge by officials, if by policies is meant particular methods or systems for securing the objectives set by ministers. The move to establish agencies to be responsible for the delivery of government services, discussed below, reflects the promotion of individual responsibility for securing agreed objectives within the degree of freedom of action which can be given to individual managers.

These changes are often viewed as the introduction of business or commercial values and methods. If by this is meant a greater awareness of costs, including the cost of staff time, recognition of the need to streamline working methods, devising and using adequate information systems to assist decision-making and managerial control, and promoting personal responsibility, it is correct. But the provision of public services has to meet objectives which do not constrain private business, notably public accountability through ministers, and equitable treatment of individual citizens in their dealings with the state.

One manifestation of this new thinking was the efficiency studies instituted by Sir (now Lord) Derek Rayner which examine in depth specific activities with a view to cutting costs and staff and tightening methods of work without detriment to results. These studies are now carried out by small departmental teams under the guidance and supervision of the Efficiency Unit of the Cabinet Office, responsible to the Prime Minister.

Another important development was the financial management initiative. The public expenditure survey, Ministers' decisions thereon, periodic policy reviews and the discipline of cash limits should suffice to determine and control the total of public spending and its allocation between competing services. The vote accounting system and the associated Parliamentary and audit procedures should guard against spending without constitutional authority and misappropriation of the public funds. But essential as they are for these purposes these arrangements are insufficient to secure maximum efficiency and cost-effectiveness in day-to-day management in departments. The government's financial management initiative (FMI) was designed to meet this need. It was first described publicly in 1982 in the government's reply to a report from the Parliamentary Treasury and Civil Service Committee on efficiency and effectiveness in the Civil Service (Cmnd 8616). It is both a financial and a management initiative. Its object is to promote in each government department an organization and a system in which civil servants in a managerial capacity at all levels have a clear view of their objectives, well defined responsibilities, and the necessary information to help discharge them. Clearly the nature of these responsibilities will vary greatly according to the particular job. Senior officials in the Treasury, responsible for advising on matters of monetary policy, may have virtually no expenditure under their direct control and few staff. A principal in the Department of Social Security may supervise the distribution of millions of pounds in benefits and have scores of people working on their detailed administration. A project manager in the Ministry of Defence may be in charge of the development and procurement of a complicated weapons system for whose success a variety of military, scientific, industrial, financial and administrative skills have to be satisfactorily combined. The management approach, and allocation of budgetary and other managerial tasks, must be adapted to the reality of each such situation.

Adequate, timely and relevant financial information is clearly one important requirement for successful management. The annual appropriation accounts obviously cannot meet it. Nor for that matter can the commercial accounts produced by departments which operate as trading funds. Even if their structure was fully consistent with the allocation of responsibilities within departments, these accounts could not display the necessary degree of detail, and in any case they are produced only annually some time after the end of the year to which they relate.

The Treasury's internal financial information system provides prompt expenditure figures throughout the year, but it was designed to meet broader objectives than those of middle managers responsible for specific parts of departmental programmes. Their need has to be met by the development and use of additional management information and accounting systems. They can vary in form from a full costing of a specific activity, say the acquisition, nurture and training of police dogs, to set against the outputs of these particular public servants, to the enumeration and costing of the multiple activities of a large department, such as the MINIS system (Management Information for Ministers) developed in the Department of the Environment. The aims of this type of analysis are to know what is being done in the pursuit of policy objectives, what it costs, and whether an alternative procedure could produce efficacious results more cheaply: better value for money, not a poorer standard of service. But value cannot be judged without some measure of assessment of what is produced. Sustained effort is therefore necessary and is being applied to the development and improvement of measures of output and performance. The greatly improved reports of some departments, for example the report *The Health Service in England* published by the Department of Health, contain numerous examples. More of these may now be confidently expected.

The FMI is not, however, simply a collection of financial and management techniques, however sophisticated. It also sets out to promote people's self-reliance and enthusiasm and to increase their job satisfaction, by giving them as much independence and personal responsibility for the achievement of their objectives and the management of their staff and budgets as is consistent with accepted policy and with their individual freedom of action. Granted that there are inevitable constraints on such freedom in large public service organizations, which have to operate within set policies and procedures and often with wide internal and external consultation, the FMI in practice is nevertheless demonstrating that there is more scope for it than had previously been thought. Progress on the FMI and its application in all the main government departments has been made public in successive White Papers.

Civil service management: agencies

Early in 1988 a report by the Efficiency Unit to the Prime Minister was published: *Improving Management in Government: The Next Steps*. It summarized the progress made under the financial management initiative and related developments, criticized some continuing aspects of Civil Service organization, ethos and approach, and made recommendations for further change, including the setting up of agencies to deliver governmental services to the public.

In a statement to Parliament on 18 February 1988 the Prime Minister announced that the government had accepted four of these recommendations:

(a) That to the greatest extent practicable the executive functions of government, as distinct from policy advice, should be carried out by units clearly designated within departments, referred to in the report as agencies, with responsibility for their day-to-day operations delegated to a chief executive within a framework of policy objectives and resources set by the responsible minister in consultation with the Treasury;

(b) That the government should commit themselves to a progressive programme for attaining this objective;
(c) That staff should be properly trained and prepared for the delivery of services 'inside or outside central government';
(d) That a 'project manager' at a senior level should ensure that the programme of change takes place.

These decisions represent an experiment in the development of units of accountable management within central government. Of the first twelve candidates for treatment as agencies, which include the Employment Service of the Department of Employment, Her Majesty's Stationery Office, the Royal Parks and Historic Royal Palaces and the Passport Department, three or four will be initially designated, including the Driver and Vehicle Licensing Directorate and the Vehicle Inspectorate of the Department of Transport, and the Companies Registration Office of the Department of Trade and Industry. It remains to be seen how far other proposals for introducing greater flexibility in such matters as Civil Service pay and grading structure, perhaps with regional differenti-ations, will be found workable and acceptable.

The promotion of management as an important skill, with as much devolved responsibility for meeting defined objectives as possible, is now widely accepted. But government services are delivered in accordance with policy decisions and within a close control of resources which the Treasury will certainly wish to maintain. Moreover, policy cannot be rigidly separated from administration; experience with the delivery of services, however efficiently managed, may well throw up problems or defects in the policy framework itself. Ministers must therefore retain ultimate responsibility. The extent to which senior officials, whether permanent secretaries, chief executives or otherwise designated, can reasonably be held accountable for their decisions and performance therefore depends on the extent of the responsiblities which can constitutionally and in practice fairly be attributed to them. In this connection it is of interest that the official heads of the new agencies are to be designated Accounting Officers, and are required to appear before the Public Accounts Committee to answer for their stewardship, though the departmental permanent secretary will also attend to answer for matters of policy reserved to the department and its minister.

Summary

This chapter has explained the government's central role in planning and controlling the expenditure of the public sector. This objective has been related to the economy as a whole, to the government's financial relations with local government and the public corporations, and to their own spending policies. The objectives and changing methods of departments in the day-to-day management of their programmes has been summarized. The framework of public accountability, the role of Parliament and of the select committees, and the supporting structure of government accounts and financial reports have been described. Important changes in the reporting system, superseding over the next few years the long standing Public Expenditure White Paper, have been indicated.

Further reading

Study of the main government documents published each year – the Public Expenditure White Paper (till 1990), the Autumn Statement, the Financial Statement and Budget Report, the departmental annual reports (from 1991) – will give a full and up-to-date picture of the presentations summarized in this book. *Government Accounting* (HMSO) describes the basic accounting system, including the Supply Estimates and Appropriation Accounts. The annual *Supply Estimates Summary and Guide* (HM Treasury) gives full details each year and explains the Parliamentary procedure. The House of Commons Treasury and Civil Service Select Committee reports on topical issues of expenditure policy and control; the Public Accounts Committee concentrates on financial management. The interplay of political, departmental and administrative aspects of public expenditure is discussed with considerable insight by Heclo and Wildavsky (1981) in *The Private Government of Public Money. Getting and Spending* (Pliatzky, 1982) gives a personal account of life in the Treasury by a former senior official who was concerned with the present author over several years in advising ministers on public expenditure matters.

Glossary*

Accounting Officer. An officer appointed by the Treasury historically in compliance with Section 22 of the Exchequer and Audit Departments Act 1866 to sign the Appropriation Accounts and any other accounts within his responsibility; and by virtue of that duty, the duty of being the principal witness on behalf of the department before the Committee of Public Accounts to deal with questions arising from those accounts, now covering financial management in its widest sense as well as matters of accuracy and regularity.

Ambit (of a Vote). The description in Part I of a Supply Estimate, or of a Supplementary Supply Estimate, of the purposes for which provision

---

* Taken from *Supply Estimates 1982–3*. Reproduced by permission of the Controller, Her Majesty's Stationery Office. Crown copyright.

is made. The ambit appears in the Schedule to the Appropriation Act
and Parliament authorizes specific sums of money to each ambit.

Appropriation Account. An end of year account of government departments' spending of monies voted by Parliament which compares the
Supply Estimate (and any Supplementary Estimates) with actual
payments made and receipts brought to account, and explains any
substantial differences. An Appropriation Account is prepared for each
Vote.

Appropriation in aid. Receipts which, with the authority of Parliament,
are used to finance some of the gross expenditure on the Vote, thus
limiting the amount to be issued from the Consolidated Fund to the net
Vote.

Capital expenditure. Expenditure on new construction, land and exten-
sions of and alterations to existing buildings and the purchase of any
other fixed assets (e.g. machinery and plant) – including vehicles –
having an expected working life of more than one year, and stocks. Also
includes grants for capital purposes and lending.

Cash limit. The limit on the amount of cash that can be spent on certain
specified services during one financial year.

Class. A group of Votes which broadly correspond to the voted expenditure element of one of the main programmes in the public expenditure
survey.

Consolidated Fund. The Exchequer account into which are paid gross tax
revenue, less repayments, and all other Exchequer receipts not
specifically directed elsewhere. Issues from the Fund include issues to
meet Supply services shown in Supply Estimates.

Contingencies Fund. A fund which can be used for urgent expenditure in
anticipation of provision by Parliament becoming available. The Fund
is limited to 2% of the previous year's total authorized Supply.
Drawings on this fund must be repaid when Parliament has voted the
additional sums required.

Economic classification. An analysis of public sector accounting transactions according to their economic character. It is based on the
classification used by the Central Statistical Office for compiling the
accounts of national income and expenditure.

Extra receipts by the Consolidated Fund. Receipts related to expenditure
in the Supply Estimate which Parliament has not authorized to be used
as appropriations in aid of the Vote.

Financial year. The year from 1 April one year to 31 March the next.

General administrative expenses. Current expenditure, other than pay,
directly related to administration such as post and telephones, stationery, etc.

Grant. Money voted (i.e. granted) by Parliament to meet the services
shown in Supply Estimates. Also used in individual subheads of Supply
Estimates to describe an unrequited payment to an individual or body,
in the private or public sector (see also Subsidy.)

Grant in aid. A grant from voted monies to a particular organization or body where any unexpended balances of the sums issued during the financial year will not be liable for surrender to the Consolidated Fund. In such cases the chief official of the grant-aided body normally accounts in detail for expenditure, and the Accounting Officer of the department issuing the grant has the broader responsibility of ensuring that the conditions of grant are met.

Main programme. One of 20 departmental functional programmes within the public expenditure survey, for example defence, housing, social security. Most main programmes are further divided into sub-programmes.

National Audit Office (formerly Exchequer and Audit Department). The department of the Comptroller and Auditor General. Officers of this department carry out the audit of Appropriation and Trading Accounts (other than that of their own department), many related accounts, and by agreement a number of international accounts such as those of some of the specialized agencies of the United Nations.

Net subhead. A net subhead is created when receipts are offset against expenditure in a specific subhead, rather than appropriated in aid of the vote as a whole. In most cases the receipts equal or exceed the expenditure and only a token £10 is shown to be voted.

Outturn. Actual expenditure, normally in a financial year.

Planning total. The aggregate used by the government for public expenditure control purposes.

Programme. See Main programme.

Section. A group of subheads in the same programme and Vote. Sections provide a means of summarizing a Vote if, for example, it covers more than one programme.

Subhead. Expenditure within a Vote which is separately identified in the Appropriation Account. (See also Net subhead.)

Subsidy. A grant (i.e. an unrequited payment) to a producer or trader which is deemed to benefit the consumer by reducing the selling price of the products. (See also Grant.)

Supply Estimate. A statement presented to the House of Commons of the estimated expenditure of a department during a financial year (i.e. 1 April to 31 March) asking for the necessary funds to be voted.

Token subhead. See Net subhead.

Token vote. In some cases receipts of a kind that could be appropriated in aid of the vote are expected on a scale equal to or greater than the expected gross expenditure. In these circumstances, sufficient of the expected receipts are shown as appropriations in aid to leave only a nominal balance, usually £1,000, to be voted as Supply. Part IV of the Estimate shows the balance of the receipts expected which are payable to the Consolidated Fund as extra receipts (see above). In addition, a Supplementary Estimate for a token sum may be presented, for example to transfer some existing provision to a new service in the same vote.

Vote. An individual Supply Estimate.

Votes on Account. Monies granted by Parliament to carry on public services from 1 April of the next financial year until the passing of the Appropriation Act, which authorizes the issue of the amount required for the full year.

Chapter 5

Local government and its financing

Finance and accounting in local government is probably more complex than in any other part of the public sector. In a book of this kind it is therefore not possible to provide a fully comprehensive coverage of all facets of the subject. The aim of this chapter and the following one is to provide an introduction, while highlighting points of current debate.

This chapter outlines the structure of local government and goes on to examine the many aspects of the financial relationship between central and local government. The next chapter reviews the external reporting and internal control of local government.

Because local government finance and accounting have developed in a distinctive fashion, they have developed a terminology that may be unfamiliar even to those with experience of finance in either the public or private sector.

Structure and functions

The legislative programme following the 1979 general election contained a substantial amount relating to local government. But this was surpassed by the post 1987 election programme, which involved major leglislation relating to local government finance, competitive tendering, housing policy and finance, higher education, schools devolution and urban development. Because this type of legislation often leaves many important matters to be dealt with in regulations, details of the systems of local government finance are inevitably subject to regular change. These chapters are based on the systems of finance which at the time of writing (early 1989) are expected to be implemented in 1990 or earlier in some form.

It has to be borne in mind that British local government is not homogeneous. There are different systems of local government in England, Wales, Scotland and Northern Ireland. It is not possible to take full account of this variety and the material below specifically relates to England, although for most purposes this also covers Wales. Scotland has a broadly similar system of local government but a different legislative framework. Northern Ireland has, at present, a much more limited form of local government.

Parish councils (community councils in Wales) are local authorities and an important part of the fabric of local democracy – there are over 9,000 in the UK. But as they are not major spenders, they are not covered in depth.

The environment of local government

Local authorities in Great Britain provide a very wide range of services which, as with the nationalized industries, have a daily impact on almost everyone. The functions of local government are diverse and the allocation of functions between authorities as of April 1990 is summarized in Table 5.1. This is not a definitive guide, but is intended to indicate just how disparate are the activities of local government. Unlike the health service and major nationalized industries, local government does not have one broad unifying service or function. Any local authority is responsible for a range of functions, often with no apparent link except that they are provided by a single body.

Even within English local government, which forms the main frame of reference for this chapter, taking a particular group of authorities, e.g. metropolitan districts with the same basic functions, it is important not to underestimate the variety of practice and style of operation. Each has a different set of problems, of elected members and of staff. Local government is not uniform. This is the idea behind *local* government, although it is not always appreciated and certainly not always supported by those involved in commenting on, consuming or even providing local government services.

It is not possible here to devote much space to the history of local government and how it developed into present day structure and functions. It may perhaps suffice to say that local government has evolved gradually from a pre-nineteenth century system of counties, boroughs and parishes.

Local government's modern history has been dominated by a major reorganization in 1974 in England and Wales outside London (1975 in Scotland), which altered structures – amalgamating authorities – and the allocation of functions both between types of authority and between local government and other public bodies.

The most significant restructuring that took place after 1974 was the abolition of the Greater London Council and the metropolitan county councils, effective from 1986. Their services were transferred to the borough councils, to *ad hoc* bodies such as fire boards and waste disposal authorities, and in some cases outside local government altogether. To handle the after-effects of abolition, Residuary Bodies were set up in each area. The legislative programme that followed the Conservatives winning

Table 5.1 Main functions of local authorities as at 1 April 1990

Function	Metropolitan		England and Wales non-metropolitan		London		Scotland	
	Joint	District	County	District	Joint	Borough	Region	District
Community charge collection		x		x		x		x
Consumer protection	x		x			x	x	x
Education		x	x			x	x	
Environmental health		x		x		x		x
Fire service	x		x		x		x	
Housing		x		x		x		x
Industrial development		x		x		x	x	x
Libraries		x	x	x		x		x
Passenger transport	x		x				x	
Planning								
Strategic plans		x	x			x	x	
Development control		x		x		x		x
Police	x		x		(Central Government)		x	
Recreation		x	x	x		x		x
Refuse disposal	x		x		x			x
Social services		x	x			x	x	
Transport and highways								
Policy and principal roads		x	x			x	x	
Non-principal roads		x	x	x		x	x	
Water							x	

The aim of this list is to give a brief summary of the distribution of the main functions. There are many footnotes possible in a list of this type and a detailed summary can be found in Byrne (1981). In London and the metropolitan counties joint boards, committees or authorities carry out a number of county-wide functions.

the 1987 general election contained a very substantial amount relating to local government. The major structural change was the abolition of the Inner London Education Authority (ILEA), with its services being transferred to the Inner London Boroughs from 1990.

However, other proposals would remove, or threaten to remove, significant parts of services from local government. The extension of compulsory competitive tendering to more services represented a potentially *ad hoc* loss of services. In education, the Education Reform Act led to the polytechnics and certain higher education colleges transferring to independent status from 1989. In housing, the creation of housing action trusts involved the government transferring some large estates to the trusts. Then after refurbishment properties can be sold or passed to other landlords. The extension of urban development corporations further eroded local authorities' scope for discretion. In both housing and education there were mechanisms developed for tenants and schools respectively opting out of local authority control.

The only area potentially identified for growth was the personal social services, where the 1988 report on Community Care by Sir Roy Griffiths recommended transfer of prime responsibility for certain clients to local authorities from the health service, although even here he envisaged the role as facilitating rather than of necessity always as a service provider.

Internal organization and structure

Of the over 500 principal local authorities in the UK, probably no two have exactly the same internal organization and structure. *Local* authorities will be organized to best reflect *local* situations. But, in practice, there is considerable similarity in terms of the general principles of organization and structure, which tend to group around a few broad types.

One of the distinct features of local government, which has widespread implications for both financial policy and operations, is the predominant and often detailed role played by elected councillors (or elected members as they often are also called) in management. This has few parallels in central government where most ministers cannot, by reason of time, become over-involved in detailed operations.

But in local government the committee, composed of elected councillors advised by officers, not only performs a monitoring role but also has executive powers. Although the roles of committees may have gradually changed, it would be unwise to underestimate their continuing importance. And although the relative 'strength' of officers and members is as lively a topic of debate now as it was in the nineteenth century, there is little indication that local authorities are becoming more dominated by their full-time paid officers.

The Widdicombe Committee (1986) reviewed the roles of councillors and officers in some depth, and recommended a number of changes to previous practice, including the clear identification of the chief executive as head of the paid service. But only a small number of the Committee's recommendations were eventually accepted by the government.

Approaches to management

The dominant management theme in the 1970s and early 1980s was the idea of corporate management, which gathered momentum in local government in the 1960s. It was stimulated by the Maud Management Committee Report (Committee on the Management of Local Government, 1967), which was critical of the lack of a corporate approach by both members and officers. The tradition of separate committees and departments was strong, and indeed continues to be so. Maud's well thought out but radical ideas found favour only in a few authorities initially and it has to be said that much of his critique still holds true today. But by the time the Bains Report (1972) was published, there was at least acceptance of the need to set up a structure which could promote corporate management even if the structure alone was not enough. Such structures included a chief executive with a clear brief to coordinate and lead a management team of directors to provide a vehicle for coordination, and a greater number of interdepartmental working groups to promote closer working between staff at a variety of levels.

Authorities today do tend to have corporate management structures. The policy and resources committee, recommended by Bains as a central unifying influence, is found almost universally. So, too, is the chief executive. He or she is no longer the old town clerk, *primus inter pares* with fellow chief officers, but clearly head of the paid service. Almost all authorities now have chief officer management teams chaired by the chief executive (perhaps also now with elected members present) to coordinate the council's day-to-day affairs. Whether or not these structures do lead to effective corporate management is quite another matter and they certainly do not guarantee it.

At the time of the 1974 reorganization there was much concern among chief financial officers that corporate management would put them in a subordinate position, subject to consensus decision-making, and even to the lowest common denominator. This has happened in some places and it has been felt to happen in others; but overall a tremendous amount depends on the calibre and personality of chief financial officers and their staff. And corporate management has brought advantages to the finance department because they are at the centre of the system. Problems of overlap do occur, e.g. 'What is the role of the chief executive or director of personnel in budgeting?', but in practice the advent of corporate management has not usually weakened the influence of a good chief financial officer.

From the mid-1980s onwards a new managerial theme for local

government developed, namely an increased emphasis on explicit accountability and greater devolution of managerial power and responsibility. This was not necessarily in sharp contrast to corporate management, which had often worked in loosely 'federal' systems. But it did represent a very different type of culture and required a different set of attitudes, perhaps particularly from the chief financial officer, whose systems and procedures are essential components of greater devolution.

The need for local government

Though virtually all developed countries have a system of local government, some systems involve considerable local autonomy, while others involve less. On a spectrum, the English and Welsh systems probably involve less, rather than more, autonomy.

But why have local government at all? This question and the answers are important because they reflect the type of financial framework required. One summary of the case for local government is L. J. Sharpe's (1970):

To sum up: the participatory value, if not the liberty value, still remains as a valid one for modern local government. Not perhaps in the full glory of its early promoters, but as an important element in a modern democracy nonetheless. But as a coordinator of services in the field; as a reconciler of community opinion; as a consumer pressure group; as an agent for responding to rising demand; and finally as a counterweight to incipient syndicalism, local government seems to have come into its own.

The Layfield Committee (1976, p. 53) listed the following points in local government's favour:

(a) It provides democracy;
(b) It acts as a counterweight to the uniformity inherent in government decisions. It spreads political power;
(c) It embraces accountability because it brings those responsible for decisions close to their electors;
(d) It is efficient because services can be adjusted to local needs and preferences, and because responsibility can be more decentralized;
(e) Central government would be overloaded by more functions;
(f) It provides a vehicle for formulating new policies and pioneering ideas. Scope for these are limited in centralized organizations concerned to apply policies uniformly.

It is noticeable that at a time when many inside local government felt that constitutional and financial developments were challenging the traditions of local government, there was a growth in publications justifying the bases of local government (Stewart, 1983, and Local Government Training Board, 1984).

Local authority associations

One aspect of local authority structure that is particularly important is the role of the local authority associations. In Scotland there is a single association representing all authorities – Regions, Islands and Districts – particularly in relations with central government. An equivalent to this single Confederation of Scottish Local Authorities (COSLA) does not exist in England, where the different types of local authority have their own associations, namely:

ACC: Association of County Councils (non-metropolitan counties);
ADC: Association of District Councils (non-metropolitan districts);
AMA: Association of Metropolitan Authorities (metropolitan counties and districts and London Boroughs).

In London political differences led to the splitting of councils into two groups:

LBA: London Boroughs Association;
ALA: Association of London Authorities.

Some authorities belong to no association.

The associations play a key role in representing and advocating their members' interests, particularly with central government. They are convenient to central government who would find difficulty negotiating with a large number of individual authorities. The associations are political bodies with a majority party, whose view will generally predominate in major policy issues. Since at any one time the English associations may be under differing political control, this has often made it difficult for local government to present a common stand on major financial issues. United opposition to the passage of the 1980 Local Government Planning and Land Act through Parliament was diffused when the Association of County Councils in essence agreed with the government to reduce the scale of their opposition to the legislation.

The legislative basis of local government

Almost all local government's powers are derived from legislation and, in contrast to the arrangements in some other countries, local authorities do not have the power to spend on any purpose they see fit, except for a 2p rate 'in the interests of their area' under Section 137 of the 1972 Local Government Act. (After 1990 it is proposed to alter this to £5 per head.) The legislative framework is of great importance to the finance, accounting and audit of local government, and local finance has become increasingly subject to the legislative decisions of Parliament.

In some of the major current issues surrounding local government, there is a close link between constitutional, legislative and financial matters and it is therefore necessary to examine the background to these and indeed to touch on the rationale for local government, as it is difficult to make judgements about the efficiency and effectiveness of local government and its finance merely by examining structure and functions.

The legislative framework covers three broad areas:

(a) Duties or powers to provide **services**;
(b) Specification of the **structure** of local government;
(c) Specification of the arrangements for **financing** local authorities.

Some Acts of Parliament have touched on all three areas; for example, the 1972 Local Government Act restructured local government boundaries and functions in England and Wales, consolidated legislation relating to powers and duties, and contained some financial clauses. But the 1972 Act did not in fact reflect a simultaneous and systematic review of services, structure and finance. It was really about structural review. One of its great faults was that it did not also reform finance.

Financial changes were made in 1948, 1958, 1966, 1976, 1980, 1982, 1984, 1986 and 1988, but were concerned only with parts of local government finance, such as rating or grants, and were in no sense comprehensive measures of financial reform. And when it comes to powers and duties, these have accumulated through literally dozens of Acts of Parliament passed over many years. Powers and duties are also affected by secondary legislation – regulations and statutory instruments – which are also extensive in scope.

Even though Acts of Parliament may contain reference to financial implications, there is no close or necessary relation between the powers and duties which have accumulated over many years and the equally *ad hoc* financial framework which has developed.

Two aspects of the legislative basis of local government need to be highlighted because of their far-reaching implications. The first is the degree to which legislation categorizes local authority powers between 'mandatory' powers, which impose a duty on local authorities to do something, and 'discretionary' powers, which allow them to provide a service at their own discretion. If it were possible to separate powers, and hence expenditure, into such categories it would assist in the clarification of many important aspects of local government finance. The Layfield Committee (1976) reviewed this question in some depth, and the review is contained in Annex 12 of their Report. It repays reading in full.

The conclusions reached were of great significance and the key aspects, summarized below, demonstrate the complexity of the influences on local government spending:

The respective responsibilities of central and local government for local services could not at present be expressed in terms which could form a reliable base for the allocation of financial responsiblity.

The difficulty we encountered throughout was that the categories of local government expenditure which are manifestly either totally discretionary or totally mandatory are very limited; the bulk of local government expenditure falls somewhere between the two extremes, being determined not by formal requirements alone nor by free local choice alone but by a complex mixture of pressures and influences. Informal advice and exhortation from government departments, inspection, nationally accepted standards, accumulated past practice, professional attitudes, political influences and actions by various pressure groups, national and local, all play a part in determining local government expenditure, along with the statutory provisions. (Layfield Committee (1976) pp. 403–404.)

The second aspect of local government legislation which has become a matter of note is the marked extent to which topics relating to a local authority expenditure have become the subject of dispute in the courts. Up to the late 1970s this was a rare occurrence, but by the late 1980s there had been a variety of court cases on local authority expenditure, the best known being the case brought by Bromley LBC against the Greater London Council over the legality of a supplementary rate levied primarily to enable a fares reduction to be made on London Transport. But there were also cases brought by industrial firms and ratepayers' groups over rates and expenditure being too high, as well as by consumer or pressure groups over failures to provide services. Local authorities also began to use the courts to try to reverse decisions of the Secretary of State for the Environment which were, in their opinion, unreasonable. The variety of this litigation demonstrated the extent to which local government finance had become a matter of confrontation rather than consensus.

Local authority income and expenditure – a summary

Local authority income and expenditure can be categorized in a variety of ways, and each of the most important categories is highlighted below. In most cases, these categories have significance either for resource allocation at the national level or locally or for control mechanisms. To make the summaries readily comprehensible, concepts and definitions have been presented in a simplified form, and fuller details will be found in the original sources.

Because at the time of writing the only actual data available related to rates not community charge, this is shown in the following tables. Where community charge or other aspects of the new system of local government finance have a significant effect, additional data based on estimates are shown. One problem of terminology is that both the pre-1990 grant system (Rate Support Grant) and the post-1990 system (Revenue Support Grant) have the initials RSG. At several points they will be referred to generically as rate/revenue support grant.

The first major subdivision is between capital and revenue expenditure. In the 1980s, capital expenditure bore the brunt of the cuts in local

Table 5.2 Distribution of gross capital expenditure

Service	% of gross capital expenditure
Education	9
Housing	53
Environmental Services	21
Police and Fire	4
Transport	11
Social Services	8
	100

Source: *Local Government Financial Statistics 1985/86* (1988), DOE, by permission of the Controller, HMSO. Crown copyright.

government services, particularly those falling on housing capital expenditure (Table 5.2).

Turning to gross revenue expenditure, this is summarized in Fig. 5.1 and the sources of gross income in Fig. 5.2. It can be seen that revenue expenditure is dominated by the education service.

Turning to the sources of revenue finance, it can be seen that, in the pre-1990 situation, rates were a minority source of finance. Central government grants of one type or another represented about half total income. It is perhaps hardly surprising that central government takes so much interest in the details of local authority expenditure. The importance of sales, fees, charges and similar types of income is sometimes overlooked and this is an area that has received increasing attention. The relationship between grants and local tax (rates or community charge) means that relatively small changes in government grant received can have a quite dramatic effect on local income requirements.

The Housing Revenue Account has a quite different type of financial profile from other services. Its revenue expenditure is dominated by loan charges, representing the cost of borrowing to create the housing stock. Government subsidies are reducing in importance and rents have generally been increased substantially in real terms in consequence. From 1990 housing revenue accounts will be 'ring-fenced', to eliminate subsidies from and contributions to general council resources. For some councils and their tenants this will mean dramatic changes in rent levels.

Local authorities' past borrowing is reflected in the very large volume of debt outstanding – over £30,000 million. This does not represent authorities being in deficit on revenue account – there are only very limited powers to borrow for this purpose – but instead reflects the creation of social infrastructure. The loans financing this debt derive

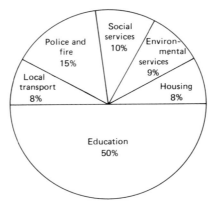

Fig. 5.1 Where the money goes. Derived from *Local Government Financial Statistics, England and Wales 1985/86* (1988), DOE, by permission of the Controller, HMSO. Crown copyright.

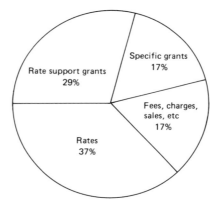

Fig. 5.2 Where the money comes from. Derived from *Local Government Financial Statistics, England and Wales 1985/86* (1988), DOE, by permission of the Controller, HMSO. Crown copyright.

from a variety of sources (Table 5.3) with the Public Works Loans Board – part of central government – being the major source. In any one year, local authorities will use funding other than loan, and the major sources of capital finance are shown in Table 5.4.

Local and central government – financial relations

The sections above outlined the way local authorities are structured and managed, and briefly indicated sources of finance and types of expendi-

Table 5.3 Summary of debt outstanding by source of finance (England)

Source of loans	% as at 31 March 1986
Public Works Loans Board	78
Banks and financial institutions	16
Other	6
Total	100

Source: *Local Government Financial Statistics 1985/86* (1988) DOE , by permission of the Controller, HMSO. Crown copyright.

Table 5.4 Methods of capital finance

	% of gross capital financing resources
Net borrowing	40
Capital receipts – Rate Fund	20
Capital receipts – Housing Revenue a/c	30
Capital receipts – Other	3
Government grant	7
Total	100

Source: *Local Government Financial Statistics 1985/86* (1988) DOE , by permission of the Controller, HMSO. Crown copyright.

ture. Attention is now directed to probably the single most important topic in local government finance and accounting – the relations between central and local government. This topic has, directly and indirectly, been the subject of a large and increasing literature, including the report of a major Commission of Enquiry (the Layfield Committee).

The very magnitude and complexity of the subject makes it difficult to summarize in an introductory text. It has also latterly been an area subject to frequent, if not over-frequent, policy changes and legislation. This means that not only points of detail, but also points of principle can rapidly become outdated. In general, therefore, the discussion below tries to emphasize general principles. These are accompanied by relatively brief descriptions of the grant and resource allocation systems in force at the time of writing (early 1989). For those requiring a more detailed and up-to-date explanation of a particular area, further sources are indicated in the bibliography, at the end of this book.

Three areas are examined to illustrate the nature of the central–local relationship, and how it is changing. They are the main areas in which central government sets finance targets, either for local government as a whole or for individual authorities:

(a) The Public Expenditure White Paper;
(b) Revenue support grant;
(c) Capital programmes.

Other areas of importance with their own particular legal or policy context, but which are not examined here, are housing and transport finance, education pooling, borrowing controls, charging policies and direct labour organizations.

The question of the central–local financial relationship has been a source of concern on both sides for the hundred years that modern local government has existed. Formal and informal reviews and reports have been produced, typically with few changes actually arising from them. In 1974 the then government set up a Committee of Enquiry into Local Government (the Layfield Committee) which was to undertake the most thorough review of local government finance and its report discusses many areas of local government finance and its report discusses many areas of local government finance. A few key points relating to the central–local relationship are outlined below, discussing the three types of financial target.

An early discovery of the Layfield Committee was that:

We were asked to consider the whole system of local government finance and we have come to the conclusion that there is at present no coherent system. (p. 49).

Layfield categorized the requirements of a coherent financial system as (Layfield Committee 1976):

(a) Accountability
(b) Fairness between individuals
(c) Fairness between areas
(d) Balance between consumption and investment
(e) Efficiency
(f) Stability
(g) Flexibility
(h) Comprehensibility

and also pointed out that finance could not really be reviewed in isolation from the structure and functions of local government.

The role of central government

Central government's perception of its role in relation to local government was set out clearly in its response to Layfield:

Because of their responsibilities for the management of the economy, central government must concern themselves with total local government expenditure and taxation. They also have responsibility for the development of policy for particular services. Central government's role is therefore:

— to ensure that the local services (education, personal social services, housing, etc.) reflect national priorities and national policies and are provided at broadly comparable standards;
— to ensure that, in aggregate, local government's spending plans are compatible with the government's economic objectives;
— to ensure that activities of one authority do not have adverse effects on the area of another;
— to promote cooperation between local authority and other complementary services;
— to ensure that the financial arrangements promote efficiency;
— to safeguard the interest of vulnerable minority groups whose intersts may get a proper hearing only at national level;
— to encourage and maintain local democracy.

(Reproduced from DOE Green Paper *Local Government Finance* (1977) by permission of the Controller, HMSO. Crown copyright.)

The government's response to Layfield's 'central' and 'local' options was to define a middle way – which Layfield had rejected as a possibility. It proposed to develop a block grant and to 'strengthen' financial machinery for four reasons:

(a) **Expenditure control** – central government needs to be able to exert more effective influence over total local authority expenditure;
(b) **Equity** – ratepayers should pay a similar rate poundage for a comparable level of service wherever they live;
(c) **Accountability** – local electors need to have some improved way of assessing local spending decisions and of requiring local authorities to account for them;
(d) **Policy control** – in some services the government needs to have additional financial powers to promote particular policies.

In Layfield's terms, these conclusions probably represented an implicit move towards a more centrally based approach, and with the coming into effect of the legislation for 1990 this centrally based approach became even more pronounced.

The macroeconomic case for controlling local government spending

The Layfield Committee supported the government's objective of controlling the total of local authority expenditure – neither local authorities nor local tax payers being in a position to assess the competing claims on national resources or the pressures which local authority expenditure may generate.

There are, however, other views, as Barlow (1981) describes in his useful review of the various Keynesian, monetarist and structuralist arguments for macroeconomic control. He concludes:

If local democracy is to be valued highly, then this freedom (to make choices about the provision of services) is essential to local government, and if local government is to be preserved, local authorities should not longer accept unequivocally the argument that control over their levels of expenditure by central government is essential to economic management. (p. 12)

There is not space here to consider these macroeconomic questions in more depth, but it is certainly the case that within local government there is no longer the near-unanimous agreement to the government's right to control total local spending that there once was. Most local authorities do take note of the government's broad wishes, but the essence of local democracy is to be able to act according to local needs and preferences, if necessary. This is why there is widespread hostility to specific controls even by authorities who would generally have no need to worry about the adverse impacts of such controls themselves.

The public expenditure white paper

The production of the Public Expenditure White Paper is discussed in Chapter 4. For local government, a body formally involved in the public expenditure process is the Consultative Council on Local Government Finance (CCLGF). This was set up in 1975 to promote regular consultation and cooperation between central and local government on major issues of common concern, with special emphasis on the deployment of resources both in the long and short term. The CCGLF is the forum for all ministerial-level meetings on the RSG and is supported by various groups of officials representing both central government and the local authority associations.

Some of the topics regularly discussed at the Consultative Council are set out below. Approximate timings are shown but latterly experience has shown that there are no 'normal' years:

March	– Setting the terms of reference for the officer working groups on grant and expenditure for the ensuing year;
May	– Consideration of the DOE/CIPFA return of expenditure;
July	– Local authorities' input into the Public Expenditure Survey Committee (PESC);
October	– Negotiations on expenditure considered relevant for RSG;
December	– The statutory meeting on RSG.

The local authority associations pressed for over a decade for more involvement in the public expenditure survey process because:

(a) Local authorities only provide an input in describing the policy implications on different funding levels. They play no part in the actual decisions on plans;

(b) Local authorities are actually responsible for a very significant section of public expenditure;

(c) If the central government were to win local government's confidence and support in pursuing national policies, local government would have to feel it had participated in the deliberations whereby those policies are fixed;

(d) Local authorities are directly in touch with the real needs of the public and are best able to assess the impacts of government policies on their own environments.

The CCLGF does enable local authorities to put their views to a variety of ministers but whether it, and the subsidiary committees, really provide effective two-way consultation is another matter. During the economic constraints which have characterized most of the period since 1974 local government reorganization, central governments of different political persuasion have often been seen by local authorities as directing rather than consulting.

In the absence of what they regard as genuine consultation, it is perhaps hardly surprising that the local authority associations refuse to frank the government's detailed decisions. For example, in one RSG Report (Local Authority Associations, 1981) they pointed out:

Annexe A to the RSG Report, 1980, sets out a breakdown of expenditure between services, which is stated to be tentative, and one which will be affected by individual local authorities' decisions taken in the light of their judgement of local needs and conditions. The associations do not endorse this or any breakdown of local authority expenditure (p. 33).

Having noted the local authority associations' misgivings about their own role in the public expenditure survey, there is no doubt that the White Paper has been an important document for local authorities for several reasons:

(a) Given the importance of central government decisions on rate support grant and over capital expenditure allocations, any indications of the government's intentions will assist planning;

(b) The relative priority given to local government spending as opposed to other areas of public expenditure can be seen;

(c) Though there is a general feeling in local government that they retain the right to make their own decisions, local authorities are responsible bodies which will often wish to take the government's wishes into account in finalizing their expenditure plans;

(d) The breakdown of expenditure for services is useful in this context for deriving *overall* charges for different types of authority.

There were, however, problems of both principle and latterly of practice which tended to reduce the relevance of the Public Expenditure White Paper to local government. In particular, the move to cash planning in the 1982/83 White Paper and the complete absence of constant price forecasts reduced the usefulness of the White Paper for most kinds of planning in the local government sector. Despite their own reservations, the local authority associations pressed for more involvement in the PESC process, but it was increasingly being argued in local government circles (see Raine, 1981) that, in fact, local authorities' own expenditure should be removed from the Public Expenditure White Paper, which should be concerned only with the expenditure directly under the control of central government (e.g. grants and loans to local government). This is because local authorities are autonomous bodies with a right to set their own local tax and responsible for carrying out legislation in the ways felt to be necessary by them in relation to local interpretation of needs. It will only be a coincidence if the totality of local government expenditure, arrived at by hundreds of local decisions, equates to a national planning figure over which local government has no real influence.

In the summer of 1988, central government eventually conceded to this point in the White Paper (Cm 441) and, as described in Chapter 4, local authority expenditure funded from local sources was to be removed from public expenditure plans. Only central government grants and the borrowing approvals on capital were to be included.

This could be treated, as the White Paper suggested, as consistent with increasing the accountability of local government. Alternatively, it could be considered that because only a relatively small proportion of local government net expenditure was to be locally funded from 1990, the new definition would still cover the great bulk of local authority spending.

Sources of income

The government's reaction to Layfield, set out in a May 1977 Green Paper (DOE, 1977), foreshadowed major changes. It proposed moving forward in areas such as Unitary Grant and an Advisory Committee on Audit. The main proposal on a new grant system was subject to great hostility from the local authority associations and was dropped. The incoming government of 1979 introduced both the block grant and new controls on capital and direct labour organizations in the Local Government, Planning and Land Act of 1980. Further alterations to block grant and a new audit system were brought in with the Local Government Finance Act of 1982. These measures were intended to secure greater control by central government on the one hand and greater accountability to local communities on the other. It was agreed by individual members of the Layfield Committee (Raine, 1981) that this outcome intensified the confusion inherent in the old system. And with another Green Paper *Alternatives to Domestic Rates* (DOE, 1981c), again concentrating on just one aspect of local govenment finance in isolation, there was powerful evidence that the lessons of Layfield had not been learnt.

In order to clarify the central–local relationships the Layfield Committee had set out two alternative systems of local government finance:

(a) **Based on greater central responsibility** – under this, both the total of local expenditure and the priorities between local services would be decided by the government, which would be seen to carry the main responsibilities for expenditure control;
(b) **Based on greater local responsibility** – the responsibility for control of expenditure would rest primarily with local authorities. They would be responsible to their electorates for expenditure incurred and revenues raised. Grants would not play a dominant role and the local tax base would need to be widened. The government's powers would only operate to meet the needs of national economic management, of which local authorities should have full understanding.

The Committee did put a strongly-held view among their members that the only way to sustain a vital local democracy was to enlarge the share of local taxation to make councillors more accountable to local electorates. A local income tax for this purpose would be justified.

Since Layfield reported, the local income tax has been rejected by government, though it has been argued that it could have been viable (Bennett, 1981). Most of those involved in local government in England would argue that the incoherent system of finance discovered by Layfield was becoming even more incoherent in the 1980s.

A further review was set in motion in 1984 with a view to reporting during 1985. This was set up as an internal departmental review by junior ministers at the Department of the Environment. The government's belief was that this would lead to more chance of useful progress than would occur through the full panoply of a formal enquiry.

From this emerged the Green Paper *Paying for Local Government* published in January 1986. Its key theme was the need for increased local accountability:

Effective local accountability must be the cornerstone of successful local government. All too often this accountability is blurred and weakened by the complexities of the national grant system and by the fact that differences arise among those who vote for, those who pay for and those who receive local government services.

The present local government finance system does not strengthen local

accountability. Local authorities' main income sources are non-domestic rates, domestic rates and Exchequer grant. All of them are unsatisfactory.
— Non-domestic rates are paid by businesses and public institutions to whom local authorities are not directly answerable.
— Domestic rates are paid by a minority of local electors, and vary in a way that now has little or no regard to the use made of local authority services. The burden of rates is carried on too few shoulders.
— Central government grants are calculated in a very complicated way that conceals the real cost of local services from the local electorate.

So in almost every respect the existing local government finance system makes it almost impossible for local electors to relate what they pay to the services provided.
   We must put this right. If people can understand the costs of the different services provided to them, and if the costs are fairly distributed, they can then make sensible choices not only about the balance between local priorities but also about the overall level of spending.   (DOE, 1986)

   The Green Paper proposed:

(a) The abolition of domestic rates and their replacement by a community charge, with effect from 1 April 1990 in England and Wales, payable by all adults. There would be three types of community charge:
     (i) **Personal** – falling on virtually all adults;
     (ii) **Collective** – primarily for people living in multiple occupation rented accommodation and institutions;
     (iii) **Standard** – for second home owners, up to a maximum of two individual charges;
(b) Community charge registration to be a district function in England and Wales, and carried out on a rolling basis;
(c) All adults to pay at least 20% of the community charge, including those in receipt of social security;
(d) Government to retain the power to cap the community charge of individual councils;
(e) A Uniform Business Rate, set by central government, and reallocated to councils pro rata to population;
(f) The possibility of a small locally determined business rate was discussed;
(g) A simplified and more certain Revenue Support Grant, split into needs and standard grants, to replace Rate Support Grant;
(h) The system to be phased in over a period not exceeding 10 years, and perhaps relatively quickly in some areas;
(i) New options for capital expenditure controls;
(j) New statutory duties for the chief financial officer.

   The Green Paper was heavily criticized by local government interests, and in particular the community charge was criticized on the following grounds:

(a) The regressiveness of such a tax, particularly with the proposal in the Green Paper that all adults on social security should pay at least 20% of the community charge from their own means;
(b) The problems involved in registering all the adult population, including both the extra costs of administration and the data protection aspects;
(c) The assumption that because domestic rates were levied on households this meant that only one member of the household perceived the impact of those rates;
(d) The removal of a tax on property would eventually push up the price of that property, as had already occurred on commercial properties in enterprise zones that had been made exempt from non-domestic rates;
(e) The whole package of changes to local government finance taken together meant that the proportion of local government spending funded from local sources would fall from about 50% (22% domestic ratepayers, 28% non-domestic) to 22%. It was also proposed to retain community-charge capping to prevent irresponsible authorities from imposing excessive burdens on their taxpayers. Neither of these measures was felt to be unequivocally increasing local accountability; indeed it appeared to many that they represented reductions in such accountability;
(f) A flat rate local tax had no parallel in any developed country in the world, and had not been given serious consideration by any of the major independent studies into local government finance;
(g) The political economic thinking that analysed the relationship between adults and their local authorities wholly in financial terms on a link between local taxation and local accountability, when this logic was not, for example, also thought to be relevant to central government.

Probably the most fundamental weakness in the rationale for community charge was the belief that there would be a clear relationship between local spending decisions and the level of community charge. This was stated at its clearest by the Treasury White Paper *A New Public Expenditure Total*:

The effect of these new arrangements will be to ensure that each pound per adult more or less that a local authority spends will add to or reduce community charge bills by one pound.

Ironically, this was published in the same week as a study by CIPFA (Hale, 1988) showed that this was not likely to be the case. The Treasury had made the assumption that all other things would remain equal, but this would not be the case in reality. Among the factors that would break the direct linkage would be:

(a) Failure to increase uniform business rate or revenue support grant in line with the level of inflation actually incurred by local authorities;

(b) Changes to the formula for calculating needs assessments for RSG;
(c) Changes in the adult population that were not immediately reflected in the level of spending on services, as population would critically affect community charge, the allocation of the uniform business rate and the RSG needs assessment;
(d) Variations in shortfalls of collection of community charge and business rates from the levels assumed by the government.

The community charge and the revenue support grant passed into legislation for England and Wales in 1988 in the Local Government Finance Act, to take effect from April 1990. However, in Scotland, implementation of community charge was to take place a year earlier under the Abolition of Domestic Rates Etc. (Scotland) Act 1987. It is believed that the political outcry that had followed the 1985 domestic rates revaluation in Scotland had been a key factor in the political thinking behind abolition of rates, particularly as Scotland had had a revaluation in 1978, whereas rateable values in England and Wales had not been revalued since 1973 due to successive governments deferring the exercise.

The legislation passed after considerable political debate, and in the process some of the Green Paper proposals were modified:

(a) The proposal that everyone should pay at least 20% of their community charge was dropped. Supplementary benefit recipients would be reimbursed on the basis of 20% of a national average personal community charge; this would impact adversely on those people who lived in areas with above average levels of community charge. A number of total exemptions were also conceded;
(b) The 10 year transitional period was dropped completely. Initially the Bill envisaged that transition would only apply to 13 high cost London Boroughs. Following political lobbying this was reduced to 9, and then in particular following lobbying by the finance directors of the 9 boroughs on the impracticality of transition, transition was dropped altogether;
(c) The idea of a locally determined business rate was dropped, except in the City of London where it was necessary to avoid enormous community charges for the very small resident population;
(d) Needs and standard grant were to be merged into a single revenue support grant, based on a separate needs assessment for each major service, with a single assessment for all other services.

The community charge represents radical innovation, and it is perhaps easier to identify problems as a consequence. However, the Green Paper that introduced it took the approach of identifying all the shortcomings of the pre-1986 system, some of which were accepted by a wide range of people, particularly the shortcomings of the rate support grant system. The Green Paper also made little analysis of the potential problems of community charge, and it was striking how even before the legislation had been passed, practitioners of local government finance were forecasting the need for major revisions to the system because of the new problems and inconsistencies it was itself likely to introduce.

Rate and revenue support grants

Since the local government reorganization of 1974 there have been three very different systems of revenue support grant to local government. Each system has always involved controversy, and this heightened after 1979 as relations between central and local government deteriorated generally.

The main objective of a grant system has been to subsidize local services by redistributing central taxation to compensate local authorities for:

(a) Differences in spending needs;
(b) Differences in the local revenue base.

These objectives reflect a relatively homogeneous society. In the USA, for example, much less emphasis is placed on the second objective.

Rate Support Grant

The Rate Support Grant from 1974 to 1981 had three components:

(a) **Domestic element** – a reduction in rate poundage for domestic ratepayers;
(b) **Resources element** – to enable all local authorities to spend a similar amount per head; authorities with rateable values below a national standard received sufficient grant to bring them up to the standard;
(c) **Needs element** – the largest element in the grant. It used a statistical formula, largely based on multiple regression analysis relating to past expenditure patterns, to measure needs. It was a fixed amount, not related to the council's own level of spending.

In the Department of the Environment's submission to the Layfield Committee, they proposed to introduce a new system, namely the 'unitary grant'. A grant of this type was introduced in 1981, and called the 'block grant'. The DOE envisaged the following aims:

(a) To introduce a simple, readily understood system;
(b) To limit the extent to which a council could increase its grant by greater spending;

(c) To end the distribution of grant purely on the basis of past expenditure;
(d) To stimulate greater public interest and reinforce local accountability.

The needs and resources elements were combined, and a new system of needs assessment introduced – grant related expenditure assessment (GREA). This was calculated using a variety of statistical indicators that could be grouped into five categories:

(a) People in the area;
(b) Physical features;
(c) Social and environmental problems;
(d) Differences in the costs of providing services;
(e) Special requirements of particular services.

Block grant was organized so that once authorities spent above a 'threshold' (typically 10%) over GREA, they were subject to a grant penalty.

The new system had only just begun in 1981 when it was subject to a major modification. A new concept of an 'expenditure target' was introduced. This was calculated on a quite different basis to GREA, and councils who spent above it were subject to further and often punitive losses of grant. In some cases every extra pound spent could lead to a loss of two pounds or more in grant. The 1982 Local Government Finance Act gave legislative form to the mechanism. It was eventually abolished in 1986/87, but the idea of punitive grant loss had by then been incorporated within the GREA-based system itself.

The local authority associations were united in their opposition to block grant. They supported the government's four objectives, however, but considered block grant would only partially fulfil them. And it would be at the expense of a fundamental consitutional change in the relationship between central and local government.

The association's main objections (Local Authority Associations, 1981, p. 58) were as follows:

(a) There was no way in which *any* centrally operated formula-based needs assessment could ever be good enough to enable the government to use it to specify what individual authorities ought to be spending;
(b) Low-spending authorities would be put under enormous pressures to improve service to the level of assessed needs;
(c) Most authorities would still get more grant, the more they spent;
(d) Block grant would therefore encourage overspending and there would still need to be 'clawback'. But this would apply to all grant (not just resources element as in the past) and hence increase uncertainty;

(e) The wide powers for the use of multipliers would make it possible for the grant distribution to be manipulated in quite unacceptable ways;
(f) Block grant was so complicated as to 'make a mockery of the Secretary of State's aim of simplicity and comprehensibilty'.

The actual operation of the block grant demonstrated that the fears of the local authority associations had, in many ways, materialized. The government had failed to heed the warnings of the Layfield Committee and **had** begun to use the block grant system to exert short-term control over individual authorities. However, such control was to be even more directly achieved with rate-capping, discussed below.

Table 5.5 Audit Commission's summary of block grant shortcomings

---

1. *The effect of new uncertainties:*
   Extent of system induced uncertainties.
   Higher rates caused by councils' response to uncertainties.
2. *The impact of a potentially sound approach to grant distribution:*
   Distorting effects of grants and penalties.
   Unresolved questions with grant related expenditure (GRE).
   Unreliable information on needs and resources.
   Complexity.
3. *Lack of necessary pressures and incentives:*
   Blurred local accountability.
   Lack of positive incentives to reduce costs.
   Frustrations of detailed central intervention in local affairs.

Table 5.6 Audit Commission's proposals for reform of block grant

---

1. Central government to fix its cash support for three years ahead; particularly the percentage of relevant expenditure.
2. Improve information on needs and local property values.
3. Introduce more robust and simpler GREs and up-to-date property values.
4. If the government wants to cut total council spending it should do so primarily by reducing the percentage of expenditure met by RSG.
5. Expenditure targets separate from GRE should be abolished to reduce perverse incentives.
6. Local market forces (the electorate) should determine local spending, after strengthening local accountability.
7. Close ending should be abandoned as should mid-year adjustments to councils spending within budgets.
8. Councils should be left to change their allocation of resources without detailed intervention from central government; specific priorities to be achieved via specific grants or legislation.

The first comprehensive review of the block grant was undertaken by the Audit Commission (1984), using its Section 27 powers to examine the effects of legislation on local government efficiency. Though the review saw the basic logic of the rate support grant as 'fundamentally sound', it did highlight a variety of shortcomings of the system in practice (see Table 5.5). The Commissions recommendations for reform of the block grant are shown in Table 5.6. Although largely ignored in the Green Paper *Paying for Local Government*, they represent an essentially 'localist' response to reform.

The conclusion of the developments in block grant must be that problems that occurred did not so much arise from the theory of the grant, but from the fact that too much was expected of it in practice. In particular, the government saw it both as a vehicle for allocating grant and as a vehicle for penalizing overspending councils. Major legislative changes were rushed through with inadequate consideration and the block grant system was subjected to precisely the kind of manipulations feared by all the local authority associations. The basic problems addressed by the Layfield Committee and demanding a coherent approach were not resolved; in particular the accountability of local authorities was not, in fact, strengthened.

Rate and community charge limitation

The 1984 Rates Act enabled the Secretary of State for the Environment to limit rate increases in individual authorities or across the board. He would first designate the authorities to be capped. Specific criteria had to be used to define 'overspending' councils. In the first year of operation the criteria were:

(a) Spending more than 20% over GREA;
(b) Spending more than 4% over expenditure target.

There were rights for councils to appeal against rate capping, but authorities were reluctant to do so overtly because the Secretary of State then had the power to 'impose on the authority in question such requirements relating to its expenditure or financial management as he thinks appropriate'.

Rate capping further increased the conflict element in central–local relations and further blurred local accountability. It was very time consuming for both Whitehall and the affected council, and by 1988 the number of capped councils had fallen from about 20 to only 7. There can, however, be little doubt that rate capping did lead to reduced rates. It affected the thinking of councils who were not actually capped, but who might be so if they increased their expenditure. Some councils managed nonetheless to maintain or even increase **real** expenditure whilst being rate capped, due to a variety of 'creative' financing and accounting devices. These loopholes were gradually closed off and by 1988 several of the rate capped councils had to make large budget reductions to keep within the rate cap.

The 1988 Local Government Finance Act introduced the limitation of community charge, simplifying the process of designation and appeal and removing a scheme for general limitation, although this had never seemed likely to be used under rate capping. The prospect was also introduced that councils could be capped for a given year **after** they had set their level of community charge for that year, as was already the case in Scotland under rate capping.

Revenue Support Grant

The third system of grant since the 1974 reorganization was, as mentioned in the discussion of the 1986 Green Paper, the Revenue Support Grant. This was created in the 1988 Local Government Finance Act, but the legislation itself provided relatively little detail of how the system would work. More details of the proposals were set out in the 1988 document from the DOE *The New Grant System*. This document identified three main weaknesses in the block grant:

(a) **Over-complication**, which also makes 'the link between council spending and rate bills very difficult to understand fully';
(b) **Instability**, which makes good financial management more difficult for some authorities;
(c) **Hidden subsidy to some regions**, through the system of resource equalization, which was unrelated to ability to pay since it was based on rateable values, not disposable income.

There would be a significant difference between the English and Welsh RSG. In Wales grant would be paid to both tiers of council, counties and districts, as was the case in both England and Wales under block grant. But this would not be the case in England. The overt reasons for this were that Welsh circumstances were different, being less complex and more stable. However, the failure to split English grant between tiers appears to be a major obstacle to the increased accountability sought from the 1988 Act.

The main features of Revenue Support Grant are:

(a) It 'compensates fully for differences between areas in the need to provide local services and will provide additional support for services in proportion to each area's population';
(b) It involves much simpler needs assessments than under the GRE system;
(c) Grant entitlements are fixed at the start of each year, and will not vary with expenditure. The Secretary of State can, however, pay 'additional grant' in exceptional circumstances. It was announced in

Table 5.7 Community charge demand note (England)

	£ per head		Needs assessment
District council	75		74
County council	320		288
Parish council	3		
	——		——
		398	362
Less			
Allocation of NNDR	200		
Revenue Support Grant	75		
	——	275	
		——	
		123	
Adjustment for safety net	24		
Reconciliation – losses on collection and under-registration	−20		
	——	−4	
Net community charge		127	
		——	

1988 that fixed entitlements would also apply to the rest of the life of block grant;

(d) The method of grant distribution is intended to be more stable from year to year than with block grant, so the limits on grant changes, known as safety nets and caps will not be needed once the new system has been phased in;

(e) In England, grant and non-domestic rate receipts are not divided between the tiers of authority, but are 'paid notionally to community chargepayers themselves'. Key figures will appear on the community charge bill. The mechanism used to achieve this is the Collection Fund. Into this will be paid grant, national non-domestic rate (NNDR) and community charge. Each elected authority, including the collecting authority, precepts on the collection fund for its income. Costs of collection and administration of the fund fall on the district council not the fund. The draft of an English community charge demand note is shown in Table 5.7. This takes account of the transitional arrangements that will apply before all elements of the 1988 Act are fully phased in. It can be seen that it is not possible to calculate a spending level for each council net of grant and NNDR;

(f) In Wales, grant and NNDR are paid direct to all authorities, so the Welsh collection fund is very similar in structure to the rate collection fund which has traditionally operated in both England and Wales.

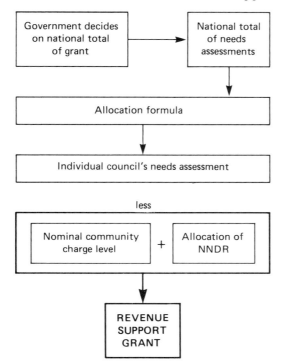

Fig. 5.3 The allocation of revenue support grant.

The actual grant calculation is summarized in Fig. 5.3. The needs assessment of each council is a key figure. It is used to calculate the notional community charge (the level that would apply if all authorities spent at the level of their needs assessment), as well as being included in the formula in its own right.

National non-domestic rate

In the 1986 Green Paper this was referred to as the 'uniform business rate', but during the passage of the legislation through Parliament it became national non-domestic rate (NNDR). This may have been because there would not be uniformity during a transitional period, otherwise there would be very significant gainers and losers overnight, depending on the type of property and region. A transition was essential as the long overdue revaluation of non-domestic property was scheduled for 1990, and coming 17 years after the previous one in England and

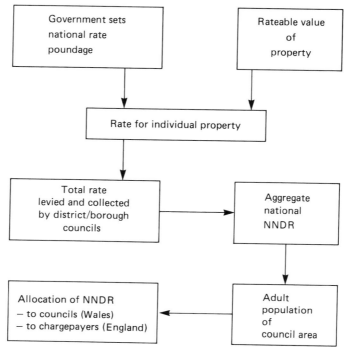

Fig. 5.4 The national non-domestic rating system (NNDR).

Wales, would inevitably involve major shifts in rateable values.

The Green Paper criticized non-domestic rates as a **local** tax on the grounds of both economic efficiency and local accountability:

— They have an arbitrary and erratic effect over time and in different areas on the competitiveness of business;
— They fall immediately on those who have no vote to influence local spending decisions;
— They are ultimately borne by people who are unaware of how these extra costs arise and may not live in the area of the authority imposing the rate;
— They conceal the true cost of local services and of marginal increases in spending from domestic ratepayers;
— They make complicated grant arrangements – which further distort the impact of changes in expenditure – inevitable.

Not all these grounds are equally persuasive. For example, businesses have no vote in national elections either. The economic case on competitiveness has not been proved conclusively by economic research. There can be little doubt that it was the penultimate reason that lay at the heart of the proposal, namely that some councils with large commercial rate bases were able to raise much more funding for growth from non-domestic ratepayers than from domestic.

The total yield of NNDR will still be hypothecated for local government, but the national rate poundage will be set by the Secretary of State. All income will be pooled, and then redistributed pro rata to population (see Fig. 5.4).

Capital expenditure – its planning and control

Major changes to the system of capital expenditure planning and control were introduced under Part VIII of the Local Government Planning and Land Act 1980. The previous system, which had been initiated in 1970, placed controls on local authority borrowing but in general allowed freedom to undertake capital expenditure not financed by borrowing. Local authorities used this freedom to supplement borrowing, particularly using leasing, capital receipts and revenue resources.

The logic behind these changes was that the government wanted greater control for macroeconomic reasons over what it regarded as high levels of local authority capital expenditure. It also wanted to reduce some of the detailed controls over individual capital projects.

The new system was detailed in Circular 14/81 (DOE, 1981b). It defined 'prescribed expenditure', which was to become the basis for control, rather than just the element financed from loan. In other words, the government sought to impose a national cash limit on total local authority capital expenditure.

The process of allocating capital resources to authorities had as its central feature the designation of five service 'blocks' – housing, education, transport, social services and 'other services'. The government's aim was that authorities could aggregate the allocations given in each of these five blocks and spend the total as they see fit – the allocations were not limited to the service blocks on which they were given.

An authority could supplement its allocation by four main methods:

(a) The application of a prescribed proportion of capital receipts from the sale of assets;
(b) Carrying forward underspendings from the previous year, or anticipating next year's allocation, up to a limit of 10% of the current year's allocation;
(c) Transfers from another local authority's allocation;
(d) Adding an amount equal to the profit of trading undertakings, as measured on a current cost accounting basis.

This last method caused significant controversy because it applied CCA principles to an area where the accounts are not kept on a CCA basis.

The procedure for making allocations for housing, education, social services and transport involved each local authority making a bid for funds to the four appropriate government departments. The bids were then analysed and allocations made to individual authorities at cash limit prices about the time of the rate support grant settlement. The 'other services' block was allocated on the basis of recommendations made by the local authority associations. The criteria for making allocations were a mixture of the political and technical – regard was paid to existing commitments, past achievement of programmes, statistical factors and pure political preference. Some blocks involved lengthy bids, in particular housing where housing investment programmes (HIPs) had to be prepared, and transport, with transportation plans and programmes (TPPs).

There were various provisos and qualifications to the operation of capital expenditure controls, explained in annually updated circulars from the Department of the Environment.

It is perhaps paradoxical that before the end of the first year of these new powers, introduced to restrain local authority capital expenditure, the Secretary of State for the Environment was making speeches complaining that local authorities had fallen well short of his forecast level of spending on capital account.

A major dilemma lay in the treatment of capital receipts. Councils could augment their block allocations by the 'prescribed proportion' of capital receipts from the sale of land and other assets. It did not matter in which year the receipts arose, as long as they had not already been used to 'justify' expenditure. On the other hand, the national cash limit only took into account the current year's receipts, and not the unused justifications from previous years' receipts, which had been of considerable significance locally.

As soon as the new system had settled down and councils were better aware of how it worked, they began to consume these previous years' justifications. And they therefore almost inevitably caused a national 'overspend' of the cash limit in 1983–84. A similar occurrence was likely in 1984–85 for the same reasons. In the summer of 1984 a system of voluntary restraint was introduced, with warnings of a full moratorium and/or deductions from future years' block allocations for those not observing the restraint.

The 1985–86 capital control system considerably reduced the percentage of capital receipts that councils could use in justification in any given year, and carried out the threat, though not in a very major way, to reduce allocations of authorities not conforming to the previous restraint.

The system of control that was supposed to put an end to the stop-go cycle in capital spending that was common before 1980 had in practice ended up having the same effects, if not worse. It was hardly surprising that the Audit Commission were as highly critical of this system's impact on local authority efficiency as they had earlier been of block grant.

The 1986 Green Paper accepted that problems existed for local government; it also voiced central government dissatisfaction with the outcomes of the 1980 system. Two alternative approaches were put forward:

(a) Control over councils' total net external borrowing, for both revenue and capital, through an external borrowing limit (EBL);
(b) Expenditure control, but over **gross** expenditure, including an allowance for capital receipts, and with revenue contributions to capital as a limited supplement to the allocations.

Following consultation, the EBL option was rejected. The local authority associations had misgivings about gross expenditure control too, and the government made further amendments to its proposals in a 1988 consultation paper (DOE, 1988a). This restated governmental objectives:

The proposals involved extending the definition of capital to include schemes where third parties actually own the assets or provide immediate funding; these were designated as 'credit arrangements' and would be treated as borrowing for control purposes. This was an attempt to discourage or even stop the numerous creative financing devices developed by brokers to circumvent the 1980 capital controls system.

Under the new system there would be three sources of finance for capital commitments:

(a) Borrowing or credit arrangements;
(b) Government grants or contributions from third parties;
(c) Local authorities' own resources, specifically revenue contributions and capital receipts not used to redeem debt or meet future commitments.

The government proposed to place limits, called 'credit approvals', on the commitments a council could enter into by borrowing or credit arrangements. Councils would be notified before the year began of their basic credit approval (BCA). This would be based on the government's view of an appropriate share of public expenditure for that council. To assist forward planning, councils would also be told of a guaranteed minimum level of credit approval for the next two financial years. Basic credit approvals might be enhanced by supplementary credit approvals (SCA) covering particular projects or programmes.

It was also proposed that government capital grants would in future take the form of a lump sum rather than contributions towards annual loan charges.

In a proposal with a new emphasis for local authority capital financing, the government considered that 'proper' provision should be made for repaying debt, namely the use of straight line repayment methods rather than the sinking fund method. This aroused considerable criticism from local government as an example of further over-detailed involvement in local authority financing methods, with a significant adverse impact on a number of councils. The government also proposed that reductions in the direct provision of services, e.g. housing, 'should be accompanied by an appropriate reduction in indebtedness'. The new system would provide that part of a capital receipt from asset sales must be applied to debt redemption or set aside to meet future capital commitments.

The Consultation Paper proposed that up to 25% of proceeds from council house sales and up to 50% of other capital receipts could, at the council's discretion, be made available for new capital expenditure. However, if a council were to dispose of all its housing stock, redemption of all housing debt would be the first charge on the proceeds of the sale.

A major concern of the DOE was the growing size of local authorities' unapplied capital receipts, which would be swollen if large housing estates or whole municipal housing stocks were sold en bloc. By enabling allocations to take account of both accumulated and new capital receipts, capital receipts were much more explicitly brought into the central government control framework.

The mechanism around which capital planning and control would revolve was the capital funding pool (CFP), into which a council would pool their borrowings, credit arrangements and money set aside for debt redemption of future capital commitments. From the pool would be met interest and principal payments, liabilities under credit arrangements, and the cost of capital expenditure. Authorities also would be required to keep their borrowing within a capital borrowing ceiling (CBC).

Conclusion

The Green Paper *Paying for Local Government*, and the major legislative programme that followed it in 1988, had as explicit objectives increasing local choice and accountability. These are important elements in any vital local democracy. However, there was widespread belief in local government circles, largely independent of political viewpoint, that the fundamental rationale for the proposals lay other than in strengthening local democracy.

Those actually in local government clearly also have vested interests, and the real test of the major programme of change in both financial and non-financial areas will be how far, during the 1990s, the changes actually do lead to the objectives overtly stated.

It is likely that whatever changes take place at central government level in the future, local government finance will be a subject of continuing disagreement and controversy. It is also likely that there will be pressure from several quarters for further structural changes. But the prospect of an integrated and coherent review of local authority structure, functions and finance, rejected in practice by the actions of successive central governments, seems perhaps more remote than ever.

Summary

This chapter has reviewed the structure, functions and financing of local government, particularly in relation to England. Particular attention has been paid to the general financial relationships between central and local government. Major changes in financing from 1990 were discussed, including their rationale and potential problem areas. The chapter concluded with a review of the planning and control of capital expenditure.

Further reading

The financing of local government is subject to continuous amendment and it is therefore essential to read *Public Finance and Accountancy* together with either *Local Government Chronicle* or *Municipal Journal*. CIPFA publishes a large quantity of relevant material both within the *Financial Information Service* and on an *ad hoc* basis. Useful summaries of developments are contained in the following annually produced publications: *Local Government Trends* (CIPFA), *Public Domain* (Public Finance Foundation).

Chapter 6

Local government: external reporting and internal control

Chapter 5 examined the environment and financing methods of local government. In this chapter attention is focused on the budgeting and control mechanisms which are the vehicles of internal control. Internal audit as a control mechanism is covered in Chapter 9. This chapter begins with a review of external reporting, including key areas of accounting that affect both external stewardship and internal management control. There is a discussion of the major area of potential innovation, namely capital accounting, as well as direct service organization accounts and service level agreements. The chapter concludes with a review of budgeting and financial management.

Local authority external reporting

Local authority external reporting has developed in a distinctive fashion, and in parallel to, rather than as a derivative of, private sector methods. It has developed its own principles, practices and terminology. Since the 1970s there has been some movement in relating local government external reporting more closely to generally accepted private sector accounting principles and practice. But there still remain many areas of importance in local government external reporting which cannot be readily discussed within the framework of private sector principles.

Whereas in private firms external reporting is almost synonymous with published accounts, in a democratically elected local authority a vast range of external reports is produced, and a rich variety of reporting mechanisms exists. (Figure 6.1 later in this chapter illustrates this well.)

Though local authority accounting has reached a high degree of sophistication, it has been argued that in its reporting to the public this sophistication may have been a barrier to comprehension. It is interesting to see what the Departmental Committee on Accounts (1907) had to say on this topic:

It is generally agreed that as wide publicity as practicable should be given to the accounts of local authorities and that they should be published in such a form as to be intelligible to ratepayers possessed of average ability but without special knowledge of accountancy. (p. 19)

It is perhaps an indication of at least partial failure that 69 years later the Layfield Committee (1976) still found it necessary to point out in almost identical language:

We believe that there is an obligation on local authorities to devise a means of providing the electorate with financial information about services in reasonably simple and straightforward terms. (p. 102)

It should be noted that the distinction between trading and non-trading accounts of local authorities is taking on increasing significance, with a very clear trend towards the former conforming as closely as possible to Companies Acts accounts.

At this stage it is important to set the formal external financial reports of local authorities in context. They are not the only source of information to users, and indeed in the present day context of British local government they are not necessarily their most important source of information. Even though local authorities publish comparisons of expenditure with that of other local authorities in their formal reports, this tends to be at a fairly broad level on a few indicators and with a relatively small groups of comparator authorities. Unions, pressure groups or researchers examining comparative expenditure on particular services will tend to use the CIPFA statistical information service which contains details of **all** authorities' expenditure on, say, education. The absence of such publicly and readily available detailed comparative information for companies is one reason why their individual company reports are more significant.

Local authority accounts – not the published external reports – are in addition uniquely openly available. The 1982 Local Government Finance Act continued the longstanding rights of public inspection:

At each audit . . . any person interested may inspect the accounts to be audited and all books, deeds, contracts, bills, vouchers and receipts relating to them.

Local government electors also have the right to question the auditor about the account. In practice those who wish to make detailed enquiries into one or more aspects of a particular authority's finances are able to use the rights of inspection to such as degree of detail that the level of disclosure in the published accounts is of no great significance to them. Recent years have seen what is felt to be a significant increase in the volume of public inspection and questioning, particularly about controversial projects or policies.

The 1984 Rates Act introduced the requirement for local authorities formally to consult on their finances with commercial and industrial ratepayers. The Access to Information (Local Government) Act provided freedom of information over a whole variety of previously unpublished documents. It further confirmed local government as the most open and accountable part of the public sector, not least in respect of financial and accounting data.

Statutory basis of external reporting

Before the Second World War, most local authorities were subject to very detailed specification by central government of the form and content of their accounts. But as local authorities became more visibly competent in financial administration – not least through the efforts of the Institute of Municipal Treasurers and Accountants (IMTA), the predecessor of CIPFA – and as specific grants reduced considerably in scope, so too did this detailed control reduce. Only with the passing of the Local Government Planning and Land Act 1980 did a greater degree of prescription again enter into external reporting, and this was for different motives than those of 50 years earlier.

The major legislation relating to local authority accounts is the 1982 Local Government Finance Act. This essentially carried the previous legislation forward without innovation. It does not itself touch on more than some very general areas of accounting. More detailed accounts regulations are made by the Secretary of State. The current accounts and audit regulations are made by the Secretary of State, and are in fact considerably shorter than their main predecessor, the Accounts (Borough and Metropolitan Boroughs) Regulations 1930. It is perhaps a direct reflection of the successful self-regulatory activities and the absence of any major structural shortcomings in local authority accounts that the regulations contain so little detail compared to, say, the Companies Acts.

A further source of guidance comes in the Local Government Audit Code of Practice. This sets out the framework for external auditors and includes reference to the more important matters to which an auditor should draw attention; these include a number of aspects relating to accounting.

Most local government expenditure and income relates to general fund services. Other accounts must, however, be kept separate under statutes relating to various services including housing revenue, housing advances, police, reserve funds, superannuation, lotteries and loan funds.

In the more general area of external reporting, as opposed to accounting, further radical changes were also introduced in the Local Government Planning and Land Act 1980 relating to the need to prepare annual reports and other documents in a format laid down by the Secretary of State. The draft legislation would have involved the Secretary of State **prescribing** the detailed form and content of annual reports but this met very hostile criticism from the local authority associations and CIPFA, not least because of the speed with which new mandatory requirements were proposed for implementation. The government then conceded the principle of a code or codes of practice, though it still warned that if local authorities were dilatory in conforming to the code it might have to take more positive action.

Codes of practice which have been published include:

(a) Information to be issued with rate demands;
(b) Annual reports and financial statements;
(c) Manpower information;
(d) Information for publication at quarterly intervals, e.g. planning applications.

The single most significant is the second on annual reports (DOE, 1981a). It was based largely on suggestions put forward by CIPFA and the Society of Local Authority Chief Executives (SOLACE). Its objectives, which are important enough to warrant further consideration, are quoted as follows:

(a) To give ratepayers clear information about local government's activities;
(b) To make it easier for electors, ratepayers and other interested parties to make comparisons of and judgements on the performance of their authorities;
(c) To help councillors form judgements about the performance of their own authority.

The objective of the annual report is, through the use of narrative and financial statistical data, to integrate the total management and financial reporting of the authority. It should also account for the resource costs implicit in the policies of the authority, and as far as practicable the performance and efficiency of the local authority. The documents should be designed as a statement of stewardship for the benefit both of members of the council and of the public (pp. 2–3) (Reproduced by permission of the Controller, HMSO. Crown copyright.)

The development of local authority accounting

The annual reports were an important innovation but did not eliminate the need for continued develoment of the fundamental vehicle of financial reporting, the financial accounts, commonly published as an 'abstract of accounts' (i.e. a condensed version). A number of authorities still formally publish detailed accounts that are effectively a line-by-line analysis of outturn. Though these will now usually be accompanied by a short abstract, it was not so very long ago that such lengthy accounts were the norm in local government.

A landmark was the publication of *The Standardisation of Accounts: General Principles* (IMTA, 1963). To develop the 'general principles' in depth relative to individual services, detailed standard analyses of income and expenditure were prepared for 17 services. The success of CIPFA in achieving uniformity in the form of account is indicated by the widespread use of the CIPFA standard form in completion of returns to central government and, of course, in the completion of returns of CIPFA's own statistical information service.

Legislation, regulations and the various audit and information codes of practice provide a broad framework for accounting but they do not wholly constrain discretion and indeed they cannot if definitions of good practice are to be allowed to change and develop. 'Proper accounting practices' as referred to in Section 15 of the 1982 Local Government Finance Act are therefore something that have gradually evolved during the era of modern local government, and which are particularly evolving as CIPFA responds to its full membership of the Accounting Standards Committee, touched on later.

Although *General Principles* was reprinted as late as 1979, it could not be expected to survive unscathed major reorganizations, service developments, computerization and the demand for more management information. A major review of the standard form was undertaken, including extensive consultation, and a more modern approach was taken (CIPFA, 1985).

In relation to the accounting principles themselves, these had moved from a topic of relative obscurity to become an issue of great political interest. Because of the financial restraint that became most acute after 1979 on both revenue and particularly capital accounts, local authorities of all types began to turn to 'creative accounting' techniques both to circumvent controls and to optimize the financial position of the council.

These techniques were often borrowed from long-standing private sector accounting practices, and were rarely capable of legal challenge. However, they were clearly a source of frustration to central government, which took direct steps to contain them, e.g. by more widely defining the description of prescribed capital expenditure. The techniques also made traditional inter-authority comparisons more difficult, as expenditure could be charged in different ways depending on the approach used in a given authority.

It was therefore perhaps not entirely surprising that in early 1984 the Department of the Environment produced a lengthy consultation paper on standardized statements of accounts by local authorities. It was subject to widespread criticism from the local authority associations, Audit Commission and CIPFA. It both ignored recent CIPFA work and, most controversially, proposed detailed pro-formas of accounts. The latter were heavily criticized, particularly given the background of successful self-regulation in local authority accounts.

The DOE effectively withdrew the consultation paper, but proposed new regulations, some elements of which were still of concern to local authorities. This put local government in a position where, unless it could deliver changed principles through self-regulation, it was very clear that change would be imposed. A joint CIPFA-Audit Commission working party was set up in response to a 1986 invitation from the Minister for Local Government to develop proposals to be in place by 1 April 1987 as an alternative to a major statutory extension to the accounts and audit regulations.

The Code of Practice on Local Authority Accounting was endorsed by CIPFA council on 20 March 1987, just before the deadline, and it was also adopted by the three major local authority associations, in terms which show the by-now heightened political sensibility of accounting principles:

We value highly the traditions of accountability and proper accounting practice which remain the hallmark of public service by local government. The Code is an important contribution to the maintenance of these ideals, and we agree that self-regulation in this area is the best way forward. We are pleased to adopt this Code, and commend it to our members.

The Audit Commission advised its auditors 'that the provisions of the Code represent best practice for the purpose of expressing the audit opinion.'

The central concept used in the code is that 'the statement of accounts shall present fairly the financial position and transactions of the authority.' Fair presentation is achieved by complying with proper local authority accounting practices, the accounting code of practice and with the broad accounting concepts of matching, consistency, prudence, substance over form and materiality. Where the requirements of the code are not met, full disclosure and, where relevant, quantification of the departure is required. The summary of the proposed content of the financial statements is set out in Table 6.1.

Table 6.1 Outline of local authority financial statements

Explanatory Foreword
Statement of Accounting Policies
Accounting Statements:
General/County Fund Account
Housing Revenue Account
Consolidated Balance Sheet
Consolidated Statement of Revenue and Capital Movements
Summary DLO Revenue and appropriation account
Superannuation Accounts

Source: *CIPFA*, 1987b.

The code stressed two particular issues:

(i) All statements of account should reflect a common pattern of present-ation, although they may not be in an identical format. One of the main aims of this Code is to narrow the areas of difference and variety in accounting treatment and thereby to enhance the usefulness of pub-lished statements of account . . .

(ii) Interpretation and explanation of the accounts is considered to be extremely important. The Explanatory Foreword should make reference to the more significant features in the accounts using plain English and avoiding technical terms or jargon.

(CIPFA, 1987b)

A great emphasis was also placed on **consistency**, avoidance of which was regarded by some of those critical of individual councils as a primary creative accounting technique. CIPFA advised:

Generally a change in accounting policy should not be made unless it can be justified on the grounds that the new policy is preferable to the one it replaces because it will give a fairer presentation of the results and of the financial position.

One area which was deliberately not covered was capital accounting, other than as a 'holding exercise' in relation to the definition, classi-fication and quantity of fixed assets. It was regarded as too large and significant to be resolved in the very tight timescale within which the code of practice had to be produced. This topic is covered in more depth below.

The code of practice was endorsed as a franked SORP in November 1987, and a few months later more detailed guidance notes on the code were published (CIPFA, 1988b). These contained detailed worked ex-amples of the code in action.

Applicability of accounting standards to local authorities

A major CIPFA statement on accounting standards (CIPFA, 1980) started off with three paragraphs that showed how far by then CIPFA had moved towards accepting the relevance of the accounting standards which had primarily been initiated for private sector trading organizations:

The Accounting Panel, through its Local Authority Accounting Sub-Group, has given consideration to the applicability of Statements of Standard Accounting Practice (SSAPs) issued by the Accounting Standards Committee (ASC) to local authority accounts in England and Wales. Local authorities, for this purpose, are as defined in the Local Government Act 1972, but excluding town, parish or community councils and meetings.

The Accounting Panel is of the opinion that there are advantages in applying these standards in the interests of good accounting practice and the general movement towards increasing standardization of financial information. CIPFA is a member of the ASC and, as such, should encourage the application of agreed standards. In practice, it is not thought likely that there will be much need for change in accounts preparation.

As SSAPs apply to accounts intended to give a 'true and fair view', it was originally thought that it was not appropriate to apply them generally to the accounts of the local authorities, which are based on 'proper accounting practices'. Following consultation with interested parties, including the Chief Inspector of Audit, there would not appear to be major difficulties in applying most SSAPs to local authority accounts. (p. 19).

The proposals to apply SSAPs reflected the changes that had been taking place anyway in CIPFA's approach during the 1970s and which had perhaps been accelerated by the exigencies of the direct labour organizations legislation. It was decided that CIPFA would state clearly for each SSAP its degree of applicability, normally:

(a) Apply in total;
(b) Apply partially with reasons, or
(c) Not apply – with reasons.

CIPFA subsequently arranged that its own observations would be fully integrated into the standard setting process, so that as SSAPs were developed a panel of local authority specialists would advise the ASC on the extent to which the standard was applicable to local government. Material departures from the standards as applied to local government need to be disclosed in a note to the accounts.

Capital accounting

Capital accounting is perhaps the most contentious of all aspects of local authority acounting. Historically local authority capital accounting has been closely related to the methods of capital finance used. The 1963 *General Principles* distinguished between two types of capital assets:

(a) **Capital outlay**. This refers to tangible saleable assets such as land and equipment, which were to be retained at cost in the accounts until disposed of;
(b) **Other long-term outlay**. This is expenditure that does not produce saleable assets, e.g. highways and sea defences. This was to be segregated in the accounts, and then written off at the end of the loan period.

In practice these recommendations were not followed in many authorities, with many authorities only showing the cost of assets net of loan repayments, with assets not financed by loan not being shown at all. This was partly expediency, as the CIPFA recommendations required full scheduling of all capital assets, which many councils simply lacked in the form necessary.

There were serious shortcomings in the overall position:

(a) It was inconsistent and arbitrary in the charges which appeared in the revenue account;
(b) It may have met basic stewardship criteria, but it could not promote accountability for efficiency;
(c) It failed to demonstrate the authority's financing policies.

For example, an authority which had made substantial use of revenue contributions to capital expenditure on a particular service will have a very different revenue charge for that service from an authority which had exclusively used loan. The accounts would therefore be misleading in respect of the consumption of capital assets, even though they would correctly reflect the pure financing transactions.

The continued failure to resolve the basis for local authority capital accounting led to reviews in both the 1970s and the 1980s. In 1975, the CIPFA Accounting Panel recommended the introduction of **depreciation accounting** (CIPFA, 1975). This was rejected after consultation. A 1983 review (CIPFA, 1983) concluded 'the weaknesses are sufficiently serious to warrant urgent changes' and proposed that charges to revenue should be based on **asset use**. This aroused considerable controversy among CIPFA members, and there was insufficient support for change. Much of the criticism reflected the simple desire, which was very understandable, to avoid changes at a time when accounting resources were very hard pressed, not least as a result of a variety of government legislation.

In 1987 CIPFA published its code of practice on local authority accounting, but it contained only interim proposals on capital accounting. The Secretary of State for the Environment then wrote to the local authority associations asking what they intended to do about capital accounting. There was a clear implication that unless local government itself reformed the system, central government would take steps to do so.

CIPFA set up an informal working party, whose work led CIPFA Council explicitly to identify the inadequacies of the existing system for accountability in the use of assets, and to identify the need for a new system. The Council then initiated a joint CIPFA-local authority associations' Capital Accounting Steering Group. This was set up in early 1988, with a high level membership including the Audit Commission and DOE, with the finance under-secretaries of the associations as observers. Price Waterhouse were appointed as technical advisors, and the group's terms of reference were to:

(a) Prepare a consultative implementation manual for a revised capital accounting system by the end of 1988;
(b) Recommend a revised system which separates accounting for financing from accounting for capital assets in the cost of services;

(c) Prepare a revised system which meets these requirements in a practical and cost effective way;
(d) Liaise, as appropriate, with any parties necessary to ensure that, in the wider context, the recommended system could be implemented properly (e.g. legal changes if required), and without hindrance.

The Group's work timetable envisaged implementation testing at six pilot sites during 1989–90, in order to achieve a definitive version of the manual in 1990, with a view to implementing the new system in 1991–92 accounts. It was envisaged the Group's recommendations would be broadly consistent with accepted accounting principles and existing best practice in other sectors. In the summer of 1988 a possible outline of the new system was presented to CIPFA Conference by the Chairman of the Working Party and a video made of the proceedings for widespread circulation among CIPFA members. The system proposed was outlined as follows:

1. The starting point is an inventory of the authority's capital stock;
2. Assets are then divided into depreciating and non-depreciating categories;
3. Charges are made in the service operating accounts for:
    — depreciation;
    — the full maintenance of all assets and – possibly – the renewal of non-depreciating assets;
    — the cost of capital, via a rate of interest applied to the asset stock.
4. 'Below the Line', i.e. at authority rather than service level:
    — the cost of capital is reversed out in the accounts;
    — to be replaced by net interest paid to external lenders;
    — residual financing costs (i.e. in addition to depreciation and renewals provisions in service accounts) are shown as 'ratepayers' contributions to capital equity';
5. In the balance sheet, assets are shown at depreciated cost or valuation.
                                                             (Parkes, 1988)

An example of the proposed system, based on a county library service, is shown in Table 6.2. It can be seen that the apparent service cost of the libraries increases, reflecting the real costs of capital, but the increase is reversed out below the line so that the authority is in an identical external financial position.

In his discussion of the possible new system, the chairman identified a number of practical considerations. First, there was the question of depreciation. Table 6.3 summarizes the likely treatment of different types of asset. The most difficult case is infrastructure such as roads which, if properly maintained, could last indefinitely, yet generally has no realizable value. There is also the question of historic cost versus current cost depreciation. The latter correctly reflects the economic cost of providing services, but as a pragmatic compromise historic cost may be acceptable for short-life assets.

Table 6.2 Humberside libraries: before and after the new capital accounting system

	Present system £000	New system £000
Operating costs	6,926	6,926
Capital charges		
— Depreciation (10% of written-down value of equipment)		43
— Cost of capital (5% real rate on replacement cost of buildings of £20.7m)		1,037
Financing charges	466	
Cost of library service	7,392	8,006
(included in Council's summary accounts 'below the line')		
Reversal of cost of capital		−1,037
Net interest payable		166
Ratepayers' contribution to capital equity		257*
	7,392	7,392

*Representing	Present RCCO	155
	Principal repayments	85
	Capital element of leases	60
	Depreciation	−43
		257

Note:
Book value of buildings   £1.5m
Replacement cost   £20.7m

Source: *Parkes* (1988).

Another practical consideration is valuation. A form of current valuation would be favoured, but to give wholly accurate signals to managers would require regular physical valuations and a consideration of alternative uses. Such an approach is unlikely to be practicable, so the most attractive approach is to use replacement cost aiming to avoid physical valuations through the use of simple formulae, such as cost per school place or square metre.

The Steering Group regarded the making of an annual charge for capital as a cornerstone of the new system. This raises two questions: the asset base to be applied and the interest rate to be used. Again, infrastructure is the difficult case, and the Group's emerging preference

Table 6.3 Possible treatment of different types of asset

Asset type	Example	Depreciation?	Cost of capital
Depreciable with realizable value	Buildings, vehicles	Yes	Real rate on net replacement cost
Depreciable with no realizable value	Specialized equipment	Yes	Real rate to reflect replacement in long term
Non-depreciable with realizable value	Land	No	Real rate to reflect opportunity cost
Non-depreciable with no realizable value	Roads with no alternative uses	No	Nominal cost of capital, e.g. abated replacement cost

was to include at least a nominal amount in relation to this. Illustrations of this are shown in Table 6.3.

Trading accounts

Local authorities have historically had a wide range of trading services, from markets to airports. It was not until the 1980 Local Government Planning and Land Act, however, that major differences emerged in the accounting treatment of trading and non-trading services. This Act required councils to set up direct labour organizations (DLOs) for the areas set out in Table 6.4. DLOs had to submit to competition on the majority of their work.

In 1985 the government issued a consultation paper proposing a major extension of the principle of competition, with a wide range of services being subject to some form of test of performance against private sector alternatives. Eventually via the 1988 Local Government Act legislation was passed extending the services subject to compulsory competitive tendering (CCT), though not quite to as many services as envisaged in the consultation paper. The generic name used to describe such services was direct service organization (DSO).

The Act prescribed in much more detail than the 1980 Act the mechanisms of the tendering process. It also gave power to the Secretary of State to add services to the list by regulation, the management of sports and leisure being the first added in this way. The services covered under the 1980 Act tended to involve a whole series of separate and perhaps small contracts, some of which might be won, some lost. By contrast, the 1988 Act services typically involved a whole service being tendered for at once; a lost tender would thus quickly lead to complete elimination of that particular function.

Table 6.4 Services covered by compulsory competitive tender

Service	Timescale
1980 Act: Construction and maintenance works to buildings, land and other structures by engineering and building trades	
1988 Act Grounds maintenance	20% 1/1/90; then in 20% phases until 1/1/94
Management of sports and leisure facilities	1/1/92, except London: 1/8/92 or 1/1/93
Refuse collection Cleaning of buildings Street cleansing Schools and welfare catering Other catering Vehicle maintenance and repairs	Phased by service from 1/8/89 to 1/1/92

There are a variety of exemptions and qualifications to the list; the coverage below concentrates on the accounting and financial management issues. In this context CIPFA had taken a very proactive role in relation to these aspects of the 1980 Act, and in response to the 1988 Act CIPFA sponsored the setting up of a Competition Joint Committee, which involved a wide range of relevant professions. One of the key roles of the Committee was to produce a code of practice on accounting and financial matters. This was published in provisional form in 1988 (CIPFA, 1988a) with the following objectives:

(a) To set out practical steps for satisfying requirements of the law;
(b) To put forward procedures that provide for fair competition and to preserve a fair balance between the interests of the various parties;
(c) To secure the best possible value for money in service delivery.

The code is voluntary, and in the words used in the code 'this gives it the strength of self-regulation.'

One of the issues that the 1988 Act highlighted was the distinction between 'client' and 'contractor' functions. The client function involved preparing and evaluating the tender, and monitoring the performance of the contractor. Typically before the Act a parks maintenance division, for example, would not have had a separation of this type; it would have been an integrated operation within a single organizational structure. CCT led to many councils physically splitting the client and contractor roles structurally. There was in fact no legal requirement to do so, although it was necessary to keep separate DSO accounts.

Table 6.5 Example of calculation of rate of return on capital

	£	£
Surplus on DSO revenue account		80,300
Add back:		
Interest charged during the year (via overheads and stores on-costs)		15,100
Principal repayments to the loans fund (via ditto)		10,500
Renewals fund contributions (via transport and plant charges)		40,800
		146,700
Deduct:		
Depreciation (calculated on a CCA basis)	32,200	
Stock adjustment	9,000	
		41,200
Current cost operating surplus		105,500
Capital employed on:		
Depot land – average of market value on 1 April (£165,000) and on 31 March (£175,000)		170,000
Stores land – average of direct service portion (67%) of market value on 1 April and 31 March (direct service portions £120,000 and £134,000 respectively)		127,000
Buildings, vehicles and plant		189,700
Stock		124,200
		610,900

Return is therefore at the rate of $\frac{105,500}{610,900} \times 100$, i.e. 17%

Separate accounts had to be kept for each type of DSO work. The financial objective set in the Act was to make a 5% rate of return on capital employed except for building cleaning where the target was to break even. If DSOs failed to make the rate of return, the Secretary of State could close them down, as had happened with some DLOs under the 1980 Act.

The calculation of the rate of return for each category of work raised a number of accounting issues. An exemplification of the calculation is set out in Table 6.5. The first point is that the DSO Revenue (Profit and Loss) Account is kept on conventional local authority lines, so the surplus derived from that account has to be adjusted to the commercial accounting framework required in the legislation. This includes allowing for depreciation, calculated on a current cost accounting basis. Secondly, the capital employed is based on market value, rather than the historic cost basis conventionally found in the local authority balance sheet.

The 1980 Act required the DSO revenue accounts to be prepared on a **true and fair view** basis, whereas the 1988 Act required such accounts **to present fairly the financial results**. The code of practice envisaged that both requirements would be satisfied if local authorities followed:

(a)   Good accounting practice;
(b)   The DSO code of practice;
(c)   The local authority accounting code of practice;
(d)   The recommendations of CIPFA generally

One of the areas which involved considerable debate within local authorities was the accounting treatment of the cost of support services (overheads). They were commonly felt by contractor departments to be higher than those faced by private sector competitors. An important part of the code of practice was therefore devoted to this area. The code first recommended that for the following areas the **client**, not the DSO contractor, should be charged:

(a)   **Core costs**, e.g. those needed even if there was no in-house contractor, for example electoral registration or statutory officers;
(b)   **Central direct services**, e.g. civic hospitality or public relations.

A key recommendation relates to all other central costs (the document referred to is CIPFA's statement on the cost of support services):

For the cost of all support services other than those forming part of core costs, the document provides for the complete allocation to users of the full costs of all of the support services which they use. DSO revenue accounts should therefore be charged with proper shares of the cost of all support services to the extent that these services would not be needed if outside contractors were employed instead of DSOs.

One of the effects of CCT has been to heighten the awareness of client, and particularly contractor, departments of the need for better management information. It has also increased the need for financial expertise and advice to be provided direct to the DSO. Finally, it has tended to promote a more secretive approach, as councils are concerned that competitors (either the private sector or other local authorities) could capitalize on detailed financial data of the type councils have provided for some time to CIPFA and in their published accounts.

The costs of support services

Despite the efforts of CIPFA over many years, one of the areas of visible lack of standardization has been the treatment of the costs of central and departmental administration, now more conveniently referred to as 'the costs of support services'. In an important statement on the topic (CIPFA, 1982) it was admitted that:

... the diversity of treatment has remained sufficient to diminish seriously the usefulness of local government's published reports and accounts and associated statistics.

Support services are defined by CIPFA as 'internal activities of a professional, technical and administrative nature'. There are five categories of support services, namely:

(a) Managerial and professional services;
(b) Office services;
(c) Office accommodation;
(d) Central expenses;
(e) Democratic processes.

The significance of accounting for support services was highlighted in the 1980s by two parallel developments. The first was government legislation on compulsory competitive tendering in 1980 and 1988, which required a standard approach to allocating overheads. The need to make commercial rates of return also meant that items of overhead in the direct labour organization account came under detailed scrutiny.

The second development was the setting up of the Audit Commission. The Commission carries out a wide range of statistical work using comparative information in particular. If the costs of support services are treated in very different ways by different councils, the Commission's task is correspondingly more difficult.

The code of practice specifies certain accounting practices required to 'present fairly' the accounts of the council. One of these is the need for a full allocation of support services costs. CIPFA's definitive guidance is contained in *Accounting for Support Costs* (CIPFA, 1987a), and the key accounting requirements of this are as follows:

Support services costs should be fully allocated to all the services that an authority provides. Allocations should be made directly to services then divisions of service. Allocations should also be made to trading accounts, direct service organizations, capital accounts, special funds and services provided for other bodies.

To encourage consistency between authorities' accounting statements, authorities must include information about the following in their statement of accounting policies:

(a) The main basis of allocation used;
(b) Where any material items of support services costs have not been allocated, details of the type and amounts of the costs not allocated and the reasons for non-allocation;
(c) Where bases have been changed from the previous year, the reasons for adopting those revised bases.

The statements of accounts must demonstrate that fair and appropriate bases have been chosen to allocate support services to the cost of services. The chosen bases must be applied consistently and fairly to each account receiving an allocation.

One of the areas of controversy was the treatment of 'democratic processes'. Some commentators suggested that these should not be treated as an overhead but as services in their own right. CIPFA rejected this view, regarding the great bulk of, for example, committee meetings as an integral part of the political and managerial style of running services.

Service level agreements

One of the issues that CIPFA investigated during the discussion on support services accounting was the need for a 'fundamental change in the relationship between providers and users of support services'. CIPFA's eventual guidance on support costs recommended the concept of a 'service level agreement':

Support service users should specify as far as possible their requirements in advance, rather than be given what the support service provider thinks is needed. The term 'service level agreement' implies that both parties know as far as possible what is expected of each other. Thus a position is envisaged where any agreement may be based on an agreed cost, a day-work rate, a unit rate for a defined service, or the cost of an agreed number of staff working on a function. Such agreements must be capable of external examination by review agencies such as audit.

(CIPFA, 1987a)

CIPFA deliberately did not make more specific recommendations on the management accounting aspects of this, but a closely related development has been the introduction of 'practice accounts', whereby the support service has a form of trading account. Under this system, should a support service fail to secure enough business through its service level agreement with its users, if it did not alter its cost structure, the practice account would go into deficit. Although the earliest examples of practice accounts tended to related to areas such as architectural and legal services, where there were already very close private sector examples, there have been developments in areas such as finance departments also (Hone, 1988).

Service level agreements raise a number of areas where judgements have to be taken in each case:

(a) Will departments be allowed freedom to choose between the internal support service or outside provision in relation to some or all work?
(b) How far will the support department lay down explicit minimum

standards, for example for quality control or stewardship, by which both its own work and that of outside providers will be judged?

(c) Will there be any penalties for non-performance?

(d) How far will the same approach be applied to support services **within** departments?

(e) Will the volume of effort required to set up such a system be matched by managerial benefits, particularly in smaller authorities?

The introduction of a concept such as service level agreements into the area of accounting for support costs shows how the greater current emphasis on performance and clarity of objectives can impact significantly on what could only be previously described as backwaters of accounting.

The development of new forms of budgeting

This section focuses on internal financial management rather than external reporting. Whereas the National Health Service has a planning system whose form is devised centrally and to some extent imposed on health authorities, in local government planning and budgeting systems are normally devised locally, albeit with regard to external needs. Before analysing present practice, it is necessary to explain the context which has influenced the practice.

Through most of the 1960s and 1970s there was continuous concern with the nature of local authorities' planning and budgeting systems, heavily influenced by American writings commending more rational planning systems, and from the implementation of planning, programming, budgeting systems (PPBS) in American federal government and some state and local governments. Advocates of systems such as PPBS pointed out that there was confusion between planning and budgeting. The essentially short-term financial process of annual budgeting was also being used for policy planning. There was insufficient strategic thinking and long-term planning. Local authorities were not clear on their objectives or local needs and had not orientated their financial information to an objective-based (programme) format. Too little attention was given to measuring outputs and to monitoring the outcomes of policies.

In place of this relatively unsystematic approach, Norton and Wedgewood-Oppenheim (1981) described how PPBS:

was a comprehensive model of integrated procedures for analyses of government objectives and activities within an output-orientated programme structure, leading to a multi-year programme and financial plan and a reformed budget which would incorporate both input and output data. There was a strong emphasis on spelling out objectives of programmes, developing alternatives and evaluating these by systematic costs and benefits. It assumed that the analysis would be carried out for the organization as a whole and was therefore essentially a corporate approach. (p. 58).

PPBS was rarely tried in a pure form, but from the Institute of Local Government Studies (INLOGOV) at Birmingham University, as well as from private sector business consultants, emerged the concept of corporate planning. The Institute of Municipal Treasurers and Accountants (IMTA) actively promoted discussion of programme budgeting. Many member of treasurers' departments became involved in developing new types of management and budgeting systems.

Just as PPBS and corporate planning had their advocates, so too had they critics (e.g. Wildavsky, 1975). Most pointedly, they referred to failures to implement PPBS successfully in America, particularly President Johnson's ill-fated attempt to introduce it in the federal administration. To local government officers and councillors, whose perspective of local government expressedly related to a single profession or service, the idea of a corporate approach carried worrying overtones. And even authorities who had had some success in introducing new management systems found that more rational systems involved a lot more work.

During the 1970s, variations to PPBS were advocated, particularly zero base budgeting (ZBB) which is an approach more geared to a climate of restraint and cutback then PPBS. Sarant (1978) defined it as follows:

ZBB is a flexible approach to budget formulation by which budget analysis and justification shifts away from *increments above* the baseline represented by existing programmes to systematic review of *decrements below* that baseline, i.e. financial requirements for both *new* and *existing* programmes or activities are justified and analysed by the decision-makers. (p. 4)

As Sarant admits, ZBB is a misnomer because in most large organizations a complete zero-base review of all elements in a budget is not feasible in a single budget period; it would result in excessive paperwork and be an almost impossible task. A base level has to be chosen usually representing the minimum level of service consistent with providing services legally.

Though very few authorities would admit to having formal PPBS or ZBB systems, there is little doubt that there has been a gradual but significant change in local authorities' planning and budgeting systems. Compared to a very extensive review carried out before the 1974 reorganization (Danziger, 1978), many local authorities restructured their budgets so that they were more policy-orientated. There was a greater use of multi-year planning, and a clearer presentation of options to committees.

There is little doubt that planning and budgeting systems in British local government have evolved out of the relatively formalistic procedures and systems contained in PPBS to more flexible systems attuned to adverse economic circumstances and indeed to the local characteristics of individual authorities (Stewart, 1983 and Holtham, 1984).

The financial cycle

Figure 6.1 summarizes the main documents involved in financial reporting. Documents are only a means to an end, but they are a visible aspect of the financial cycle. There are many similarities among all authorities, with a basic annual cycle containing most of the elements shown.

The main point at which all authorities inevitably have the same document is the one-year budget. This may be a policy budget and/or a very detailed line-by-line budget. A policy budget will tend to summarize the detailed budgets. All authorities produce periodical reports on spending to date, which go out to the relevant departments. If adverse trends are spotted a report may in due course go before members.

The final accounts show what was actually spent during the year. They are of course compulsory and an important element in stewardship, with some policy implications at the aggregate level in connection with the level of surplus or deficit achieved.

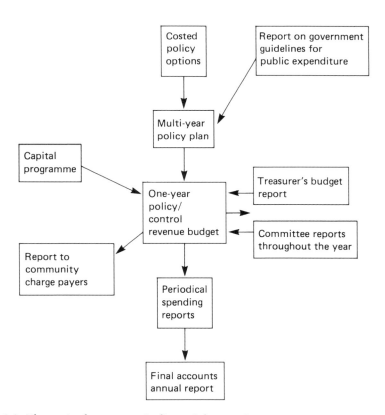

Fig. 6.1 The main documents in financial reporting.

Returning to policy-making, the multi-year policy plan may cover main political priorities only, or be comprehensive. Where there are multi-year plans, the annual budget will generally be based on the updating of the 'first year' of the plan. Virtually all treasurers now report on the government guidelines for public expenditure; this may be an important

	April	Policy Committee decides financial guidelines for policy planning purposes.
	M	Preparation of draft policy options (growth and savings options).
	J	
	J	Service Committees rank policy options in priority order.
Year 0	A	Detailed analysis of strategy and options by leadership/majority party group.
	S	
	October	Policy Committee finalizes major policies and each committee's total budget.
	N	Preparation of detailed estimates.
	D	Announcement of RSG.
	J	Estimates submitted to service committees.
	J	Policy Committee makes further growth/cutback and recommends community charge.
	F	Council debates and fixes community charge.
	April	CIPFA produces aggregate forecast of spending from returns by councils.
	M	
	J	
	J	Policy Committee: summer review.
	A	*All year*: monitoring actual expenditure against budget; requesting supplementary estimates and virement approvals.
	S	
Year 1	S	
	October	
	N	Preparation of revised estimates.
	D	
	J	Revised estimates submitted to service committees.
	F	Policy Committee: revised estimate of balance at year end influences decision on further growth/cutback in Year 2.
	M	
	April	
	M	
Year 2	J	Preparation of final accounts.
	J	Policy Committee: Forecast of Year 1 outturn influences summer review.
	A	
	S	Accounts published.

Fig. 6.2 A typical financial planning and control timetable

element in a policy or financial planning process which begins in, say, April. Of great importance also is the treasurer's report on the annual budget itself.

The capital programme is typically a separate document from the revenue budget. In some cases in the past there was an almost complete policy and even financial split between capital programmes and revenue growth or savings. But now the capital planning process is increasingly integrated as fully as possible with revenue planning. The capital programme follows from general policy decisions on financial priorities within the framework set by central government, rather than being considered entirely separately.

The budget timetable

No two councils have identical financial processes, though there are inevitably major areas of similarity. Figure 6.2 sets out a budget time-table which is increasingly common. The main point of this example is that planning, spending and accounting for Year 1's budget is spread over no less than 30 months.

Year 0 is taken up with the policy planning and finalization of the budget. Year 1 is devoted to spending the money, but at the policy level there is a summer review and the revision of estimates in the autumn; either could in theory lead to revised policies, and hence revised financial allocations. During Year 1, there is continuous monitoring of actual expenditure against budget. The preparation of final accounts begins in earnest at the end of financial year 1 and should be completed within six months of that year end.

The main variants on this cycle are really only related to Year 0. Traditionally, there have been no budget guidelines, and committees' estimates have been bids, which the finance committee has usually had to prune. This process neither suits a climate of restraint, nor promotes policy planning. A half-way house between the 'traditional' cycle and that illustrated is to issue budget guidelines in the autumn, but not to have gone through a policy planning process earlier in the year. This still leaves relatively little time to implement policies at the start of the coming year.

Balancing the books

Having undertaken all the work of detailed budgeting, the time comes when the books need to be balanced, i.e. the final decisions on expenditure made, with the consequent community charge being fixed. The key factors in budget preparation can be easily summarized in a very

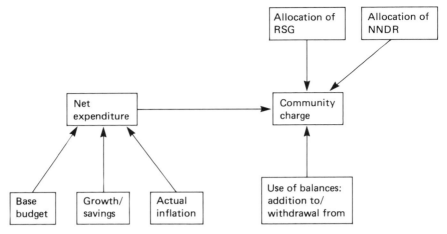

Fig. 6.3 The key factors in budget preparation.

simple diagram (see Figure. 6.3); each factor will then be considered in turn.

The allocation of government grant is a factor which is largely outside an authority's control. Once the RSG settlement has been announced in December, the degree of uncertainty involved is reduced, but not eliminated.

The term 'balances' is capable of a number of meanings, but is here shorthand for the surplus on the community charge fund account. As far as this fund is concerned, the decisions on the use of balances are wholly within the control of the authority, though account has to be taken of legal, quasi-legal or good financial management considerations surrounding surpluses and deficits.

Net expenditure is all community charge fund expenditure to be financed by community charge, RSG and balances. There are, in summary, only two types of variation to the base budget – growth/savings and inflation. The forecast level of inflation, already discussed above, is almost wholly outside the control of any individual authority. This is not to say that there is no action which councils can take in consequence; they can alter their mix of goods and services or they can take explicit or implicit policy decisions not to provide for the full effect of inflation (i.e. cut the real level of service provision). Simpifying all the many elements that make it up, therefore, the area over which the local authority does have control is the 'growth/savings' policy decision component. Hence the importance of the policy planning process to budgeting and also the need for the budget to enable fine tuning (or in extreme cases, coarse tuning) of the policy plan.

Of the four key factors in budget preparation – government grant, use of balances, net expenditure and community charge – it is if anything the latter which is the balancing factor of the four. The two single largest influences are usually the level of government grant allocation and the actual level of inflation suffered. Broadly speaking, neither is directly within the authority's control. The two factors that are – use of balances and real/growth savings – are all the more likely to reflect political decisions.

It was sometimes the case in the past that elected members would decide on a rate poundage and then set expenditure allocations for committees based on these predetermined poundages. This was known as 'rate rationing'. But the now inevitable uncertainties over inflation and RSG do not encourage such rationing in its purest form. Expenditure alone does not determine the community charge. Indeed it is perfectly possible for councils to follow broad government expenditure guidelines, yet have charge increases greatly in excess of the national average. Reasons for this include:

(a) Changes in grant or NNDR allocation;
(b) Balances have been run down and now have to be budgeted for;
(c) The council may have provided for a 'realistic' level of inflation higher than the government's assumption in the RSG settlement.

Budgetary control

The basic principles of budgetary control do not vary significantly across the public and private sectors. The need is to define a structure of accountable management, produce budgets which are as realistic as possible, and set up a monitoring system to provide the managers with relevant and timely information to help them make decisions. However, the problems encountered and the major issues in budgetary control can vary from organization to organization, even within local government. There is ample discussion in Chapter 3 on the general problems of accountable management and budgetary control much of which is equally relevant to local government.

To summarize briefly the position in local government: once the budget has been fixed by the council, officers responsible for spending it receive detailed figures of their budgets, against which the actual trends in spending can be monitored on a periodic basis, usually monthly. Local authorities invariably use computerized systems to handle the large amount of data involved. The 1988 Local Government Act introduced a new dimension because under Clause 114 a Treasurer had a new duty, not only to warn councillors if the council was likely to overspend, but also to prevent new commitments being undertaken. This further highlighted the need for reliable financial monitoring systems.

Councillors may become involved in this process when some adverse trend is discerned at a detailed level, e.g. if income from a particular council service is considerably below forecast, a policy change may need to be considered. Alternatively they may become involved at a global level, e.g. if pay awards have exceeded the provision in the contingency fund, the policy committee must consider the options open to the council.

The responsibility for budgetary control usually lies with service chief officers, with the treasurer's role relating to the collation of data and global monitoring and forecasting. Since it is physically impossible for individual chief officers to control all details of spending, except in the smallest departments, there should ideally be a formal structure of accountable management, defining the roles of resource and service committees, the treasurer, chief officers and the named line managers directly responsible for controlling spending. Accountable management is often introduced with the aim of delegating responsibility to those nearest the actual provision of services, e.g. headteachers, officers-in-charge of residential homes, area superintendents. Whatever the extent of delegation – and some authorities permit remarkably little – the principle of accountable management should still be promoted. Improved financial information systems are now increasingly paying attention to ensuring that data can be presented flexibly to meet the wide needs of different types of manager.

One of the most significant issues in budgetary control is the way inflation is treated. Some authorities budget at outturn prices, i.e. allocate out inflation at the beginning of the financial year. Others may allocate the sums in respect of inflation on request from committees. If actual spending is to be compared with something comparable, then generally some element of inflation must be allocated, unless there is an overriding reason, e.g. if no cash is available to allocate!

Another area receiving increasing attention is the attitude of the authorities permit no virement at all. Others allow almost unlimited virement. Two points need to be stressed. The first is that fortuitous savings are not appropriate for use in virement. Second, increased commitments should not be generated by virement. Having said that, with an increasing climate of restraint, a flexible approach to virement – which in many authorities still needs to be sanctioned by elected members – can act as a powerful motivation to seek value for money and should be encouraged.
members – can act as a powerful motivation to seek value for money and should be encouraged.

Budgetary control has tended to relate solely to financial information. But a number of authorities are introducing systems which integrate financial and non-financial data. This may involve the production of unit-cost information, e.g. cost per resident-week in homes, cost per swimmer in baths, cost per square yard of road patched, and so on. Such data are more concerned with the measurement of efficiency and effectiveness than a purely financial system which relates to stewardship and to ensuring that cash limits are not exceeded. This leads on to the broader question of performance measurement, which is discussed in a later section.

Decentralized resource management

During the 1980s there began to develop a significantly greater interest in moving from a narrow interest in budgetary control to a wider concept of decentralized resource management. This was identified in an INLOGOV survey of management innovation (Stoker *et al.*, 1988), and has been analysed in Holtham and Stewart (1986). Table 6.6 summarizes the growth found in decentralized resource management from 1980 to 1988, although it is noteworthy that only a quarter of authorities claimed to be working in this area.

Decentralized resource management has been promoted by two parallel influences. The first has been the growing managerial belief in both public and private sectors that delegation, decentralization and devolution were both valid and necessary. Since these concepts were not widely found in local government, innovations in the area tended to be well publicized.

Secondly central government began to see devolved management as one of several methods of transferring power from local authorities as institutions to other bodies. The most explicit area where this has occurred is in education, where the 1988 Education Reform Act required local authorities to prepare schemes for financial delegation to schools.

Such schemes brought into focus the difficult question of splitting up previously largely centralized budgets for individual establishments. It is interesting that this involves councils in precisely the same kind of problems faced by central government in RSG allocations.

Cambridgeshire County Council was an early innovator in the local financial management of schools, and prior to the Reform Act had

Table 6.6 Local authorities giving devolved budgetary control to managers in units, sections or cost centres 1980 and 1988

Year	In some departments		In all departments		Totals	
	%	No.	%	No.	%	No.
1980	8.9	20	3.6	8	12.4	28
1988	15.6	35	10.7	24	26.2	59

Source: *Stoker et al.* (1988).

Table 6.7 Elements of the formula for allocating budgets to secondary schools (Cambridgeshire County Council)

Formula element	Example
1. Items to be managed centrally	Careers Service
2. Items to be managed centrally, but funded by schools	Supply cover for long-term absences
3. Managed by schools, but funded by direct allocation on the basis of historic costs	Fuel
4. Relative special needs managed by school and funded by formula	Socio-economic factor to reflect low income
5. Age-weighted pupil units	Teachers
6. Protection for individual schools	Safety net

introduced a formula for allocating budgets to secondary schools using the elements shown in Table 6.7.

Performance measurement

As part of the development of improved planning and budgeting systems during the 1970s, quite a lot of effort was devoted to improving the measurement of performance in meeting authorities' objectives. These objectives are largely non-financial in nature. Unlike the nationalized industries, few key performance measures can be reduced to a financial basis, perhaps an exception being the rate of return for direct labour organizations. Most objectives laid down by statute are of a general nature such as 'to secure efficient education to meet the needs of the population', and explicit performance measures cannot be readily derived from them.

Considerations of performance measurement tend to focus on two issues: efficiency and effectiveness. Effectiveness relates to how far authorities are actually meeting their ultimate objectives. Efficiency concerns whether, for a given level of achievement, the use of resources is being minimized. Considerable effort has been put into examining the measurement of effectiveness and into how, if at all, the 'outputs' of services can be measured. In particular, IMTA's Output Measurement Working Party published an important series of reports and articles. The main conclusion of these reports (*IMTA Output Measurement Working Party*, 1974) was that it was not possible or desirable to incorporate output measures into planning and budgeting systems in the precise and regular way possible with financial measures. Successful use of output measures requires the establishment of a recognized management process, and does not present a total picture of the organization's output

Table 6.8 Categories of output data

Type of decision	Type of output data	Frequency of decision
Introduction of new policy or major change in existing policy	Quantified final output measures where possible and other sorts of quantitative assessment (usually produced by detailed studies)	*Ad hoc*
In-depth review of existing policies	As above, plus opinion of staff and clients	Periodic
Budget	A few key statistics on need for, and use of, services Simple performance measures Unit costs	Annual
Routine implementation of policies	Workload and throughput data targets and simple achievement measures	Regular, but frequency depending on the subject
Review of management performance	As above, plus evidence of effectiveness available from other types of decision-making	Periodic

Source: IMTA Output Measurement Working Party (1974), *Public Finance and Accountancy*, **10** (October), pp. 339–42. Reproduced by permission.

at one time. The Working Party developed a simple categorization of different types of output data (see Table 6.8).

Given the problems of measuring effectiveness, latterly more attention has been directed to measuring efficiency, particularly by central government. In local government, as elsewhere, **comparison** is at the heart of measurement of efficiency. Inter-authority comparisons have been the subject of much interest, and in the Code of Practice on Publication of Information an annex is devoted to 'performance statistics'. Authorities are asked to provide comparisons with the average for their class of authority, and with other authorities chosen by the authority as having similar characteristics.

The Code of Practice recognizes that the performance statistics listed need to be interpreted with care, and often provide only a starting point for analysis of relative performance. Also the statistics measure different aspects of performance, including the cost, scale and quality of service, the demand for service, a degree of client satisfaction, relative efficiency, and so on. Most of the list relates to the cost and scale of service, which is a somewhat limited aspect of performance.

A broader perspective has been taken in the study by Hatry *et al.* (1979) which, in addition to undertaking a number of in-depth studies, also proposes a general approach to comparison for performance measurement, suggesting:

(a) Comparisons over **time**;
(b) Measures compared **between** geographical areas or institutions **within** an authority;
(c) Comparison of actual performance with '**standards**', particularly in relation to standardized procedures;
(d) Comparison of actual performance with performance **targeted** at the beginning of the year;
(e) Comparison with similar **private sector** activities;
(f) **Inter-authority** comparisons.

This range of comparisons highlights the importance of performance measures as internal tools of control rather than just as measures for an external audience. A number of local authorities have been developing improved internal performance measurement systems. One example of this is Bexley LBC, where chief officers present to committees a 'Quarterly Operations Report'. Typically this might include:

(a) Service demand and deliveries – general;
(b) Key performance indicators for the last quarter;
(c) Finance: latest position for the current year;
(d) Manpower;
(e) Capital programme monitoring.

Value for money

Considerable attention has been devoted to the question of value for money in local perception in recent years, not least because of a perception that local government is not giving value for money. A large number of recommendations have been made to promote its achievement. These include strengthened external audit, a greater use of management consultants, more publication of more information, more participation of the public and of industry and commerce, privatization of services, and the development of zero base budgeting. The problem with most such recommendations is that they tend to treat value for money as an extra – achieved by a particular approach – rather than as a basic aspect of management. Many approaches such as those outlined have a contribution to make, but as integral parts of the management structure, process and performance of an authority.

In developing an overall framework for action (Holtham and Stewart, 1981), the following themes have been identified as critical:

(a) Value for money involves comparisons, not as ends in themselves, but as a means of developing beyond the apparent necessity of the present;
(b) Value for money involves changes in individual activities, but changes will not be achieved without adequate management processes which are dependent on the working environment;
(c) Management processes must clarify accountability and promote the managerial initiative that achieves real value for money;
(d) Over-detailed control systems can prevent the search for value for money;
(e) Selectivity is the key to tackling value-for-money work. The resources are there for such work but they have to be realized, and an action plan can structure the overall process.

Since its inception the Audit Commission has played a very valuable role in promoting the achievement of value for money. It has done this by:

(a) Reports on good practice in specific services;
(b) Recommendations on good management practices;
(c) Special studies of individual authorities;
(d) The institution of a monitoring system to review the actual achievement of value for money in individual authorities.

Conclusion

Local authority external reporting was the subject of intense scrutiny in the 1980s, particularly in relation to the capital accounting area from a technical viewpoint. The failure to achieve consensus within the profession exposed local government to the prospect of detailed governmental regulation. There was no doubt that it was more convenient to the majority of practising accountants to retain the traditional system of capital accounting. However, it was also equally clear that this system did not generate the type of management information needed for modern asset management. It also did not necessarily send the correct signals to line managers.

The internal control of local government became a much more critical area in the 1980s, as most councils adjusted to levels of revenue funding that were lower in real terms than they were used to, and much lower than needed to fund both council and consumer expectations. The need to keep within externally imposed limits such as rate capping or below expenditure targets meant that precise budgeting and financial control were needed. Many authorities invested substantial amounts in the hardware and software needed to run a sophisticated computerized budgetary control system.

Actually achieving better value for money is a more problematic task, but the Audit Commission has been very actively promoting the cause of value for money, albeit from the side-lines.

Summary

The chapter reviewed the general aspects of local authority external reporting before going on to look at the main issues in accounting, particularly the question of capital accounting. There was a review of topics such as direct service organization and service level agreements. The final section outlined the basic issues in financial management and budgetary control, including the question of decentralized resource management which is a topical issue across most parts of the public sector.

Further reading

External reporting is an area heavily influenced by CIPFA recommendations and guidance notes, and by regulations made by the Department of the Environment. The budget process is often analysed in general journals such as *Local Government Studies, Policies and Politics, Public Administration* and *Financial Accountability and Management*. Decentralized resource management is covered in a variety of ways, particularly the output of the Local Management of Schools project, of which CIPFA is a co-sponsor. Some of the most useful publications on value for money are produced by the Audit Commission, relating to specific topics as well as general management issues.

Public Finance and Accountancy, Local Government Chronicle and *Municipal Journal* all publish articles relevant to this area on a weekly basis.

Chapter 7
Nationalized industries

This chapter deals with a group of industries which, although significantly diminished in number by the privatizations in the 1980s, remains an important part of the public sector. The policy framework for their control and financing is examined first, together with the dilemmas which have arisen from the attempts over the years to establish the framework. The internal mechanisms of control and performance measurement are explored next, and finally the chapter examines the mechanisms and problems in external reporting by the industries.

Introduction

Despite major privatizations (denationalizations) in the 1980s, the nationalized industries covered in this part of the book are, socially and economically, a major part of the British economy. Industries such as British Rail and the Post Office are household names because they deal directly with the public, while others such as the Civil Aviation Authority (which supervises the country's air traffic) or the British Waterways Board (which manages many inland waterways) are less familiar. The industries are often regarded as a group, and are usually treated as such in planning the country's financial and economic policy. But it is important to remember that they vary in many ways:

(a) Some, such as the electricity industry, are monopolies (at least in electricity, though not in energy) while others, such as British Shipbuilders, are subject to national or international competition;
(b) The industries vary greatly in size. British Waterways employs about 3000 people, British Coal 100 000;
(c) Some have a record of profitable operation, while others have been consistent lossmakers.

Table 7.1 lists those industries which have their own identifiable and separate financing from central government. It is from these industries that the examples in this section of the book will be taken. There are a large variety of other publicly owned organizations which are funded by government departments. These include organizations as diverse as the

Table 7.1 The main industries

British Coal	London Regional Transport
British Railways Board	North of Scotland Hydroelectric Board
British Shipbuilders	Post Office
British Waterways Board	Scottish Transport Group
Civil Aviation Authority	South of Scotland Electricity Board
Electricity Council	Water Authorities (England and Wales)

National Film Finance Corporation and the Royal Mint. A full list is given in Appendix 7.1 at the end of the chapter. There are also organizations which are not formally nationalized, but where the state has a majority shareholding, as with the Rover Group before the company was sold to British Aerospace. These are not included because for most financial purposes they can be treated like private sector organizations which happen to have a controlling state interest.

There have been many changes in these lists of organizations. British Steel has been in and out of the public sector. British Aerospace was nationalized in 1977 only to have the shares sold back to the private sector in 1981 and 1985. In the 1980s a whole range of industries were privatized. So this is a group whose members are liable to change at any time as a result of changes in government policy towards public ownership. The industries covered in this section of the book may therefore be joined at any time by others or may be reduced in number by privatization. Indeed, as this edition of the book went to press, discussions on the privatization of the electricity and water industries were in full swing.

The privatization programme has been driven by a number of motives. There has been the political impetus to reduce the size of the public sector and to spread private shareholding more widely. There have also been a number of economic motives. These have included the desire to move the commercial risk to the private sector, a drive to improve efficiency and an interest in increasing competition where possible. Finally, there has been the financial motive of raising extra revenue for the government from the sale.

The privatization programme has been important for those industries remaining in the public sector, even though privatization is outside the scope of the chapter. On the plus side they have felt the effect of the general drive for greater efficiency and reduced reliance on government financial support. Their relations with government departments too are better, mainly because of the emphasis on the economic rather than social role for the industries. On the other side there has been little incentive to make progress on developing a control framework from that set out in the 1978 White Paper which is still the basis of procedure. More prosaically there has been a tendency to make sure that the accounts of industries which are scheduled for privatization should show a suitably favourable picture.

Quite separately from privatization developments, the system of parliamentary and government monitoring and control described in the following sections also changes over time, so developments need to be watched carefully to make sure that what is described and analysed still applies. As the previous edition of this book went to press, for example, the government was considering proposals to 'tidy up' various aspects of nationalized industry statutes, including provisions on borrowing and guarantees, accounts, report and audit, and financial targets. But such was the opposition to the proposals that they were dropped.

The organization of the electricity and water industries before privatization needs some additional explanation. Until the industry is privatized, the Electricity Council acts only as an 'umbrella' policy-making body covering England and Wales. Power generated by the Central Electricity Generating Board is transmitted in bulk to the 12 area Electricity Boards. Industrial and domestic consumers are supplied by these Area Boards through their own networks. Scotland and Northern Ireland have their own arrangements. As for the water industry, the Water Act 1983 replaced the National Water Council with the Water Authorities Association in which the ten regional Boards discuss national issues but it is not an 'umbrella' body like the Electricity Council. The Water Authorities are therefore effectively individual nationalized industries. Again Scotland and Northern Ireland have their own arrangements.

Finally, a note on abbreviations. Those who work in or with an industry often refer to it by its initials, but apart from abbreviating some titles (British Railways Board to British Rail, etc.) initials have not been used in the text in order to maintain clarity and avoid jumbles of letters.

Policy-making

Government and Parliament

Public ownership means that the basis of all policy is the legislation which covers each industry. The Acts which contain the most important passages as far as finance and accounting policy are concerned are listed in Appendix 7.2 and the main details of what is in the legislation are examined in the section on external reporting.

It is the minister who is formally responsible to Parliament for implementing the legislation and this responsibility means, for example, that the auditors report not to the management of the industry or to Parliament, but to the minister.

In practice, this responsibility is not exercised entirely personally. Although the minister answers certain questions relating to an industry

Table 7.2 Sponsoring departments

Department of Energy	British Coal, Electricity Council
Department of the Environment	British Waterways, Water Authorities (England)
Department of Industry	British Shipbuilders, Post Office
Department of Transport	British Rail, Civil Aviation Authority, London Regional Transport
Scottish Office	North of Scotland Hydroelectric Board, Scottish Transport, South of Scotland Electricity Board
Welsh Office	Welsh Water Authority

in the House of Commons, the day-to-day work is done under his authority by officials of the government department that 'sponsors' a particular industry. The sponsoring role means that the department is primarily responsible for government policy in relation to the industry and looks after its interests in discussions with the Treasury and other government departments. These discussions will generally be between senior officials from the sponsoring department and senior management of the industry, but for matters concerning financing, capital expenditure monitoring and the accounts, Treasury officials are also likely to be involved. Table 7.2 gives a list of sponsoring government departments.

Parliamentary control is rarely exercised through the House of Commons as a whole, although on occasions there may be problems with an industry of such magnitude that there will be a debate on its position on the 'floor' of the House of Commons. Normally, however, parliamentary control over an industry is exercised through a select committee. Until the 1978–79 parliamentary session, all industries were covered by the Select Committee on Nationalized Industries (SCNI), but in 1980 the SCNI was abolished and a system of select committees was set up so that a committee covered each of the main government departments. The select committee responsible for an industry will be the one covering its sponsoring department.

Select committees are in general more likely to be interested in general policy (including finance) than accountancy issues, though the Transport and Energy Select Committees have undertaken a specific investigation of the reports and accounts of certain industries. The Treasury Select Committee has also taken an interest in financial policy for the nationalized industries as a whole. Otherwise, finance and accounting matters come up at various times when chairmen and other board members of an industry are giving oral or written evidence before select committees. Because they are often spontaneous, some of the answers given in oral evidence are revealing and make fascinating reading. But these investigations are not conducted primarily to provide entertainment. The select committee draws to the attention of the House of Commons as a whole those matters the committee feels require action. Often, however, a report itself will be enough to produce any changes which the industry's management or the government may agree to be necessary.

Policy through White Papers

The formal control mechanism through the minister and Parliament has, since 1961, been supplemented by White Papers outlining government policy towards the industries. The White Paper *The Nationalised Industries* (Cmnd. 7131) issued in 1978 is still the basis of policy. Its predecessors were:

(a) *The Financial and Economic Obligations of the Nationalised Industries* (Cmnd. 1337) issued in 1961;
(b) *Nationalised Industries: A Review of Economic and Financial Objectives* (Cmnd. 3437) issued in 1967.

In practice, while some of the policies set out in the 1978 and earlier White Papers have become firmly established, others have been varied by successive governments because of changing ideologies or economic circumstances. So although the White Papers provide important guidelines on government policy, day-to-day decisions will be based more on the needs of the moment. The effect of rapid changes in policy and the resulting conflicts are dealt with in greater detail later in this section.

The 1978 White Paper itself was the government's response to a report issued in 1976 by the National Economic Development Office (NEDO) called *A Study of the UK Nationalised Industries: Their Role in the Economy and Control in the Future*. This criticized some of the ambiguities in government policy, and although the government rejected some of the recommendations of the report, it accepted the need for greater clarity on financial and other objectives. So the White Paper laid down a financial and economic framework within which the industries were to work. This is still the foundation of the policy, not least because of the difficulty of finding a suitable alternative.

Key areas covered by the White Paper were as follows:

(a) **Financial targets**. After confirming that each industry would work to a specific financial target, the White Paper stipulated that 'the level of each financial target will be decided industry by industry. It will take account of a wide range of factors. These will include the expected return from effective, cost conscious management of existing and new assets; market prospects; the scope for improved productivity and efficiency; the opportunity cost of capital; the implications for the public sector borrowing requirement; counter-inflation policy; and social or sectoral objectives, for e.g. the Energy and Transport Industries.' For those industries not likely to make a profit, the White Paper said that the target would be set in terms of the amount of grant or deficit. The financial target was also said to be the 'primary expression' of financial performance;

(b) **Investment criterion**. The legislation covering an industry gener-ally requires that the minister approves programmes of major capital expenditure. The White Paper supplemented this by stating that the industries should earn a required rate of return (RRR) on new investment as a whole of 5% in real terms before tax. This figure was based on 'the pre-tax real returns which have been achieved by private companies and the likely trend in the return on private investment. The cost of finance to the private sector has also been taken into account along with considerations of social time prefer-ence.' The 5% figure was to be reviewed every three to five years and an appendix in the White Paper gave details of how the link between the financial target and the RRR was to be made;

(c) **Non-financial performance indicators**. To supplement the finan-cial targets, the White Paper also stipulated that each industry should publish non-financial indicators of performance and service standards, to ensure that an industry should not be able to improve its financial performance simply by increasing prices or lowering standards of service. It was explained that the government had 'asked each industry, in consultation with its sponsoring department, to select a number of key performance indicators, including valid international comparisons, and to publish them prominently in their annual reports. They would be supported by an explanation of why they had been chosen and of significant trends ... There will probably be some indicators common to most including, for example, labour productivity and standards of service where these are readily measurable.'

Financial targets, the RRR and non-financial performance indicators were designed to be the three major elements of the control mechanism for nationalized industries. The White Paper also covered many other aspects of the relationship between industries and government of which other important financial and accounting elements included:

(a) **Corporate plans**. Financial targets and investment strategies were to be part of the framework of the corporate plan whose importance was underlined by the statement that 'the government considers that the corporate plan, and the examination of strategic options, should have a central place in the relationship between the nationalized industries and their sponsoring departments';

(b) **Audit committees**. The development of audit committees within the industries' own boards was welcomed, and their role in looking at efficiency and performance was emphasized;

(c) **Pricing policy**. Prices were to be the result of the level at which the financial targets were set rather than of following the principle in the 1967 White Paper that the nationalized industries should price to cover their long-run marginal costs;

(d) **Inflation accounting**. The importance of inflation accounting was emphasized and the White Paper stated that financial targets 'should be put on some suitable inflation-adjusted basis';

(e) **Cash limits**. Flexibility was to be allowed on cash limits in view of the fact that, 'like private sector companies, their revenues and expenditures depend on trading conditions.' But while acknowledging that there might be conditions in which the cash limits should be increased, the White Paper also emphasized there was no guarantee that this would be automatic;

(f) **Disclosure**. The White Paper provided that a large amount of information should be published in the annual report and accounts including:

   (i) The main points in the corporate plan and any government response to them;
  (ii) The financial target and the accompanying parliamentary statement explaining it, including any sectoral and social objectives set for the industry as well as how financial performance compared against target;
 (iii) The cash limit (later known as the external financing limit) set and how well the industry had performed against it;
 (iv) The performance indicators and how well the industry had done against them.

It can be seen from this list that the White Paper was an attempt to provide a comprehensive financial and economic framework, and to ensure that the public was informed about what was going on through disclosure in the annual report and accounts.

Changes since the 1978 White Paper

Three changes have taken place since the 1978 White Paper which have significantly altered the emphasis of the control mechanism:

(a) The relative importance of the various control measures has changed, with what is effectively a cash limit on each industry's ability to obtain funds from the government assuming primacy over the other elements in the White Paper's control mechanism. This limit, known as the external financing limit or EFL, is set each year for each industry;

(b) As a means of providing external assessment, there are regular reviews of each industry by the Monopolies and Mergers Commission at the government's request;
(c) To add to the measures of control and act as a stimulus to greater efficiency, cost reduction targets have been set for a number of industries.

Each of these changes is discussed in greater detail later in the chapter but meanwhile it is worth briefly assessing how the White Paper proposals have turned out in practice, bearing in mind that it has been Conservative governments since 1979 that have been operating a policy introduced by a Labour government.

In terms of the Conservative government's stated aims there is no doubt that the industries have become more efficient. Their calls on public funds have also been greatly reduced. But the success here was primarily due to the change of emphasis towards greater efficiency and the adoption of a more limited commercial, rather than any wider social role. These changes were greatly helped by the appointment of chairmen much more prepared to implement change. The White Paper certainly helped in some measure, but a number of flaws were quickly evident.

The corporate planning mechanism was of much less use than had been hoped. The plans were difficult to put together – in part because of the industries' desires to maintain some ambiguity in public about their plans – they were not as forthcoming as they should have been, and the process was not well understood by sponsoring departments. The investment appraisal process too was difficult to operate and the non-financial performance indicators turned out to be the weakest of the parts of the control system and not a real balance to the financial elements. Furthermore, for each of the elements it was difficult for sponsoring departments to know whether targets, both financial and non-financial, were set at realistic levels.

Some of these factors are discussed in more detail later in the chapter.

Financing the industries

Almost all the funds provided for the industries by the government are in the form of loans from the National Loans Fund administered by the Treasury. Interest is payable on these loans at the rate prevailing when the loan is taken out. The industries are also able to borrow on the home or overseas capital markets if they consider the terms more favourable and if government policy allows them to do so. These loans are usually guaranteed by the government and therefore count as part of government financing, even though the money may not come directly from public funds. In the case of overseas borrowing, the Treasury has a scheme whereby the industries are insured against losses that might arise for them if the pound depreciates against the currency in which the loan has been taken out. The industry pays the Treasury a premium for this service, exactly as it would do on any insurance policy.

A few industries have been partly financed by a form of share capital known as public dividend capital (PDC). Dividends are payable on PDC on a basis which reflects trading profits, so PDC has generally been made available only to industries which were thought to have a reasonable chance of paying dividends in good trading years. It was therefore most relevant to those industries with cyclical, competitive businesses such as British Airways and British Aerospace, many of whom are now in the private sector.

The total of grants, net borrowing, leasing and PDC make up the industry's cash limit which is determined each year, taking into account the capital requirements of the industry and the internal resources which it can generate. Table 7.3 gives an example of how an EFL is built up for the Water Authorities. Some points to note from the table are:

(a) 'Other capital requirements' means mainly working capital;
(b) The capital value of leases is included both under 'capital re-quirements' and also under 'net borrowing, etc.' This treatment of leases is an attempt to stop industries leasing assets in order to get round the government's cash constraints.

EFLs are first published before the beginning of the financial year, usually in November, and the full table can be found in the *Financial Statement and Budget Report* (FSBR) published each year at the time of the Budget. Details of cash actually provided in the year are published

Table 7.3 Water authorities' EFL for 1987–88

	£ million	Total
Capital requirements:		
Fixed assets in the UK	1,026	
Other	(3)	1,023
Financed by:		
Internal resources:		
— current cost operating profit	573	
— interest, dividends, tax	(584)	
— depreciation	900	
— other receipts and payments	97	988
External finance:		
— government grant, net borrowing and leasing		35

Source: *Forecast in 1987 Public Expenditure White Paper*. Reproduced by permission of the Controller, HMSO. Crown copyright.

with the following year's FSBR and also in the reports and accounts of each industry.

EFLs are by no means as severe a constraint as an overdraft limit for a private sector organization at a commercial bank. This is because the government does not have statutory powers to force the industry to keep within its EFL for the year, so the limit can only be maintained by agreement. In practice the government has a great deal more muscle, since ministers can withhold agreement for major investment decisions or borrowing. Nevertheless, in recognition of the fact that it is often difficult for an industry to keep within a fixed target set up months before the beginning of the financial year, there is some flexibility if, on the basis of discussions, there is a danger of a major departure from the industries' medium-term commercial interests or damage to explicit government objectives. An additional 'fine-tuning' formula was also agreed so that additional borrowing of 1% of the total of the turnover and capital expenditure for the year over and above the EFL would be allowed. The sting in the tail is that this amount is deducted from the limit for the next year.

The level at which the EFL is set will be determined by a large number of factors but will usually be a compromise between the claims of the industry for the cash to finance its current programme and the needs of governments to balance individual spending programmes, as well as keeping public expenditure as a whole under control. Starting from those two bargaining positions, there will be a great deal of discussion about the 'appropriate' level to be set for the coming year.

Policy issues

Conflicts between objectives

In theory there ought to be no difficulty in reconciling the objectives set out in the White Paper. The corporate plan should be the mechanism by which financial targets, non-financial performance indicators and the RRR are reconciled. In theory, too, the corporate plan ought to include sufficient provision of cash to ensure that the plan can be carried out. However, there are both theoretical as well as practical difficulties in reconciling the objectives.

Taking the relationship between the RRR and the financial target first, the White Paper suggests that an industry's revenue requirement should be the link between the two, the financial target on all assets being set to reflect the need to earn the 5% RRR on new investment. But one difficulty in linking them is the difference in the time scales involved. The financial target is supposed to last three to five years. The RRR, on the other hand, is assessed over the life of a project as a whole and indeed may be altered by the time a project with a long lead time comes on stream. With a regular ordering pattern, timing may not be such a problem, but if there is 'lumpy' investment, it is likely to be difficult in practice to match the two year by year. The calculation will be made even more difficult because estimates have to be made for the rates of return on 'old assets' and because the RRR is an average of 5%, so that in any one year the return is unlikely to correspond to the average even if it is exactly as planned.

To take an example, a new nuclear power station, costing hundreds of millions of pounds, may be planned. If it takes, say 7 years to build and has a life of 25 years, the average rate of return may be calculated at 10%. But the return may never be 10% in any one year and may have to be very high in the first few years of operation to balance out lower returns later in its life, when maintenance costs are likely to increase.

Meanwhile, the financial target will be calculated taking into account not only this new power station, but all existing stations. It can be seen that there will be difficulties in combining, in any one year, the return from the new station with the returns from all other stations to reconcile a financial target figure. These difficulties will be compounded in practice because of the uncertainties surrounding the construction times and costs of each station, the relative costs of coal, oil and nuclear fuel as well as many of the other factors involved in energy planning.

A further problem is the reconciliation of financial and non-financial performance measures, and there may well be difficulty in succeeding both financially and against non-financial performance measures, particularly those on standards of service. For example, projects to improve British Rail's financial return may cause a deterioration in standards of service, so that running down the maintenance staff may save money, but may also result in more trains being cancelled. A similar conflict may arise between better performance against non-financial performance indicators and achieving a 5% RRR. It may be necessary to improve standards of service, but only by accepting projects that cause the industry to fail to meet the 5% target.

In theory, too, the primary position of the financial target should mean that, in case of any conflict, the non-financial performance criteria will have to take second place. In practice, the problem has not turned out to be reconciling the three targets, but reconciling all three with a target not given any prominence within the White Paper – keeping within the EFL. This was originally seen as a constraint rather than a target, but is as important as financial and non-financial targets. That this is so continues to provoke debate. For example in 1984 the Select Committee on Energy in their report on electricity and gas prices was highly critical of the Electricity Council's EFL which, it said, was imposed without due consultation and was not consistent with the other elements of its guidelines.

The use of the 5% RRR

The idea of taking a standard rate of 5% RRR on new investment as a whole for all industries is conceptually difficult to justify. It is also difficult to apply in practice. Financial targets are supposed to be set in a way which mirrors the differences in the circumstances of each industry. But, curiously, the White Paper fails to follow the logic through and gives a standard RRR, no matter how risky each of the projects might be. It would seem more appropriate, at a time when capital is rationed, to take different rates of return depending on the risk. The idea behind taking a standard rate may well have been that capital should be rationed across all the industries using the same rate of return, to enable comparisons to be made between competing projects from every source. But without more information on the reasons it seems very difficult to justify the use of a standard rate on these grounds, and more probably the standard rate was included to avoid the difficult and embarrassing job of quantifying risk.

Methods of financing

The industries have often argued that using loan capital financing through the National Loans Fund as virtually the only way of providing funds is far too inflexible, and that the industries should be allowed to borrow directly from the market. On the face of it, this argument would seem to be very reasonable, bearing in mind the very different circumstances of each industry, but there are some powerful arguments against a greater variety of financing methods. First, loan capital may be the only way by which a return can be assured on the money provided by the government. PDC has on the whole fallen into disrepute because industries financed in this way have often not been able to pay dividends. And even those able to pay have been generally unwilling to do so because, with controls on external borrowing, they needed the cash for the internal financing of investment. Second, the justification for borrowing through the National Loans Fund (which means that the source is the money raised by the government for all its purposes) rather than letting the industries go straight to the market to borrow is that the industries with no independent credit standing would then be competing with central government. It is argued that it is therefore more economic to go through a central mechanism to ensure that rates are not bid up as public sector institutions compete with each other to raise funds. Third, the argument has also been that since an industry's borrowings are guaranteed by the government, it would be wrong for them to go separately to the market and commit the government in such a way that it might break its overall financial limits.

A separate argument on financing has been whether interest should be payable when the project being financed has not yet come 'on stream'.

Certain industries, notably British Coal, have argued that with very long projects the interest ought to be deferred until the projects being financed are ready to generate revenue and thereby pay off the accumulated interest charges. Successive governments have rejected these arguments, mainly on the grounds that to give in to them would mean less financial discipline and a loss of control over their ability to get any return on the money which has been provided. Over the years the government has made some concessions, such as allowing the industries to borrow for varying periods of time, but the central arguments against greater flexibility have been upheld.

Flexibility in the control mechanism

Industries have also regularly complained that the system by which they are financially controlled is far too inflexible. This has applied both to the setting of financial targets and to EFLs.

In the case of financial targets, it has never been clear what the appropriate circumstances are for changing them. For example, will the target be adjusted if any industry consistently beats it or consistently fails to beat it? And what circumstances (domestic recession, world trade recession, bad weather) mean that the industry has to adjust to the target or that the target has to be adjusted? This is obviously an important issue in the way in which an industry responds to changing circumstances. After all, if the financial target has got to be maintained at all costs, this may mean that big savings have to be made and services may be cut with severe consequences for the consumer and maybe the economy. On the other hand, if it is entirely flexible, if could be argued that, once again, discipline is lost. In practice, the financial targets have rarely been adjusted in order to take account of changed circumstances, and there seems to be an 'unofficial' adjusted target for any year, which operates on the basis of an agreement between the industry and its sponsoring department but which is not published.

The second major area where the issue of flexibility has arisen is in the operation of EFLs. The nationalized industries have regularly complained about the difficulty of aiming at a precise target figure for financing which is a very small difference between large amounts of income and expenditure (both on current purchases and on capital expenditure). The chairman of one industry likened it to trying to land a jumbo jet on a postage stamp. The agreement reached in 1980 on increased flexibility for the industries meant that they had at least some margin of safety for financing. But even this formula has not satisfied many industries on the grounds that EFLs are not really a suitable method for controlling the industries anyway. Indeed, it has been argued that it is beyond the capability of any industry to forecast its capital requirements with such precision, bearing in mind not only the normal commercial uncertainties of the market place, such as an unexpectedly steep recession, but also many factors outside their control, such as political turmoil in a key market or major currency fluctuations. The industries' difficulties are increased because even if they want to increase prices to meet the EFL, they often have to go through a lengthy enquiry procedure before they can do so.

In practice, EFLs have really not turned out to be such a harsh discipline because successive governments have either allowed the industries to overspend their EFL or have raised it when it has become clear that commercial circumstances have dramatically changed. So the system has been operated on the basis of an implicit ambiguity. The government has not officially been willing to be seen to give much away to the industries, because they have not wanted it to be seen that the control mechanism has become slack. On the other hand, they have acknowledged by their action in raising limits that industries cannot in reality be controlled down to a very small amount.

Control using EFLs as the main instrument

The system of cash control through EFLs has been condemned for a number of reasons. First, it has been argued that EFLs unjustifiably push up prices; second, that they are simply a means of keeping down pay demands; and third that they burden today's consumers with the cost of investment which is for the benefit of the consumers of tomorrow.

None of these arguments carry much weight. Taking them in turn, EFLs of themselves do not necessarily mean increased prices for the consumer – an argument which can anyway only apply to those industries which are monopoly suppliers, since the effect of the others raising prices to a level which is higher than private sector competitors will be that they lose business. But even monopoly suppliers do not have complete freedom of action. If British Rail's prices are too high, consumers can and indeed do switch to bus, car or air transport. There are also a number of mechanisms to ensure that the industries do not automatically pass on the full burden to the consumer. These include statutory consumers' councils and the government's power to refer an industry to the Monopolies and Mergers Commission to investigate its efficiency.

As to whether EFLs constitute an unofficial incomes policy for an industry, when an EFL is set, an industry will make an assumption about the level of wage settlements for a coming year. This means that if an industry exceeds the assumed level of wage increase for a year, it has a number of options, including raising prices or making a trade-off between wages paid and the numbers of people employed. The government itself may respond by increasing the EFL, or by acquiescing in overspending. This means that although EFLs are a **guide** to wage settlements, there is enough flexibility for the system of itself not to constitute a pay policy.

Finally, the argument that, if EFLs are set at a level which means that the industries have got to raise money to finance capital investment from charging their customers more, this will mean that today's customers are paying for the benefits which will be enjoyed by customers in future years, confuses cause and effect. EFLs do not in themselves shift the burden. They are simply one means of carrying out a policy decision about how public expenditure should be controlled. Indeed, there is no guarantee that an industry will not cut its capital expenditure, thereby depriving future customers of their coal or electricity.

What all three arguments have in common is that the mechanism for controlling expenditure is taken as the cause of a lack of funds, a continuation of the long and honourable tradition of executing the messenger bringing bad news.

The status of government minority shareholdings and 'golden' shares

As a result of its privatization programme, the government retained minority or 'golden' shareholdings in a number of former public corporations. The purpose of having minority shareholdings has never been completely clear though the explanations put forward have included:

(a) A desire not to overload the market with too many shares when the organization was originally privatized;
(b) An attempt to reassure the public/the unions/the employees that the government would still exercise influence over those that enjoyed monopoly status;
(c) A means of protecting the organization from unwanted takeover, particularly by a foreign predator.

The 'golden' shares, on the other hand, were specifically designed to give the government power to outvote all other shareholders on specific issues, such as takeovers. Jaguar, Britoil and British Telecom were among the industries to receive one.

However, the government has in practice made it clear that it has little interest in intervening in the affairs of the privatized organizations. With experience it is also clear that they have the means to intervene in other ways, for example through threat of referral to the Monopolies and Mergers Commission or through the time-honoured means of discreet ministerial arm-twisting. Although the timing of the sale of huge numbers of shares has to be judged with great care – witness the debacle of the BP offering in October 1987 when the market price dropped below the offer price in the Stock Market crash – minority shareholdings are likely to be sold as a means of raising revenue.

Internal control and performance measurement

This section concentrates on performance measurement rather than internal control because the details of how to operate the control mechanism, including budgeting, financial management, capital investment and internal reporting, are left very much to the individual industries.

There is no common system covering internal control, and practice varies between industries as much as it does between private sector organizations. This means that there is a fundamental distinction between the well-established rules and constraints for external reporting, which are common to all industries, and internal mechanisms which are a matter of individual management style.

The measurement of performance links what the organization decides to do internally with how other people measure it. So while each industry has its own way of deciding how well or badly it is doing, in general it will tend to watch more closely those performance measures which the outside world is using. This section therefore deals with those measures of performance that are commonly used to assess the industries.

Determining performance measures

The legislation

The legislation which set up each of the industries contains some statement about a financial objective. Often that objective is to break even (without the basis being specified) taking one year with another, although some are set profit targets. Table 7.4 summarizes the financial objectives of the industries as set out in the legislation.

In most cases, the legislation also gives the industries a variety of non-financial tasks. These may be expressed as obligations or duties, and some examples are:

It shall be the duty of the Railways Board . . . to provide railway services in Great Britain . . . and to provide such other services and facilities as appear to the Board to be expedient and to have due regard . . . to efficiency and economy and safety of operation.

(British Rail: Transport Act 1962)

To have full regard to the requirements of national defence [and] to promote industrial democracy in a strong and organic form.

(British Shipbuilders: Aircraft and Shipbuilding Act 1977)

Such statements are of course only very vague and do not provide clear indications about what constitutes a good performance for an industry. Nevertheless they are important in establishing the background against which an industry's decisions are taken. It is also easy to see how these

Table 7.4 Financial objectives in the legislation

British Coal
The revenues of the board shall be not less than sufficient for meeting all their outgoings properly chargeable to revenue account . . . on average of good and bad years.

British Railways Board
The combined revenues of the Board and its subsidiaries must be sufficient to meet the combined charges to revenue taking one year with another.

British Shipbuilders Board
The financial duties . . . shall be such as may from time to time be determined by the Secretary of State with the approval of the Treasury and after consultation with the Corporation.

British Waterways Board
As for British Railways Board.

Electricity Council
Revenues not less than sufficient to meet their outgoings properly chargeable to revenue account taking one year with another.

Civil Aviation Authority
Revenue is not less than sufficient for making provision for the meeting of charges properly chargeable to revenue taking one year with another.

London Regional Transport
So far as practicable the combined revenues of London Regional Transport and any subsidiaries of theirs are not less than sufficient to meet their combined charges properly chargeable to revenue account, taking one accounting year with another.

North of Scotland Hydroelectric Board
As for Electricity Council.

Post Office
To secure that its revenues are not less than sufficient to meet all charges properly chargeable to revenue account taking one year with another.

Scottish Transport
As for British Rail.

South of Scotland Electricity Board
As for Electricity Council.

Water Authorities
As for Electricity Council.

---

general objectives may clash with financial objectives, with an industry required to break-even while providing loss-making services.

The corporate plan

An industry's corporate plan, which will be seen and approved by the minister and the sponsoring department, usually contains a statement of broad objectives as well as a variety of specific objectives, some financial and some non-financial.

Performance targets and aims

Almost all industries have a financial performance target, set by the minister in one of the three main forms:

(a) Return on assets.
(b) Profit as a percentage of turnover.
(c) Target profitability or loss.

Some actual examples are:

(a) **British Rail**: Public Sector Obligation (government subsidy for maintaining socially important but unviable services) down to £555 million (in 1986–87 prices) by 1989–90;
(b) **Electricity (England and Wales)**: 4.75% return on capital employed on CCA basis in 1989–90.

Most of the targets have been set as a percentage return on net assets, as set out in the 1978 White Paper.

In addition to the financial targets, non-financial performance aims may also be set by the minister. The Post Office, for example, had the target of a real reduction in unit costs in the three years to 31 March 1989 of 6% for letters, 5.4% for parcels and 3.7% for counter services, giving a 5.5% reduction overall.

Such aims are in addition to the performance measures/indicators described in the section on policy-making. Both will be published in the report and accounts and Table 7.5 gives an illustration of some published indicators for British Rail.

Internally set targets

Most of the industries also set themselves targets as a means of measuring their performance. These are sometimes made public in the annual report and accounts and include a wide variety of different measures. One which appears again and again and is certainly regarded as important inside each industry is the self-financing ratio defined as either:

(a) That proportion of capital expenditure over a period which is financed from internal resources, or;
(b) That proportion of the total funds required for a period financed internally.

The 1978 White Paper specifically rejected this means of measuring performance, perhaps because there are so many different ways of defining it and of interpreting what the ratio means (see 'self-financing

Table 7.5 Performance indicators for British Rail InterCity

InterCity		1984/85	1985/86	1986/87	1987/88
1. Grant per passenger mile	pence	2.97	1.71	1.42	1.60
2. Grant as a percentage of other receipts	%	41.0	22.6	18.1	20.2
3. Receipts per loaded train mile	£	11.19	12.23	13.02	13.86
4. Receipts per train mile	£	10.80	11.84	12.60	13.42
5. Receipts per passenger mile	pence	7.24	7.58	7.87	7.91
6. Passenger miles per loaded train mile (average train load)	passengers	155	161	165	176
7. Train operations and train provision expenses per train mile	£	2.92	2.96	2.73	2.56
8. Train maintenance expenses per train mile	£	2.63	2.88	3.10	2.74
9. Terminal expenses per train mile	£	1.25	1.27	1.26	1.25
10. Loaded train miles per passenger vehicle	miles	16,207	15,994	16,637	18,273
11. Percentage of trains arriving within 5 minutes of booked time	%	71	73	77	78
12. Percentage of trains cancelled	%	n/a	n/a	0.8	0.5

Source: *1988 Annual Report and Accounts.*

ratio', page 176). But there is no doubt that most of the industries see their ability to generate their own funds as an important indication of how well they are doing. It is also a measurement of how dependent they are on public funds and therefore the amount of pressure they perceive the Treasury will be able to exert on them.

Types of financial performance measure

Return on net assets

The 1978 White Paper confirmed that this would be the 'main form' of target for profitable industries. The target level is set to reflect the different circumstances of each industry and is normally calculated on a current cost basis. In general the return is calculated before interest and tax since the management is not responsible for the way in which the industry is financed and therefore for the proportion of finance provided by interest-bearing loans. Table 7.6 shows the calculation for the South of Scotland Electricity Board, together with the calculation of two of the other measures.

Profit margin

The 'profit' figure may be the same as that used in calculating the 'return for return on net assets, or may be a variation of it. Such variation might exclude income from investments, or include interest.

Table 7.6 Profit margin, return on net assets and self-financing ratio: South of Scotland Electricity Board

	£ million
1. Income	782.5
2. Expenditure	611.4
3. Profit before interest	171.0
4. Interest	154.9
5. Profit after interest	16.1
Profit margin $\frac{16.1}{782.5} \times 100 = 2.1\%$	
6. Fixed assets less depreciation	1,577.4
7. Net current assets	201.9
8. Net assets employed at year end	1,779.3
9. Average net assets during year	1,598.8
Return on net assets $\frac{171.0}{1,598.8} \times 100 = 10.7\%^{1}$	
10. Financing from internal resources	187.3
11. Net external borrowing	248.6
12. Capital requirements during the year	435.8
Self-financing ratio $\frac{187.3}{435.8} \times 100 = 43.0\%$	

[1] *Note:* This ratio differed from that published in the accounts (12.4%) because the Board deducted supplementary depreciation from expenditure to arrive at the profit before interest.
Source: Derived from *South of Scotland Electricity Board Report and Accounts* 1983–84, pp. 60–61.

Profit margin is much more rarely used as a financial target by the government than return on net assets, but it is almost always used within an industry as a measure of performance.

Self-financing ratio

Although not acknowledged by the government as a proper measure of performance, there is no doubt about its importance to the industries, and examining a series of ratios over a few years helps to build up a useful picture of an industry's ability to finance itself. Industries themselves vary in the way in which they use the ratio, referring sometimes to the proportion of its capital expenditure which it is financing internally and sometimes to it as the proportion of funds as a whole. The South of Scotland Electricity Board in Table 7.6 used the former.

In assessing the ratio, it is necessary to take into account many factors, including the capital expenditure required to fulfil the industry's plans and the government's financing constraints, as well as their policy on prices and the level of the financial target set for the industry. These factors may mean that a high self-financing ratio is not necessarily 'good' and a low ratio not necessarily 'bad'.

Achieving a target of profit or loss

The requirement to achieve a certain level of profit or to contain loss to a certain figure is often, though not always, given to industries which are loss-making.

In assessing what an industry with this kind of target has achieved, once again changes in government policy and trading conditions since the target was set need to be taken into account. Either may change very rapidly and make it easier or more difficult for an industry to achieve the planned performance level.

Operating within the EFL

The importance of the EFLs and the problems surrounding their operation have already been discussed in the context of policy making, and Table 7.3 has given an example of how the EFL is built up.

Measuring performance – an assessment

It can be seen that it is likely to be difficult to avoid conflict between different types of performance measures. The problem of reconciling non-financial with financial objectives in the legislation has already been mentioned. Combining these with the targets set by the minister, an industry may well have a set of objectives which are not reconcilable with each other. In this respect, the industries are very different from private sector organizations even though most private companies rarely have a single, 'profit maximizing', target and have other targets as well as acknowledging their obligations as members of the community and employers. Nevertheless, in terms of the sheer diversity of the measures, public sector enterprises generally have a more complex job to achieve satisfactory performance than those in the private sector. And it is because different groups in the community perceive success for the industries in very different ways that many of the industries' managers complain that they are being asked to do a task in which they cannot possibly succeed in everything required of them. This has an adverse effect on their morale and may make it more difficult to attract capable managers into the industry. It has certainly been a factor encouraging those in the industry to support the principle of privatization.

Another problem in measuring performance is that many of the industries are unique inside the UK; so there are no organizations with which they can be closely compared. In this respect also, therefore, nationalized industries differ from private sector organizations where comparisons between similar organizations are often regarded as the key indicators of success and failure. So the emphasis almost certainly has to be on the analysis of trends over time, or international comparisons and performance against target. But analysis of each of these has to be handled with great care.

(a) Trends need to be interpreted in the light of changing commercial circumstances and government policies;
(b) International comparisons are fraught with difficulty because of circumstances particular to each country and the fact that the organizations are rarely comparable in what they do, so adjustments have to be made to the figures;
(c) Targets may not be a good guideline because the level is to some extent the result of bargaining between the industry and the sponsoring department.

Of the three, the comparison between target and actual performance is probably the least complicated to interpret, and international comparisons are the most complicated.

External reporting

Accounting and external reporting in nationalized industries is much closer to private sector practice than for most of the other parts of the public sector.

The rules governing external reporting

The starting point for nationalized industry accounting is that it should follow best commercial accounting practice, and indeed this phrase is sometimes included in the legislation. For the Electricity Council the relevant passage reads:

The central authority and each Area Board shall keep proper accounts and other records ... being in a form which shall conform with the best commercial standards.

(Electricity Act 1947)

This means taking into consideration (though not necessarily being bound by) four broad categories of regulation:

(a) **The 1985 Companies Act**;

(b) **Stock Exchange requirements**. Even though the industries are not quoted on the Stock Exchange, they will normally be expected to follow the disclosure requirements for quoted companies;

(c) **Professional regulation**. The industries are covered by the work of the Accounting Standards Committee (ASC) and will be expected to follow Standard Statements of Accounting Practice (SSAPs);

(d) **General accounting practice**. The industries are covered by normal accounting conventions and will generally follow the latest practice of the accountancy profession.

Legislation

There is no standard wording in the legislation covering each industry (Appendix 7.2), but a number of items are always included, such as the appointment of auditors, the need to present information to the minister and the power of the minister to give directions on the form of the accounts, with the approval of the Treasury. Some examples are as follows:

British Rail, British Waterways, Scottish Transport

Each Board:

(a) Shall cause proper accounts and other records in relation thereto to be kept, and

(b) Shall prepare an annual statement of accounts in such form and containing such particulars compiled in such manner as the minister may from time to time direct with the approval of the Treasury.

(Transport Act (1962)

Water Authorities

(a) At each audit of the accounts of a Water Authority under this schedule any local government elector for any area to which the accounts to be audited related may inspect those accounts and all books, deeds, contracts, bills, vouchers and receipts relating to them and make copies of all or any part of the accounts and those other documents.

(b) At the request of any such government elector, the auditor shall give the elector, or any representative of his, an opportunity to question the auditor about these accounts or to draw the auditor's attention to any matter on which he could make a report . . .

(Local Government Finance Act 1982)

Some passages in the legislation are open to differing interpretations, and this has led to trouble on occasions between the board of an industry and its sponsoring department. On the other hand the ministerial directions, which most industries have received in the past few years, cover highly detailed items (particularly on the accounts) very precisely. The 1987 Direction for the Civil Aviation Authority, for example, includes the following as one of many requirements:

The Group profit and loss account or notes thereto shall include:

a. analyses of turnover, expenditure, and profit and loss on ordinary activities before interest and tax over the following activities:
  Airport air traffic services
  North Atlantic air traffic services
  UK airspace traffic services
  Economic regulation
  Air safety services
  Miscellaneous services
  Highlands and Islands airports services
                              (Annual Report and Accounts 1986–87)

Further detailed stipulation on how this analysis should be done is also provided.

Self-regulation

A mechanism peculiar to the nationalized industries has grown up over the past few years using the Nationalized Industries' Chairmens' Group (NICG). The NICG has acted as a forum for discussion on a number of important policy issues, including European Community matters, which concern the industries collectively, and financial affairs are dealt with by their Finance Panel. The Panel has been particularly active in the field of inflation accounting. It was responsible for compiling a code of practice and a response to the Byattt Report (see below).

Looking at this system of regulation, it might be thought that the industries would be very constrained in what they could do. But one of the major problems in developing a framework of regulation for the industries as a whole is the sheer diversity of their activities. This means that the industries themselves are not likely to be agreed about what constitutes best practice, and it is clear from the way they report that there is much more flexibility than might at first appear possible. Furthermore, while ministers might seem to have almost total power over the industries in this area through their ability to issue directions, in practice there is a good deal of discussion and negotiation between an industry and its sponsoring department before a direction is issued. An example is shown in Figure 7.1. This shows an agreed form of analysis for the accounts of water authorities. Although the direction setting out this form of accounts was issued by the Department of the Environment, there was preliminary discussion and consultation with the water industry itself.

	Water Resources	Water Supply	Sewerage Services			Environmental Services	Total of Services other than Land Drainage and Flood Protection	Land Drainage and Flood Protection	Total 1987/88	Total 1986/87
			Sewerage	Sewage Treatment and Disposal	Total					
	£000	£000	£000	£000	£000	£000	£000	£000	£000	£000
Unmeasured charges	—	116,983	*	*	133,392	5,067	255,442	—	255,442	238,320
Measured charges	—	71,013	*	*	56,690	—	127,703	—	127,703	117,003
Precepts	—	—	—	—	—	—	—	12,872	12,872	12,320
Abstraction charges	426	—	—	—	—	—	426	—	426	431
Trade effluent charges	—	—	—	20,432	20,432	—	20,432	—	20,432	19,332
Miscellaneous charges	—	5,634	—	—	—	464	6,098	—	6,098	5,935
Government grants	85	940	2,290	1	2,291	10	3,326	—	3,326	428
Other income	1,095	9,659	2,018	1,658	3,676	195	14,625	295	14,920	11,464
Total income	1,606	204,229	*	*	216,481	5,736	428,052	13,167	441,219	405,233
Operational costs	564	84,837	22,932	34,624	57,556	1,765	144,722	6,140	150,862	152,433
Operational support costs	210	7,522	207	3,167	3,374	1,829	12,935	696	13,631	11,013
Non-operational support costs	239	25,423	3,341	13,318	16,659	1,986	44,307	1,733	46,040	43,627
Total Operating Costs	1,013	117,782	26,480	51,109	77,589	5,580	201,964	8,569	210,533	207,073
Depreciation and other amounts written off	160	18,447	7,051	11,728	18,779	377	37,763	1,248	39,011	34,804
Operating Profit	433	68,000	*	*	120,113	(221)	188,325	3,350	191,675	163,356
Interest							(112,432)	(2,015)	(114,447)	(114,932)
Profit on ordinary activities							75,893	1,335	77,228	48,424

* Note: Unmeasured and Measured Sewerage Services income is not allocated over services.

Fig. 7.1 An agreed format for analysis purposes: North West Water turnover and profits by class of business. Source: *1988 Annual Report and Accounts*.

Differences between the accounts of nationalized industries and of private sector organizations

There are two kinds of difference: the first in the underlying purpose of producing a report and accounts document, the second in the more detailed differences in the financial information shown.

The most obvious difference in the purpose of producing accounts is that while private sector organizations do so to conform with the Companies Acts, each nationalized industry has to conform with the legislation specific to that industry. This is not merely a technical difference, since it means that responsiblity in the private sector is to the shareholders, while for the industries it is through the minister to Parliament. But behind these formal differences are the differences in the practical needs of users. *The Corporate Report* already referred to in Chapter 2) took the view that reports, including those for nationalized industries, should be based on satisfying the information needs of users identified as:

(a)   The equity investor group
(b)   The loan-creditor group
(c)   The employee group
(d)   The analyst-advisor group
(e)   The business contact group
(f)   The government
(g)   The public

Using this classification, it is clear that there are important differences between the user needs of the private sector, where the seven groups represent seven different interests, and the nationalized industries. Parliament can be said to be ultimately both the equity investor group and the loan-creditor group through its power to control funds, as well as having an important role to play as a watchdog over the interest of the public, but the government's role also spans these three functions. Moreover, through the sponsoring department the government is also to a large extent acting in the role of the analyst-advisor.

Apart from Parliament and the government, the public's interests are served by bodies set up specifically to look after consumers of a particular industry such as the Transport Users' Consultative Committee on behalf of the transport industries' customers and the Post Office Users' National Council for those of the Post Office. But it is the media which probably act as the most influential watchdogs, though their influence is generally more idiosyncratic than systematic.

It can be seen that the relative importance of groups using the accounts is very different compared to those concerned with the accounts of large private sector organizations. There are also great differences in how much information is available to the users. Unlike the private sector, where the report and accounts document is virtually the only source of information to all except the loan-creditor group (who need to have detailed financial projections directly from the organization to which they lend in order to safeguard their own funds), the sponsoring government department already has very detailed information. This includes not only information on past performance but also short- and longer-term projections, both financial and non-financial. The report and accounts document, therefore, may provide some additional useful information to the government but in practice it is Parliament, the media, consumer and employee organizations and the public at large for whom the document is crucial. Apart from answers to parliamentary questions, select committee investigations and other *ad hoc* reports, it will be their only public source of financial information. For this reason alone, the industries tend to regard a major purpose of the document to be to express their views about current problems and achievements, partly for public relations purposes, partly as a means of exercising indirect pressure on the government.

The difficulty of combining a campaigning and opinion-forming document with one which also provides a clear and dispassionate view of the industry to enable users to make up their own minds is obvious enough. Some of these more dispassionate purposes include helping the reader to:

(a)   Evaluate an industry's performance over time;
(b)   Establish its liquidity and possible future requirements for funds;
(c)   Assess future prospects and the vulnerability of the industry to outside forces;
(d)   Have a basis for comparing it with other organizations;
(e)   Act as a staring point to assess the effectiveness of the management;
(f)   Find facts and figures about the industry.

The user group having rather different requirements is that represented by the employees who may well want the document for any of the purposes outlined above, but are likely to be primarily interested in the information as a means of establishing a wage-bargaining position.

Turning to the specific accounting differences between private sector organizations and nationalized industries, anyone comparing the main financial statements will find most of the items and the way they are presented to be very similar. But there are differences, and these are outlined below.

Profit and loss accounts

The major difference from the private sector is the prominence of current cost profit and loss accounts either as the main or as supplementary statements. Figure 7.2 shows a profit and loss account for the Electricity

		£ million
	1986/87	1985/86
Turnover		
Electricity supply	10,385.1	10,092.7
Contracting	183.8	168.7
Appliance marketing	549.7	481.2
	11,118.6	10,742.6
Operating costs		
Electricity supply	9,266.7	9,158.7
Contracting	174.8	161.4
Appliance marketing	510.9	449.2
	9,952.4	9,769.3
Operating profit before monetary working capital adjustment		
Electricity supply	1,118.4	934.0
Contracting	9.0	7.3
Appliance marketing	38.8	32.0
	1,166.2	973.3
Monetary working capital adjustment	16.5	29.1
Profit on ordinary activities before interest and taxation	1,149.7	944.2
Interest payable	436.3	529.8
Profit before taxation	713.4	414.4
Taxation	126.5	—
Profit for the year transferred to reserves	586.9	414.4

Fig. 7.2 Current cost accounts as the main accounts: Electricity Council Consolidated Profit and Loss Account for the year ended 31 March 1987.
Source: *1986–88 Report and Accounts.*

Council. This was the main profit and loss account for the industry and the basis for its financial target.

The rules for the format of the current cost profit and loss account were set out in 1981 in the Code of Practice on Inflation Accounting issued by the Finance Panel of the NICG. The contentious issues concerning this important area are set out later in this chapter.

The other main difference from private sector practice is in the amount of detail available in the profit and loss account and the treatment of grants. Because of the importance of accountability, the amount of detail given by the nationalized industries to support the profit and loss account is much greater than that available in private sector accounts. Many industries provide details of profitability by types of activity or even by location. The Post Office provides complete sets of financial statements separating counter services from letters and parcels. Even when industries do not go so far, the amount of supporting information is often extensive, covering the breakdown between different types of expenditure and other information not normally provided in the private sector. Figure 7.3 shows a breakdown of this kind for British Waterways. Note the separation of grant-aided and other activities and the increasing importance of property transactions.

This information may not necessarily be attached to the profit and loss account, and may be in separate statements elsewhere in the report and accounts document. British Coal, for example, has for many years provided a particularly useful table analysing results by area. This shows how some areas cross-subsidize others.

Balance sheets

There are no major differences between private companies and nationalized industries here, though the balance sheets will reflect the prominence or otherwise of current cost accounts and differences in the form of capital structure with loans as the main permanent means of finance.

Auditors' report

The form of statement reflects the fact that while auditors in the private sector report to the shareholders, nationalized industry auditors report to the minister. Assuming that the auditors have not qualified the accounts, their report will confirm to the minister that the accounts comply with the relevant legislation and any directions given. The complexity of the rules as a whole means that qualifications are more common for nationalized industries than for private sector organizations (see below).

Other statements and notes

As made clear above, in general far more information is available in the statements supplementary to the accounts than is shown in the accounts of private sector companies. The greater detail may not only be the result of initiatives by the industries or ministerial direction, but also the product of encouragement by a parliamentary select committee or of discussions with the sponsoring department. This requirement for greater public disclosure has not gone unchallenged. Some industries operating in competitive markets have objected to the amount of information they have to disclose.

	Waterways Operation and Maintenance		Other Activities		Total	
	1987/8 £000	1986/7 £000	**1987/8 £000**	1986/7 £000	**1987/8 £000**	1986/7 £000
Turnover	**10,102**	10,288	**10,520**	9,323	**20,622**	19,611
Grants receivable	**43,177**	44,194	—	—	**43,177**	44,194
Total revenue	**53,279**	54,482	**10,520**	9,323	**63,799**	63,805
Operational costs	**48,224**	48,399	**5,735**	5,524	**53,959**	53,923
Gross contribution	**5,055**	6,083	**4,785**	3,799	**9,840**	9,882
Administrative expenses	**6,915**	6,549	**958**	946	**7,873**	7,495
	(1,860)	(466)	**3,827**	2,853	**1,967**	2,387
Other operating income	**213**	118	—	—	**213**	118
Operating profit/(loss)	**(1,647)**	(348)	**3,827**	2,853	**2,180**	2,505
Income from investments	—	—	**327**	170	**327**	170
Profit/(loss) on ordinary activities before interest	**(1,647)**	(348)	**4,154**	3,023	**2,507**	2,675

	1987/8	1986/7
Interest payable and similar charges		
Short-term interest payable less receivable	**105**	49
Interest on capital debt	**2,826**	2,835
Total interest	**2,931**	2,884
Loss on ordinary activities	**(424)**	(209)
Investment property transactions	**5,745**	2,089
Extraordinary items	—	(562)
Profit for the year	**5,321**	1,318
Transfer to realized capital reserve	**5,287**	1,290
Retained profit for the year	**34**	28

Fig. 7.3 Identification of subsidized activities: British Waterways Profit and Loss Account year to 31 March 1988.

Source: *1987–88 Report and Accounts.*

Other items

In almost all other respects, the structure of the report and accounts document is similar to the private sector and items other than statistical material in the report and accounts will include the following:

(a) The letter signed by the chairman formally submitting the report and accounts to the minister;
(b) The chairman's statement, the length, style and content of which varies as much as similar statements for private sector organizations;
(c) A summary of key figures or highlights at the beginning of the report – in some cases this may be purely financial, in other cases it may cover all aspects of the year's operations;
(d) A review of the past year, usually covering finance, organization technical aspects, marketing and sales;
(e) Performance, the economic and social environment and recent research developments;
(f) Prospects for the year ahead, either as part of the chairman's statement or as a summary of the corporate plan;
(g) Members of the board and some details of the organization of senior management.

Most of this information is provided in a form which is at the discretion of the industry, though, as already described, the 1978 White Paper required publication of certain information, including the financial target for the year and the outturn, the cash limit and outturn, performance indicators and the main points of the corporate plan.

Interpreting the financial statements

The immediate impression gained from reading the commentary accompanying the financial statements of most industries is that all is not only well but **very** well. 'Considerable further progress . . . prospects for the current year are good', 'another successful year', 'continue to build on our recent successes' are typical phrases from recent reports. Even if things do not go so well, the tone is determined ('a difficult year') or euphemistic ('tensions in the past year' – a strike), or there is the implication that those things which went wrong were outside the control of management ('despite industry problems', 'despite turbulent conditions', etc.). It is unrealistic to assume that managements will not seek to blow their own trumpets, but the analyst of nationalized industries, as of private sector organizations, needs to interpret the figures with great care. Public relations statements can only be regarded as an opening bid on behalf of the management.

In interpreting the figures, a number of factors need to be carefully considered. Some of these factors are peculiar to nationalized industries, others apply to all commercial organizations but are more acute than for private sector organizations because of their size, complexity, history or position in the economy. For example, the statutes of most of the industries stipulate that they should 'break even taking one year with another'. Yet for a number of reasons (other than those which would apply anyway, such as the impact of inflation) it is unwise to rely on the profit and loss account to show whether the industries fulfilled that obligation or not.

In the first place, the magnitude of extraordinary and exceptional items and provisions for some nationalized industries may make it difficult to know how 'break even' should be calculated. Taking two examples:

(a) **British Coal**. Strike recovery costs of £342 million provided in the profit and loss account for 1984/85 were found not to be required, and so were written back in the following year. Neither of the profit and loss accounts included the costs of various government schemes, such as the redundant mineworkers' payments scheme, which cost over £500 million in 1985/86 alone;

(b) **British Shipbuilders**. £248 million was charged as an extraordinary item for 1985/86 for loss on sale of companies. (It is clear from the auditor's statement that the value of the businesses had been previously overstated.)

Second, for some industries the grant which forms a major part of income is not always clearly distinguished from trading operations. British Rail includes its grant as part of its turnover. In the case of British Coal, the deficit grant totalled over £4 billion over the period 1979 to 1987, a figure which itself understates the public subsidy because of the amounts which were paid direct to the industry referred to in (a) above. Yet for both industries, the profit and loss account is shown in a conventional format.

Third, other, special attributes of the industries make it difficult to evaluate the profit figures. In the case of the electricity industry, for example, there is the need to provide adequately – in practice on a highly uncertain basis – for the costs of decommissioning nuclear power stations and for the reprocessing of irradiated fuel. The problems of interpretation are well illustrated in Table 7.7. This shows, for the year 1987/88, the impact on both profit and loss account and the reserve of changes in assessing the amount to be put aside for decommissioning and the abandonment of supplementary depreciation. Profit and reserve are dramatically affected by these changes.

Finally, the levels of depreciation charged on a conventional historic cost basis are, in many cases, a matter of historical accident. For some industries – British Waterways for example – there is a justifiable assumption that all assets will not be replaced. In others, such as the

Table 7.7 Problems of interpretation: North of Scotland Hydroelectric Board 1987/88

	£ million	Note
Profit (before exceptional item)	15.7	
Exceptional item	(25.9)	1
Transferred to reserve	(10.2)	
Balance of General Reserve 31.3.87	87.2	
Prior year adjustment	(53.7)	2
	33.5	
Supplementary depreciation written back	86.4	3
	119.9	
Loss for year from profit and loss account	(10.2)	
	109.7	

Notes
1 Nuclear decomissioning and reprocessing (including backlog).
2 Change in nuclear accounting policy.
3 Discontinuing charging supplementary depreciation (accumulated balance).

Source: *Annual Report and Accounts* 1987–88.

electricity industry, depreciation on power stations is charged on the basis of modern equivalent assets, with all the uncertainties of what those might be.

Issues in external reporting

Uniformity of presentation and accounting treatment

There have been calls at various times to standardize the terminology used by the industries, the format of their accounts or the way in which items are treated within the accounts. The three cannot be treated entirely separately since in each case there is a question of whether the industries **ought** to be similar to each other as a matter of principle, rather than following the private sector practice of leaving it to the individual organization to decide, together with the auditors, on 'best accounting practice'.

Taking terminology first, the industries use a large number of different terms, particularly to describe profit or loss. The words surplus, revenue, income and profit are used to cover various concepts, no doubt in part reflecting different views about the objectives for a nationalized industry, bearing in mind that they are not generally trying to maximize their profits. Indeed, the objective may just be to break even over a number of years.

The question of these differences in the use of terminology is probably only important because profit is most often used to describe how well an industry is doing, and a large variety of terms may well confuse the reader. On the other hand it could be argued that it is for the industries themselves to decide what terms they should use and terminoloy is not a proper matter for anyone else.

But terminology is not nearly as significant as questions of whether there should be uniformity in format and accounting treatment. Following evidence to the Treasury and Civil Service Select Committee in the 1980/1 session, the Treasury submitted a memorandum on nationalized industry accounts. The Treasury stated that 'it has been the policy of successive governments . . . to reduce, so far as practicable, unnecessary diversity in the accounts of different industries.' It is clear that this is not going nearly as far as suggesting uniformity, and such a softly-softly approach seems appropriate, since accounting rules covering not only the nationalized industries but also private sector organizations are essentially a compromise between the desire to show uniformity where possible and the need to show diversity where essential. It is then up to the analyst to make adjustments when comparing organizations for particular purposes. The danger in a common format is that it would result in a distorted picture being presented because the diversity of the industries' activities could not be reflected in the financial information. The industries have also asserted that since it is normal to allow differences for private sector organizations, there is no reason why they should be treated any differently.

There have also been calls for uniform treatment of similar items, for example for the industries to depreciate similar items at the same rate. The fear that lies behind some of these calls is that accounting differences will distort policy decisions or that the industries will try to use accounting manipulation to meet a financial target. These fears should not be taken too seriously. The differences in accounting treatment are clear from the report and accounts, even though expertise may be needed to find and interpret all the relevant figures, and in general the figures are subject to far more public scrutiny than those of a private sector organization. The sponsoring department obviously also plays an important role in ensuring that accounting differences do not lead to distortions of policy, but as a more practical point it is doubtful in any case whether the government or Parliament has the right under existing regulations to impose strict uniformity for the accounts.

Auditing and value-for-money audit

Public sector audit as a subject is covered elsewhere in this book, but two issues are worth noting here. First, there is the difficulty faced by some auditors in being able to give an assurance that the accounts present a 'true and fair view'. Second is the need for a value-for-money audit.

A far higher proportion of nationalized accounts are qualified than is common in the private sector. This does not mean that the industries do not adhere to the rules but it illustrates the complexity of their commercial circumstances and the difficulties of fitting them into some parts of the framework of accounting rules.

Perhaps the most extreme example of such difficulties has been British Shipbuilders, whose lack of work and loss-making shipbuilding contracts have led to yard closures and major problems for the auditors. At one stage the 1984 audit report went from:

We are unable to express an opinion as to whether the accounts, which have been prepared under the historical cost convention, give a true and fair view of:

  (i) the state of affairs of the Corporation and of the Group at 31 March 1984;
 (ii) the loss of the Corporation and of the Group for the year to 31 March 1984;
(iii) the source and application of funds of the Group for the year to 31 March 1984.

to give an impressive catalogue of reasons. For example:

As referred to in Note 16, the outcome of contracts depends on a number of factors the effect of which cannot be foreseen with reasonable certainty . . .

and

There is a continuing shortage of profitable work in the merchant shipbuilding and composite division and in certain other companies which together have fixed assets with an aggregate net book value, after taking into account the provision referred to below, of £114 million (1983 £141 million). Consequently there is uncertainty regarding the extent to which the net book value of these assets will be recovered.

(Annual Report 1984)

Two other examples are indicative of the kinds of difficulties faced by auditors in giving an unqualified audit report. In the case of British Coal:

As stated in Note 13, the recoverability out of future earnings of the total value of net tangible fixed assets is dependent upon the future competitive situation of the industry.

(Annual Report 1988)

And for the British Waterways Board:

> The Board have statutory obligations for maintenance and remedial work on tunnels, reservoirs and road bridges . . . the level of expenditure in this respect is dictated by the finance available to the Board . . . the Board's Engineering Department has prepared an estimate of the liability for maintenance tasks which are required . . . but for which no provision has been made . . . as at 31st March 1988 [this] was £200 million.
>
> (Annual Report 1988)

Turning to value for money, in recent years there has been increasing interest in extending the scope of audit to cover this aspect. The argument is that the financial audit cannot go far enough in establishing whether the industries are efficient and how well they have used the assets under their control. With this in mind, it has been argued that a value for money audit is needed to monitor their use of resources and efficiency in producing goods or services. The main issues to be decided for such an audit are the choice of the body to carry out the investigation, the frequency with which it should be done, the nature of the investigation to be carried out and the body to whom the report should be submitted.

Nationalized industries are specifically excluded from investigation by the National Audit Office under Section 7 of the National Audit Act 1983, which covers examination into the economy, efficiency and effectiveness with which bodies mainly supported by public funds use their resources. However, there are two other mechanisms for conducting audits of efficiency. One is the Monopolies and Mergers Commission. The Commission has a programme of investigations initiated by government, which should include each nationalized industry every four years. These investigations can also cover formal accounting procedures; a report on the London Electricity Board, for example, recommended that a more detailed breakdown of the Board's financing of retail showrooms should be shown in the Annual Report. The other mechanism for conducting efficiency audits is for the government to hire commercial consultants to conduct the work such as that for British Gas a few years before privatization.

Following an efficiency review, the minister in the relevant sponsoring department has the power to require the industry to take remedial action. In practice this power is not used and differences of view about the Commission's report will be settled behind the scenes of discussion after the industry responds to the findings. After about a year the industry reports on progress in implementation and a final report is made after three years. But the scope of any investigation is limited and in 1987 the role and efficacy of the Commission's work was questioned by the House of Commons Public Accounts Committee. While agreeing with some of the criticisms, there were those who said that the comments had to be seen in the context of the Public Accounts Committee's claim for the nationalized industries to be made more directly accountable to Parliament. This has been resisted as a matter of principle by the government and on practical grounds by the industries who have said that they already have quite enough monitoring mechanisms and it is unreasonable to add detailed Parliamentary scrutiny to what is already in place.

Chapter 9 discusses the issues in this area in more detail with specific reference to the role of the National Audit Office.

Inflation accounting

No subject has aroused more controversy in the field of accounting in the nationalized industries than the introduction of accounting for inflation. The magnitude of the problem can be seen from the fact that for the financial year 1985/86 a historic cost profit of over £2 billion after interest and tax for all the industries combined would have been transformed into a profit adjusted for inflation on a current cost basis of only about £100 million.

There have been a large variety of methods used over the years, including:

(a) Current costs on a CCA basis as the only accounts;
(b) Current cost accounts as the main accounts, with supplementary historic cost accounts;
(c) Historic cost accounts as the main accounts with supplementary current cost accounts;
(d) Historic cost accounts incorporating additional depreciation as a form of inflation adjustment.

These variations have included some industries providing only partial cost accounts (a proft and loss account or statement) and some including – and others not – a gearing adjustment (see Glossary at the end of the chapter) in the current cost accounts. The list is so varied because until 1981 there was no agreement on what form of inflation adjustment should be made by the industries. But in the NICG code of practice they were given three presentation options:

(a) Historic cost accounts as the main accounts with prominent supplementary current cost accounts;
(b) Current cost accounts as the main accounts with supplementary historic cost accounts;
(c) Current cost accounts as the only accounts accompanied by adequate historic cost information.

although there is a general provision allowing the industries additional flexibility.

The result has been confusion. By the mid 1980s all industries were producing current cost information, though with varying degrees of prominence and a lack of uniformity. Most produced historic cost accounts with supplementary current cost accounts; of these, some also produced current cost accounts with supplementary historic cost accounts, while others produced only current cost accounts, though with some additional historic cost information.

Despite the confusion, readers of these accounts at least had the opportunity to have inflation-adjusted figures if they wanted to use them. Acceptance of the implications of these changes by the industries was a different matter. Some, notably those attacked for 'excessive' profits, embraced current cost accounting with enthusiasm. Others, especially those with poor profits, made clear their resentment that the government had insisted on the adoption of supplementary current cost accounts, usually by ignoring such accounts altogether in commenting on their own performance. Overall there is circumstantial evidence that the industries used the flexibility available in their choice of method to give the picture which they thought put their performance in the best possible light.

Nevertheless, willing or not, as far as inflation accounting was concerned, the nationalized industries could reasonably claim to be well ahead of the private sector. However, the basic problem, common to industrial and commercial companies generally, but particularly acute for the nationalized industries with their long-lived assets and dominant positions, remained: how to reconcile backward-looking accounts with forward-looking investment criteria? In 1986 a government advisory group, led by a senior Treasury official, Ian Byatt, put forward a possible solution in a report which amounted to a comprehensive framework for adjusting accounts for inflation and reconciling the economic concepts used by the government with the accounting measures used by the industries.

The report confirmed that adjustments for inflation should be made using the current cost accounting system that had already been developed within the accounting profession, provided that additional financial information was made available. This information should not only use changes in an industry's operating capacity as the measure of financial performance. The report argued that the nation as an investor should also be able to assess changes in the real value of the industry's financial capital. The analysis covered pricing, the required rate for return on investment, the valuation of assets in the balance sheet, and the need for an interpretative section explaining the significance of the valuations.

The report's own summary was:

(1) Current cost accounting (CCA) is particularly important in nationalized industries because of the long lives of their assets and because their economic performance has to be assessed in the absence of fully competitive markets;
(2) The accounts of these industries should be in a form consistent with the economic framework in which they are being regulated and should identify the continuing costs of supply, including the costs of capital;

(3) The required rate of return on new investment in nationalized industries is part of these capital costs. This has been set by the government at a rate estimated to be the normal return on capital earned in the private sector;

(4) The CCA principle of valuing assets at their current value to the business is the right principle for measuring continuing capital costs. However, the report suggests revisions to the methods currently used for estimating asset values and depreciation;

(5) If assets are appropriately valued on this CCA basis, whether or not the required rate of return is be earned on investment can be shown in the accounts in the form of a comparable return on total capital employed, taking one year with another;

(6) Where there is no Stock Exchange giving a continuous valuation of the business it is desirable that the return on investors' capital should be visible in published accounts. This special requirement argues for accounts in nationalized industries that show the return being earned after maintaining the real value of the financial capital invested in the business, as well as the profit available after providing for maintenance of the physical operating capability of the business;

(7) Further work is required with individual industries to develop the practical application of the accounting principles identified in this report.

If adopted, the report would lead to far greater consistency in the presentation of accounts, and would make evaluation of the industries' performances much easier. But in the event, despite the government's announcement in 1987 that discussions with the industries on the report had been satisfactory, there was no impetus to implement it. The report had received a lukewarm response from an accountancy profession embarrassed by failure to agree on overall adjustments for inflation. To this was added hostility from some nationalized industries which wanted to be treated as far as possible like the private sector and to be free of constraints. The importance of the report may be in the model it offers once the unresolved issue of accounting for inflation is again actively on the agenda, not only for the nationalized industries, but for the accountancy profession as a whole.

A major issue on inflation accounting has been the treatment of the **gearing adjustment**. The arguments have probably been more strongly rooted in differences about policy than principle – industries tended to advocate whichever course of action would put their results in the best possible light. The main argument for having a gearing adjustment was that the industries benefited from the falling real value of their loan capital in exactly the same way as private sector organizations and that this should be reflected in an allowance for that proportion of their net operating assets financed by borrowing. The main argument against was that although the industries are financed by a combination of loans and equity, the relationship between the two was much less clear than for private sector organizations because all the funds were derived from a single central source. Since these loans were the normal form of finance, treatment should not be the same as for the private sector where finance was through a combination of equity and loans, so a gearing adjustment was not appropriate. The compromise struck in a statement issued by the government in 1979 was that the gearing adjustment should go in a note, so that the information was available to make a calculation of profit including the adjustment while the profit would be declared without it. This decision meant in practice that industries were indeed treated differently from the private sector, though in practice some industries have found reasons not to provide the information agreed.

Another major issue arising from the adoption of current cost accounting is the implication it has for the industries' ability to fulfil their statutory obligations. The financial requirements in the legislation were generally drawn up at a time when historic cost accounting was the accepted form of financial reporting. It is unclear whether these obligations should be restated in current cost terms, quite apart from any financial target stipulated by the government. This may not be as simple as substituting one figure for another – there are complex technical problems involved in the calculation. Power stations, railway lines and airport runways are just some examples for which difficult decisions have to be made. Two key decisions are on the length of life of the assets and whether they will be replaced by assets of a similar kind. The importance of the technical decisions is magnified because many of the industries which have these 'difficult' assets are highly capital intensive, and the results of the decisions will have a major effect on profitability through the valuation of the asset base and the determination of current cost depreciation.

What are acknowledged to be unrealistic assumptions are built into the calculations of several industries, often because there is no more realistic valuation method. The Electricity Council, for example, values power stations on the basis of modern equivalent assets, but uses the convention that stations will be replaced by stations with a similar fuel source (coal by coal, nuclear by nuclear, and so on). The industries deserve a good deal of sympathy in having to grapple with these difficult technical problems, and while they do so readers of the accounts need to look carefully at the basis which has been used to make sure they understand the implications of the decisions which have been made.

Deciding the framework of accounting rules

The framework of rules, incorporating legislation and ministerial direction, accounting practice and self-regulation, ought to mean that the industries have a clear basis for compiling their acounts. But over the years there has been a great deal of controversy about whether the framework is too loose and whether they should not be more closely controlled, as well as what the answers should be to some of the more contentious accounting issues already described. The industries themselves have been adamant that they should not be treated as 'special cases', but should be covered by the Accounting Standards Committee. What is clear from looking at the way in which the industries have presented their accounts over the years is that they have as much discretion as private sector organizations in applying the rules, and compliance with the requirements of White Papers and the self-regulation mechanism has been frankly patchy. It has also become apparent that there are few effective sanctions for non-compliance.

Suggestions on how to achieve closer control have involved using Parliament, the sponsoring departments or the Accounting Standards Committee. But simply setting rules is not enough, as the history of the debate on inflation accounting shows, and agreement may not ensure compliance unless the industries enter into the spirit of any new arrangements. Here, progress will probably be determined by developments in the whole relationship between nationalized industries and the government. Seen in the perspective of this wider picture, problems over accounting rules are just one manifestation of a difficult and often ambiguous relationship. It may well be that clarity in the framework of accounting rules will only come with less ambiguity in the relationship as a whole, something which is not necessarily seen as wholly desirable by the industries or the politicians.

Summary

The chapter, after introducing the context within which nationalized industries operate, dealt with the policy framework for controlling and financing them, then with internal mechanisms of control and performance measurement, and finally with external reporting. Analysing the issues and dilemmas of operating as a type of organization more akin to private sector organizations than most of the rest of the public sector, the chapter makes clear that there are a number of dimensions of the accounting and control framework which are not present in the private sector. It also pointed to the areas where dilemmas remain largely unresolved. The continuing programme of privatizations has made these dilemmas of less national significance, but recent developments in how nationalized industries account for inflation may turn out to be important for future developments in the private sector in the future.

Further reading

There are three major sources for further reading on nationalized industries: the reports and accounts, official reports and other sources.

Because of its importance, the second group is given fuller treatment than normal in this section. As with the other chapters, the third group is included in the bibliography at the end of the book.

Annual reports and accounts

These are invaluable as source documents for facts about the industries as well as indicators about government policy and the industries responses. The majority of the industries make a small charge for the document and most must be ordered from HMSO or through bookshops, though some are available from the industry's head office.

The industries have a March year-end and publish their reports and accounts in July or August.

Official reports

Listed below are some important recent reports. Almost all are available through HMSO. Additional material will be found in other reports of House of Commons select committees, the Monopolies and Mergers Commission and other relevant official bodies such as statutory Users' Councils.

HM Treasury (1979) *The Test Discount Rate and the Required Rate of Return on Investment*. Government Economic Service Working Paper No. 22.

HM Treasury (1984) *Nationalized Industry Legislation: Consultative Proposals*. Reproduced in Energy Select Committee, Session 1983/4, HC 302. (Also in the first edition of this book.)

HM Treasury (1986) *Accounting for Changing Costs and Economic Prices* (Byatt Report). HMSO.

House of Commons Committee of Public Accounts, Session 1980/1. 15th Report, Appendix on 'Nationalized Industry Accounts'. HC 349.

House of Commons Public Accounts Committee, Session 1983/4. *The Monitoring and Control Activities of Sponsoring Departments – Departments of Industry, Transport and Energy*. HC 139.

House of Commons Public Accounts Committee, Session 1987/8. *Efficiency of Nationalized Industries: References to the Monopolies and Mergers Commission*. Fourth Report, HC 26.

House of Commons Select Committee on Transport, Session 1981/2. *The Form of Nationalized Industries' Reports and Accounts*. Third Report, HC 390.

House of Commons Treasury and Civil Service Select Committee, Session 1980/1. *Financing of the Nationalized Industries*. Eighth Report, HC 348.

National Audit Office (1983) *Departments of Energy, Trade and Industry and Transport: Monitoring and Control of Nationalized Industries.* HC 553.

National Economic Development Office (1976) *A Study of the UK Nationalized Industries: Their Role in the Economy and Control in the Future.* NEDO.

Price Commission (1978) *South of Scotland Electricity Board – Price Increases in the Supply of Electricity.* HC 535.

Glossary

Cash limit. The limit on the amount of cash that can be spent on certain specified services during one financial year.

External financing limit (EFL). A form of cash limit for a nationalized industry used as a means of controlling the amount of finance (grants and borrowing) which an industry can raise in any financial year from external sources. The limit is the difference between an industry's capital requirements and its internally generated funds.

Gearing adjustment. Either: (a) that part of the adjustments made to allow for the impact of price changes on the net operating assets (including the depreciation, cost of sales, monetary working capital, fixed asset disposals, minority interest and extraordinary items adjustments) that may be regarded as associated with items that are financed by net borrowing; or (b) those parts of the total adjustments made to allow for the impact of price changes on the net operating assets, including the net surplus on the revaluation of assets arising during the period, that may be regarded as associated with items that are financed by net borrowing.

Public dividend capital (PDC). Capital provided as permanent finance on which a dividend is expected to be paid to the Exchequer. This dividend will normally be related to the industry's profitability in that year, though on average dividends are expected to be not less than the interest which would be payable on government loans.

Self-financing ratio. Used to mean, often without specifying which, **either** the proportion of the capital expenditure which is financed internally over a period, **or** the proportion of the funds required for a period which are financed internally.

Appendix 7.1   Other public corporations

Audit Commission
Bank of England*
British Broadcasting Corporation*
British Technology Group

Cable Authority
Commonwealth Development Corporation
Covent Garden Market Authority
Crown Agents
Crown Agents Holding and Realization Board
Crown Suppliers
Development Board for Rural Wales
English Industrial Estates Corporation
General Practice Finance Corporation
Her Majesty's Stationery Office
Highlands and Islands Development Board
Housing Action Trusts
Housing Corporation (Scotland)*
Independent Broadcasting Authority*
Letchworth Garden City
Local Authority Public Transport and Airport Companies
National Dock Labour Board*
National Film Finance Board
New Town Development Corporations and the Commission for the New
  Towns*
Northern Ireland Electricity Services
Northern Ireland Housing Executive
Northern Ireland Public Trust Port Authorities
Northern Ireland Transport Holding Company
Oil and Pipelines Commission
Pilotage Commission
Public Trust Ports*
Royal Mint
Royal Ordnance plc
Scottish Development Agency
Scottish Special Housing Association*
Urban Development Corporation
Welsh Development Agency
The Welsh Fourth Channel Authority

Note: Other than those marked with an asterisk, external finance is included in the planning total. The treatment of those with an asterisk varies – the last Public Expenditure White Paper gives details.

Source: Public Expenditure White Paper 1988, Vol. I, p. 79.

Appendix 7.2 Important legislation covering each industry

British Coal
Coal Industry Nationalization Act 1946
Coal Industry Act 1980
Coal Industry Act 1983

British Rail
Transport Act 1962
Transport Act 1968
Railways Act 1974

British Shipbuilders
Aircraft and Shipbuilding Industries Act 1977
British Shipbuilders Act 1983

British Waterways
Transport Act 1962
Transport Act 1968

Civil Aviation Authority
Civil Aviation Act 1971
Civil Aviation Act 1982

Electricity Council
Electricity Act 1947
Electricity Act 1968
Energy Act 1983

London Regional Transport
London Regional Transport Act 1984

North of Scotland Hydroelectric Board
Electricity Act 1947
Hydroelectric Development (Scotland) Act 1954
Electricity Reorganization (Scotland) Act 1954
Electricity (Scotland) Act 1979
Energy Act 1983

Post Office
Post Office Act 1969
Post Office (Banking Services) 1976
British Telecommunications Act 1981

Scottish Transport
Transport Act 1962
Transport Act 1968

South of Scotland Electricity Board
Hydroelectric Development (Scotland) Act 1943
Electricity Act 1947
Electricity Reorganization (Scotland) Act 1954
Electricity (Scotland) Act 1979
Energy Act 1983

Water Authorities
Water Act 1973
Water Charges Equalization Act 1977
Local Government Finance Act 1982
Water Act 1983

Chapter 8

The National Health Service

Previous chapters have covered central and local government, where fundraising (e.g. by taxes or borrowing) and expenditure allocation are directly linked to the democratic political process, and also nationalized industries and other public corporations which sell goods and services on a commercial basis and which just happen to be part of the public sector by reason of past political decision to regulate monopoly or control key sectors of the economy. There is a further category of public services which through historical accident or consensus have come to be funded partly or wholly from the public purse, yet which have been allowed a substantial degree of non-political and non-partisan self-governance or autonomy. This category includes public corporations such as the British Broadcasting Corporation (BBC), universities and polytechnics, the Arts Council and the National Health Service (NHS).

Given that the NHS is the largest and most costly of these public services, and given also that it is an excellent example of a complex organization with inherent conflict between professional/service objectives and the overriding requirement to balance the books within funding primarily from central government allocations, this chapter will explain in some detail the organizational, financial and accounting arrangements for the management of the NHS.

Structure, functions and policy-making

National and regional organizations

Nearly all UK hospitals were nationalized in 1948, within the NHS. Hospital doctors and other staff became employees of the NHS, although not civil servants. Family doctors (GPs), dentists, opticians and pharmacists did not agree to become NHS employees, but their work was brought within the NHS by putting them under contract to treat NHS patients under conditions and funding arrangements supervised by NHS Family Practitioner Committees (FPCs). Community health care and ambulance services remained under the control of local government

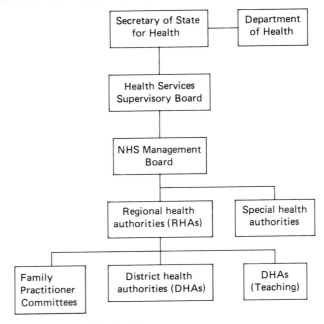

Fig. 8.1 NHS structure in England.

until the more or less simultaneous reorganizations of local government and the NHS in 1974, at which time these services were transferred to the NHS to be administered and funded on the same basis as the hospital services.

Originally there was a separate ministry for Health, but for some twenty years until 1988 a combined ministry, the Department of Health and Social Security (DHSS), supervised policy and funding for both health affairs and social security. The objective was to achieve greater integration – or certainly coordination – in policy and service delivery for these two important areas of public service. But it is not obvious that much progress towards the objective was achieved, and in the summer of 1988 it was announced that there would now be a separate Department of Health (DOH), headed by a Secretary of State for Health (see Fig. 8.1). This should strengthen the representation at Cabinet level of the case for the funding and other needs of the health care services.

Figure 8.1 additionally illustrates the relationship of the other principal organizational components of the NHS in England. The Welsh, Scottish and Northern Ireland Offices effectively provide the same higher level functions down to and including the role of regional health authorities (RHAs) in England. In Scotland and Northern Ireland the equivalent of district health authorities (DHAs) are known as health boards, and in Northern Ireland these include the administration of social services. In practice the organizational, financial and accounting arrangements for the NHS are closely similar throughout the UK, but strictly speaking the description which follows in this chapter is precise only for England unless otherwise clarified.

The Secretary of State for Health is advised in policy-making and performance review by his civil servants in the Department of Health, and by the Supervisory Board which provides a kind of umbilicus between the political and managerial levels of hierarchy in the NHS. The NHS Management Board and its staff have the role of promoting the implementation of policy and the improvement of management performance and cost effectiveness within the NHS. England is divided into fourteen RHAs whose role includes planning (including capital planning and the oversight of major projects), financial resource allocation between member districts (i.e. the DHAs), and the monitoring of the performance of the districts. RHAs also provide some common services for their districts, often for reasons of likely economies of scale or policy control, such as central computing, blood donor services, medical teaching, manpower planning, and centralized design, supplies and purchasing support services. There has been challenge to the need for RHAs, or certainly to their scale and costliness in the roles of planning and monitoring services managed operationally by DHAs, and there has been speculation that RHAs might be abolished, or at least that some of their functions and their resources might be redistributed to the DHAs.

Special health authorities include the NHS Training Authority and a few authorities managing postgraduate teaching hospitals not integrated into operational DHAs. All England is divided geographically among some 190 DHAs, with populations ranging from about one hundred thousand to nearly a million. A typical district will have a population of about a quarter of a million, some 4000 employees, and an annual budget exceeding £50 million. DHAs are comprised of a part-time chairperson and a board of members representative of local authorities, voluntary bodies, trades unions, health professions and sometimes a local university, supported by full-time management whose structure is explained in the next section below. DHAs whose boundaries include major teaching hospitals (i.e. for the teaching of medical students) are designated as teaching districts. They receive additional funding for their teaching role (i.e. SIFT, explained later in this chapter), and they differ from other DHAs in holding the employment contracts of their consultant (i.e. senior) doctors. For non-teaching DHAs the employment contracts of consultant doctors are held at RHA level, for historical reasons, and this has been criticized as reducing the quality of managerial and financial control DHAs can exert over their senior medical staff.

The levels of the NHS we have so far considered exist primarily for the purposes of policy-making, leading to resource allocation, followed up by performance review. Since nearly all forms of health care may be claimed to be a worthy use of public funds by those in need of care, their families and interested pressure groups – whilst public funds for the NHS are limited – the policy-making process becomes the management of a system of resource rationing, involving setting priorities for the use of scarce financial resources and limited management time. One NHS senior manager claimed to the author that he had a list of more than one hundred priorities specified by the (former) DHSS which had not yet been either fulfilled or rescinded. This becomes even more difficult for district level management, and its financial management, when local DHA members, local doctors and other health professionals seek to develop their own priorities for health care spending in response to local perceptions of need and of the greatest benefit from the use of limited resources.

District organization

The previous section summarized the formal hierarchy of authority and resources flow downwards from Secretary of State to the DHA, with a matching flow of accountability upwards. We now turn to the operational management arrangements within the DHA. From 1974, until after the publication and acceptance of the Griffiths Inquiry Report of October 1983, health districts (and also the RHAs and the former area health authorities phased out in 1982) were managed by a team of co-equal chief officers who reached decisions on a 'consensus management' basis without benefit of a permanent chairman or chief executive. The Griffiths Report to the Secretary of State of the (then) DHSS stated in effect that consensus management was a nonsense and that there must be one single individual at each level of organizational management who could and would be held responsible for performance – for success or failure. There should be a general manager in charge at each level, from the new NHS Management Board recommended by Griffiths, down through the RHAs and the DHAs to the new unit management structures established after 1982.

All DHAs will normally have at least two units of management, one for 'acute' hospital services and one for community care. Larger DHAs may have several units (e.g. for the main district general hospital (DGH), for other smaller or cottage hospitals, for mental illness and mental handicap, and for geriatric and other community care services). District general managers (DGMs) are responsible primarily for the overall planning, coordination, resource distribution and performance of the DHA's total programme, while unit general managers (UGMs) are responsible for the operational management and efficiency of the manpower and financial resources allocated to their units.

Within each DHA there is considerable local discretion regarding how

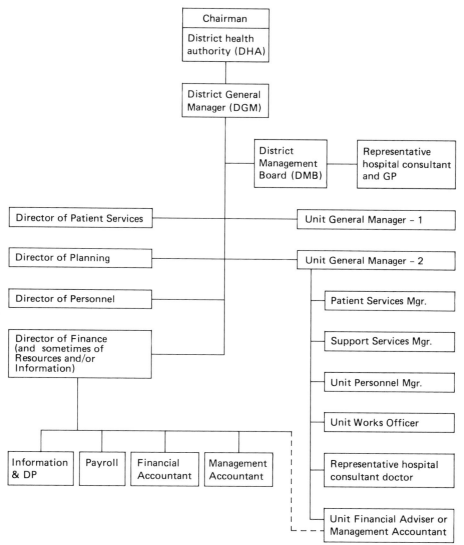

Fig. 8.2 Management structure of a district health authority in England.

the DGM organizes his internal management structure. Figure 8.2 illustrates just one of the possible variations of such structure. The DGM is supported by a district management board (DMB), which in the example includes one representative each of the district's hospital consultants (i.e. senior doctors), and of GPs practising within the district.

These medical professionals are not under the direct managerial control of the DGM. In contrast, the directors of particular managerial support services listed on the left-hand side of Fig. 8.2, and the unit general managers (UGMs) on the right-hand side of Fig. 8.2, are members of the DMB but also under the control of, or managerially accountable to, the DGM.

One exception to this, however, is that the Director of Finance, by whatever title he is called (and his title used to be 'Treasurer'), still retains separate, personal autonomy and accountability in respect of ensuring the financial probity and financial viability of the DHA's affairs. Normally he will be supported in this role by his DGM, but should the DGM be unhelpful or apparently complicit in any financial impropriety, including wilful overspending of total budgets, then it is the right and duty of the Director of Finance to go direct to the Chairperson of the DHA, or perhaps even to the RHA, to report his concern and request support.

Similarly, any accountant appointed as a Unit Financial Adviser, although ordinarily and managerially accountable to his UGM, should remain accountable to the District Director of Finance for his professional standards and performance, including the right and duty to report any financial malpractice, including wilful overspending, observed within the unit.

Financing and resource allocation

The scale of the NHS

The NHS rivals Education as the UK's most costly public service. It takes up nearly 15% of total public spending, or if we delete Social Security expenditure which is mainly 'transfer payments' for pensions and welfare income redistribution, then the cost of the NHS exceeds 20% of total public service expenditure. The cost of the NHS now approaches £22bn per annum, or over £500 per adult each year, increasing at an annual rate currently of about 6% compound (of which some 5% reflects inflation and 1% real growth). Deducting spending on health in Wales, Scotland and Northern Ireland, and deducting also the non-cash-limited spending on the family practitioner services, the residual, i.e the cash-limited, spending on the hospital and community services in England, amounts to some £12bn. Almost 75% of NHS spending is on pay, and the NHS nationally provides employment for about one million workers (including in this the staffs of Family Practitioner Services). Table 8.1 illustrates the scale of NHS hospital services, its increased workload, and its improved output 'per bed' (assisted by new drugs, new technology, and the more intensive use and productivity of staff time, especially by doctors and nurses).

Table 8.1 The scale of NHS hospital workload and acute hospital unit costs

Activity 1986/7 compared to 1981/2:

	Occupied beds	Inpatient cases (acute)	Inpatients treated per bed	Outpatient attendances	Day cases
1981/2	283,000	4,886,000	29.0	29,416,000	417,000
1986/87	252,000	5,603,000	36.2	37,241,000	895,000
% change over five years	−10.9%	+14.7%	+24.8	+26.6%	+114.6%

Resource use in large acute hospitals, averages for 1986/7:

Cost per in-patient-day	£107.32
Length of stay (LOS) in hospital (days)	7.2
Cost per in-patient-case	£767.53

Source: *Health Service Costing Return*, 1986/7.

Funding the NHS centrally

While the NHS locally may be able to obtain modest amounts of funds from donations, voluntary fund-raising and charges for private patients and for services to the private sector (e.g. diagnostic back-up services for private hospitals), in practice nearly the whole of NHS funds are provided by the government, following Cabinet agreement on total public spending and the relative resource needs of the numerous branches of the public sector. The decision on the total funding allocation to the NHS is independent of how much is raised in income from prescription charges and other fees, or from that small portion of National Insurance charges that is notionally designated as a National Health Insurance charge. Strictly, these apparently health-related sources of income have no more direct impact on determining total expenditure on the NHS than do vehicle and petrol taxes on the level of highway construction and maintenance. Currently about 4% of total NHS expenditure is met by income from health-service charges and some 12% is provided by notional health insurance levied with National Insurance contributions. The remaining 84% of expenditure is provided from the general pool of government taxation revenues.

It appears that the funding of the NHS has been the most successfully protected from economic crises, with continuous growth in real terms, even though at rates varying through time, of all the major public services (see Bevan *et al.*, 1980). Indeed this is only rational, since health care for the sick is perhaps the least postponable of services. And as the environment has improved (better education, water, sewerage, control of pollution, and improved housing and health care for at least the large majority of the population) people live longer. Thus the numbers of the elderly increase, and the increase of those over 75 years of age is especially prominent. But the longer people live, the more prone they are to diseases which are not immediately life-threatening but debilitating, crippling or otherwise destructive of the quality of life. About half the total resources of the NHS are expended on persons aged 65 or over, and it is estimated that the rising population of the elderly requires expansion of NHS resources by about 1% per year just to cope with this demographic change in the population.

But there are also other pressures for sharing in any growth moneys the NHS may secure. Technological progress in curative medicine is costly: new 'wonder drugs' are typically expensive, as are many of the newer surgical techniques, including not just the well-publicized heart and kidney transplants, but also the more numerous and much-needed interventions such as artificial joints for those crippled by arthritis but otherwise in good health and able to look after themselves.

Criteria for funding allocations to regions (RAWP)

Until the Crossman formula of 1970 and its first major reorganization in 1974, the NHS simply grew organically and incrementally. That is, generally speaking, it grew on an unplanned basis, roughly proportional in each locality to its pre-existing size, and with little coherent guidance for equalizing the scale and accessibility of health-care resources across the regions. Historically the poorer and industrial parts of the country had fewer beds, doctors and support resources, and this historical pattern was little altered in the first quarter-century of the NHS. But the matter caused increasing dissatisfaction, culminating in 'equal access to health care' as a main objective of the 1974 reorganization, and in the establishment of the Resource Allocation Working Party (RAWP). RAWP reported in 1976 and proposed that health-care funds should be allocated to the regions of England according to equitable criteria of need, as measured by objective formulae (and similar proposals were brought forward separately for Wales, Scotland and Northern Ireland). Accordingly, it became accepted that the practical policy was to progress to RAWP equalization of resources regionally by increasing the funding allocations of the best-provided regions only slowly, while using the bulk of the annual growth in funding to accelerate the expansion of health-care resources in the under-provided regions at a faster rate. At the time (in the mid-seventies) it was hoped that resource equalization might be achieved nationally by 1990 or even earlier. But as economic depression settled on Britain, and the annual rate of growth in real terms of NHS funding was cut back, the horizon date for expected equalization receded.

The RAWP formulae are based on population, adjusted for the age, sex and marital status of the resident population, for the standard mortality ratios (SMRs) locally as surrogate for the morbidity rate (i.e. measure of sickness and health need) for which no reliable information is currently available, and for the cross-boundary flows of inpatients. This RAWP approach recognizes that needs for health care are not a constant function of population, but are indeed affected strongly by social and economic factors. Analysis has shown (see Holland *et al.*, 1980) that the RAWP formula for revenue allocation is reasonably robust (i.e. little affected by possible errors in the parameters), and as a basis for resource allocation to regional health authorities the RAWP approach is now generally accepted as both equitable and efficient. RAWP and the link with planning are discussed in some detail in Bevan *et al.* (1980).

Revenue RAWP

RAWP revenue allocations are calculated from the previous year's approved expenditure, plus a percentage growth determined by **relative** under/over funding as against the RAWP targets. The allocations are then uplifted for the degree of 'pay and prices' inflation the government is prepared to fund in the NHS cash limits in the year ahead. Assuming actual pay and prices increase at the allowed rate, the allocations would result in an average increase of perhaps 1.5% in NHS purchasing power, after allowing for savings obtained from the required annual 'cost improvement programmes'. But as it is widely accepted that the NHS needs spending growth of about 1% per year simply to maintain existing standards of care for the rising population of the elderly, the supposedly 'real' increase in the cash-planning expenditure limit could become wholly absorbed in inflation above that allowed for. However, that is a statement relating to the national average, whereas the situation can have a very different impact between regions with differing rates of percentage growth. For example, the Thames regions (London and the Home Counties) do not receive a large enough allocation to cope even with a modest amount of excess inflation. Their financial reserves will be negligible, unless they actually initiate cuts in existing services for which the rising population of the elderly is inevitably causing a gradual but continuous rise in demand.

The Service Increment for Teaching

Within the regional revenue allocations is included, additional to the main block of funding determined by existing expenditure and progress to the RAWP target, a smaller amount of revenue identified as the Service Increment for Teaching (SIFT). The need for this arises because, for historical reasons, the distribution of medical schools and teaching hospitals in Britain is nowhere near proportional to the distribution of the weighted populations used in calculating RAWP targets. While in the longer term there may be some geographical redistribution of medical schools and teaching hospitals more evenly across the country, in the shorter term it would clearly be harmful to medical teaching, and to the care of patients in teaching hospitals, if some financial protection could not be given to regions carrying above-average financial burdens of teaching hospitals. These hospitals not only provide the clinical teaching of medical undergraduates, but also carry out research, innovational and developmental medicine, the training of other professions ancillary to medicine – and, in general, they provide high-quality, high-cost centres of advanced medicine.

The clearest explanation of the calculation of SIFT is contained in the *Report of the Advisory Group on Resource Allocation* (the AGRA Report, 1980). First is determined which hospitals have a significant teaching role in association with each medical school. Their actual costs for the base year are then ascertained. From these are deducted what those hospitals' costs notionally would have been had the hospitals been typical non-teaching district general hospitals (DGHs). The resultant differences, after further adjustments for the higher salaries and wages paid in London, where over 30% of medical education is concentrated, are termed the 'excess costs' of teaching hospitals. Then for the teaching hospitals associated with each medical school the 'excess cost per student' is determined by dividing by the number of clinical students expected to be in those hospitals at a date two years later.

Studies carried out by Professor Culyer and others for RAWP had concluded by regression analysis and supporting calculations that the proportion of the excess costs of teaching hospitals that might be explained by their teaching function, broadly defined, was of the order of 75%. The balance of excess costs was probably attributable mainly to a high-cost case mix arising from a concentration of regional and sub-regional specialties, such as would be properly fundable from within the normal RAWP revenue allocation as distinct from SIFT. On this background the DHSS held that the SIFT allocation should cover 75% of the median excess costs of teaching hospitals.

Capital RAWP

NHS capital allocations do not correlate well with the order of revenue allocations, revenue percentage growth or distance from RAWP revenue targets between regions. In the NHS, capital expenditure is defined to include spending on new buildings and reconstructions, on the original quota of plant, equipment and furnishings installed therein, and on the replacement of certain designated categories of equipment, e.g. computers and ambulances. Otherwise the ongoing replacement and upgrading of most furnishings, equipment, plant and fabric must be funded from revenue. The RAWP policy for capital allocation is to move towards equity of distribution of **capital stock**, on a basis of relative need related to forecasts of future population. Regions with growing population or population redeployments away from inner cities will need new hospitals in terms of locational need and of absolute level of demand. That aside, the quality (age, environment, condition, ease of access, etc.) of existing hospitals need not correlate closely with the scale of revenue-RAWP funding, and hence the overall lack of correlation between the levels of capital and revenue funding.

Alternative approaches to funding within regions

Regional health authorities have responsibilities for allocating financial resources within their regions. Their discretion is considerable: for example, they are not obliged to pass on to district health authorities containing teaching hospitals the exact amount of revenue allocation they themselves have received through the SIFT adjustment. Also, after deduction ('top slicing') for the funding of their own administration and for common services supplied to, or managed on behalf of, health districts (e.g. blood-donor services, computer and supplies-procurement services, and professional works services in support of major capital developments), they have discretion to allocate the remaining funds to district health authorities broadly on the same basis of gradually adjusting funding year by year towards resource equalization targets on the basis of the national RAWP formula (or some amended formula). Or there may be substantial additional top slicing to create earmarked reserves before the residual funds are distributed on a basis of movement towards RAWP targets.

It is widely agreed that it is not wise for RHAs to hold reserves in respect of inflation or other contingencies which might arise at the DHA level – this may leave district treasurers in uncertainty or tempt them to behave irresponsibly. But it is legitimate for RHAs to hold reserves to release as needed to DHAs as the latter bring on stream new developments as part of approved service programmes. This especially applies where new developments are linked to major capital schemes (controlled by region, with 'lumpy' expenditure, and with incremental recurrent-revenue implications for DHAs when new capital assets are actually commissioned), or where districts are developing a service (e.g. a subregional clinical specialty) where costs will be met from the funds of one district, but whose benefits may be shared with the populations of adjoining districts.

Supporters of minimizing top slicing and reserves managed at regional level and of maximizing the distribution of funds to DHAs in consistency with RAWP equalization believe their method to be better because it is consistent with policy to encourage devolution and decision-making at the local level, and because the consequential motivation combined with local knowledge could lead to better decisions and more effective implementation. This may be true, but there are questions of possible disadvantage which need to be considered. If districts obtain all revenue on a RAWP trend-line of revenue growth, how will they cope with meeting the incremental revenue needs of major new capital installations when commissioned? If they cope with this by marking time on recurrent-revenue expenditure before each new major capital (or other) development, will the resultant temporary surge of non-recurrent revenue be spent wisely, and with a better return of benefit than if it were being distributed from earmarked regional reserves only to meet the recurrent-revenue consequences of some other major development that thus might be funded to come into service sooner than otherwise?

Regional and subregional specialties

Those who are concerned about the risk of excessive replication of low-volume and/or high-cost specialties and facilities may tend to conclude that development-led revenue and capital funding, closely monitored from regions, is most likely to maximize health-service benefit to the public from the limited funds and resources available at any one point in time. There are a very few 'national' specialties with separately assessed allocations analogous to SIFT, but their cost is minute beside the total NHS budget. Also there are 'regional' specialties that may be located in only one or two hospitals within a region, e.g. for haemophilia or renal transplantation. And there are 'subregional', sometimes termed 'supra-district', specialties that may be designated at several locations within a region. But study of this problem is difficult, as the criteria for determining regional and subregional specialties are not fully consistent across regions, lower-level work in most specialties is anyway done in many district general hospitals and may develop to quite a sophisticated level without formal designation as a specialty centre, and the available methods for measuring the complexity/severity of cases treated in specialties, and for matching cost thereto, are still primitive and inadequate for rational comparison and the setting of definitive criteria. Quite aside from the cost-effectiveness of particular frequencies of replication of high-cost and/or low-volume specialties, there is a further, important problem. There is always a shortage of highly skilled staff (nursing and other support-staff, as well as medical). A high volume of complex work increases skill. Research in the USA suggests that the success rates for advanced medicine are far higher in high-volume centres than in hospitals with a low volume and frequently lower levels of skill available. All these aspects of the problem need further research in order to establish the optimal balance between quality of service, local access and cost efficiency.

Joint finance between health and local authorities

There is a need for a close relationship between health and local authorities, particularly in respect of services for the elderly, handicapped and mentally ill client groups. The 1974 reorganization set up a formal system of 'joint planning' and also brought in **joint financing** whereby a small element of health service funds was allocated to health authorities to be spent on local authority projects. In some areas joint finance has led to the stimulation of better joint planning and the introduction of innovative and imaginative projects. In other areas it has in effect served to offset the general lack of availability of funds for social services.

The whole issue of joint finance gained even greater significance with the publication of *Care in the Community* (1981). This envisaged the transfer of handicapped patients from hospitals to the community – which meant, by and large, out of the NHS and into the care of local authorities. The question of how resources were to be transferred then became of key significance and provided an interesting example of the problems of transferring cash resources between different parts of the public sector.

Accountability

Accountability for the use of resources, for the integrity and quality of service, and for constructive behaviour in community and environmental terms, has become an issue of ever-increasing importance in recent years. In the classic private-sector model, the main interest groups seeking accountability from enterprise management are identified often as comprising shareholders, major creditors, customers, employees, suppliers and the local community in which the enterprise conducts its operations.

In the case of the NHS, the government is the sole shareholder, there are no major creditors (because the government allows no borrowing, except indirectly through the extension of trade credit by suppliers), and the customers (i.e. patients) do not in the main pay for individual items of service (nor are they always in a fit state to be objective evaluators of the quality of service received). Moreover, many employees – and especially doctors – belong to professions which insist that professional standards and ethics must take first priority, at least within available resources, so that the conventional management relationships of commercial enterprises between employer and employee do not and cannot always apply in similar manner and degree in the NHS (or in universities, schools or social service departments, etc.) and without a product traded at market prices with competition between suppliers, it is difficult to evaluate efficiency – while problems in measuring the quality of health care benefit or outcomes make it difficult also to measure the effectiveness of the services provided. The various levels and forms of NHS account-ability, including accountability to Parliament in so far as this may differ from accountability to government are described briefly below.

Parliament

Parliament can draw accountability information from the same sources of reporting as government (see below) except that some forms of performance review and other accountability communications between the DOH and NHS management levels are either confidential or even unknown to Parliament and others. However, Parliament has a unique responsibility in receiving and reacting to the reports of the National Audit Office (NAO). This and other available information can provide the basis for searching enquiry by the House of Commons Social Services Committee, which recently has been very active not only in enquiring into the probity and efficiency of the use of public money in the NHS, but has also become outspoken in arguing the case for reform and improve-ments in the management, effectiveness and increased funding of the NHS. It is not clear, however, how far the views of the above Committee and of members of Parliament generally have any strong influence on the attitude of the government (with a large and secure majority) in its funding and organizational decisions affecting the NHS.

Government

Traditionally, the primary accountability concern of Government – and indeed of Parliament – has been to verify that total NHS expenditure is not exceeding the moneys voted by Parliament, and that such expendi-ture is used only for purposes and activities approved by Parliament and authorized by government. To this end there is monthly monitoring of the cash drawings of the NHS, with particular concern for the spending of the cash-limited hospital and community health services. Statutory annual financial and cost accounts (discussed in a later section), together with statistical reports on activity and patient workload, provide the basis for detailed *ex post* assessment of accountability for performance. There are also annual and sometimes more frequent performance reviews (see below), through which the discharge of accountability is monitored. Accountability is obtained additionally through the function of Audit (see Chapter 9).

Each health authority is audited annually. Most of these audits are conducted by the specialist audit staff of the Department of Health, although perhaps 10% of them are conducted by firms of chartered accountants with public sector experience. Every health authority has its own internal audit unit, or it shares this on a consortium basis with neighbouring authorities in order to make better use of specialist skills such as computer systems auditing. In some districts internal auditing has been contracted out to firms of chartered accountants. In general, internal audit and much of external audit in the NHS is expected to devote at least 40% of work time to 'value for money' issues. The NAO conducts a programme of theme audits within the NHS, with great concern for 'value for money' – or efficiency and effectiveness – as well as with concern for probity in public expenditure and for assessing the degree of achievement of policy objectives.

The various reporting and audits summarized in the two preceding paragraphs comprise largely a private, managerial and political frame-work of accountability – the exception being the NAO's published and widely publicized reports. But internal audit findings are often known only by the director of finance, the general manager and perhaps the chairman of the health authority, whilst the annual external audit reports may be seen only at RHAs and the DOH. Statutory financial and cost accounting reports do eventually become available to public access, but only a year or so in arrears and in a format not easily accessed or easily understood by laymen.

Community

There appear to be three main groups interested in NHS accountability (i.e. the disclosure of performance and intentions) at the local or community level. The first group comprises those who pay for the NHS: this includes nearly everyone, since even an unemployed person with no income tax or National Insurance to pay is nevertheless paying some-thing towards the NHS, given that VAT comprises part of the consoli-dated public revenue from which the NHS is funded. However, as there is no linkage at the local level between amount of taxes paid and amount of NHS funding and resources supplied locally, it is not surprising that most of the general public take little interest in the financial performance of their local DHA, but instead focus their attention on the national funding and performance of the NHS. This is in spite of the fact that the press have the right of attendance at the major part of health authority meetings, and that much of the local press attempts to give extensive and even critical coverage to local NHS problems.

The second group comprises patients. Those acutely sick are soon either dead, or else restored to the first group mentioned above. The long-term sick are mainly elderly, the handicapped and the mentally ill – in general they have little capacity to absorb or to take action upon NHS acountability information. The third group comprises local voluntary associations and other charities active in the health care field, together with concerned local government councillors and other local individuals committed as supporters and watchdogs of the NHS. This third group, together with the local press (and also employees – see below), make up the forum of watchful interest to which the DHA must account locally.

Health authorities discharge local accountability mainly through their main-agenda meetings being open to the press and public (although few members of the public attend). These main agendas include details of forward plans, capital programmes, current performance to budget, etc. However, they largely consist of many separate small items of resource use, examined individually and without it being easy to obtain an overview of the performance of the authority as a whole. To counter this problem, many authorities voluntarily publish local annual reports in a concise format and simplified style intended to be understandable by lay persons (and further detail on this is given in the next section below).

In addition, since 1974, there have been community health councils (CHCs) appointed with the responsibility of monitoring the plans and performance of their local health authority. DHAs typcially prepare annual reports for their CHCs, and consider the responses from the CHC in their own public meetings. A CHC representative normally attends every public meeting of the health authority. CHCs are often not sufficiently skilled or supported by any expert advice so as to be able to act as effective critics of the financial and managerial performance of DHAs, however. But CHCs do have some effective power in blocking or at least delaying hospital closures, and in some localities their vocal leadership and efficient use of the press has increased the pressure on health authorities for increased accountability, greater disclosure, and improved performance information available for public and press scrutiny.

Employees and suppliers

Leading firms in the private sector probably have a better record than most governmental and public service bodies in respect of communicating information on their performance and plans to their employees and key suppliers, if only out of self-interest to help improve motivation, commitment and cooperation – aspects of behaviour which have tended to be taken for granted in the public sector. Nor is it generally accepted any more widely in the public sector than in the private sector that employers are under any formal obligation to be 'accountable' to their employees, at least beyond specific items of information disclosure promised in formal agreements with unions.

In the private sector there are typically only two groups or cultures with whom to communicate – managers, and workers. In the public services there is often a more complex work environment. Within the NHS there are distinctly separate interest groups including doctors, nurses, managers, paramedical and other health professionals, and ancillary workers. These groups compete with each other over relativities in pay, status, influence, power and information provided. The traditional practice in the NHS appears to have been to deal with the information needs and pressures of each of these groups separately – largely privately and through their leaders. But it seems increasingly that top management aims to treat all employees as part of a common NHS team. Local annual management and financial reports are designed with staff interests in mind equally with the wider public interest, and a rising number of health authorities are providing regular newsletters for staff.

The NHS has no obligation of accountability to, nor any obvious track record of effective planning cooperation with, most of its major suppliers. The UK medical equipment industry has suffered from the stop-go purchasing programmes of the NHS. The UK drugs industry has a more stable market and demand from the NHS, however, and in recognition of this the former DHSS negotiated price limits on branded drugs, with prices being related to agreed profit margins.

Financial accounting and reporting

Financial accounting

The government's annual funding allocation to the hospital and community care services is cash-limited and divided among the 14 English RHAs on RAWP principles, as discussed earlier. RHAs then reallocate portions of their funding among their DHAs, again on RAWP principles although with regional variations and taking account of the timing of local strategic plans and new capital developments (e.g. the commissioning of a new district general hospital (DGH)). Thus each DHA gets to know its cash allocation shortly before the start of the next financial year. This cash allocation relates to cash drawn from government. However, since health authorities are required to keep minimum working cash balances in their bank accounts, in practice the cash limit defines cash expenditure almost equally with cash receipts.

It follows that the first priority in NHS financial accounting needs to be accurate cash (or, cash flow) accounting. Pay is typically about 73% of total cash flow, and it is a reasonably stable and predictable cost, once all annual pay negotiations have been completed. So perhaps the critical aspect for NHS cash accounting is control over cash payments to suppliers of goods and services. Preferably this should involve tight financial control over purchasing or supplies ordering, including the use of commitment accounting linked to budgets. But in practice it appears that purchasing expenditure controls are much more informal, with many health authorities relying on end-of-year speeding up – or in recent times more usually slowing down – the payment of creditors as the means of bringing cash expenditure more or less into line with allowable cash drawings.

Even though cash accounting is needed in order to monitor performance against cash-limit funding controls, NHS accountants have preferred for years to prepare their main accounts and reports on an 'income and expenditure' basis. Income and expenditure accounting is an approach to full accruals accounting in which either on a continuing basis or by end-of-year adjustments the account balances reflect changes in stocks, debtors and creditors. The major accruals item not included in NHS accounts is the annual cost of the consumption of capital stock, i.e. depreciation. This is because the NHS, like most other central-government funded and controlled services, is not allowed to practise capital-asset and depreciation accounting. However, this could change, as discussed in the later section on NHS capital.

The practical advantage of accrual or income-and-expenditure accounting over cash accounting is that it measures the real use or consumption of resources more accurately. This is necessary to match the financial accounts realistically with the internal management accounts and budgets. For an example, take X-ray film. The charges to the budget of the radiology department (i.e. X-ray) for film must clearly be the cost of film used, rather than the cash payments for film purchased. The latter payments will have been influenced by purchasing and bulk-buying considerations, and by the finance office's view on how much time to take between invoice date and payment date, having regard to the authority's financial position relative to its cash limit as the end-of-year cash settlements approach.

In the early years of the NHS both the financial accounting and the cost accounting of the services were based on 'subjective accounting'. This is accounting for the subject, type or category of resource input. Thus, all pay was in one category, all drugs in another, all stationery in a third category, etc., regardless of the use to which the expenditure was put, or of who caused the expenditure to happen. The cost accounting used at that time was not part of a proper management accounting and control system, but rather was analogous to the simple, mechanistic cost allocation system often used in factories largely to provide stock and cost-of-goods-sold valuations for integration in the financial accounts.

However, following the 1974 NHS reorganization, with its emphasis upon managerial authority and accountability based upon the local head of the function (i.e. profession) concerned with particular staff and services, NHS financial accounting (and costing and budgeting) became more disaggregated and more closely related to the actual management process. At about the same time came increased use of computers for payroll and general ledger, although these were located at RHAs with DHAs often in some difficulty over obtaining information outputs promptly in a form useful for management as distinct from discharging routine financial accountability and reporting requirements. This newer system, known as functional accounting and budgeting, continues in use with gradual improvement in detail and analysis, notably through the recent implementation of the Körner Reports on Health Services information for management control and reporting.

Statutory reporting

Individual health authorities are not required by statute or regulation to publish annual accounts in the manner that is expected of local authorities, water authorities or public corporations. However, district health authorities are required to submit a range of reports to the RHAs and the DOH. These include health activity analysis statistics on patients treated and workload, annual census returns on all manpower employed in the NHS at a particular date in the year, data for the financial information system operated by the Treasury to monitor public spending (termed FIS (HA) in its NHS format – see CIPFA (1980) for details), and statutory returns of both financial accounting and cost accounting data. The latter are not in the form of conventional accounts, but instead comprise detailed and lengthy schedules reporting expenditure by functional category and by detailed subjective analysis of all expenditure in the case of the financial accounts, and by institution and functional category in the case of the cost accounts. In both instances the accounting data are supplied on an income and expenditure basis, rather than on the cash receipts and payments basis involved in the monitoring and control of expenditure to cash limits. Additionally a statement reconciling income and expenditure with the cash allocations provided is supplied. Since 1988 the reporting of specialty costs (see below) has been required additionally (see NHS/DHSS, 1984).

Voluntary local reporting

At the local level the progress of expenditure against budget is reported to the monthly health authority meetings, at least in most authorities. These meetings are open to the public and are attended by the press, and certainly if there is any serious overspending or other identified problem of major import, one would expect this to be widely reported and critically assessed, locally at least and very probably nationally as well if there are any major issues of probity or of policy affecting patient care. But some health service treasurers have not been content to rely solely on this form of public reporting and accountability. They have gone further and voluntarily produced annual financial accounts and costing reports, supported by statistical and other information often including illustra-

The diagram below shows the sources of finance available to the Authority during 1983–84 and the way in which this finance was used.

There are four main sources of funds:

(a) Central funding – cash drawings approved by the DHSS and payments made centrally (e.g. income tax and national insurance contributions).
(b) Income – the amount the Authority raises itself through the provision of facilities for private treatment, supply of drugs at hospitals and prescription charges raised by the FPS.
(c) Balances – the change in the Authority's net current assets and liabilities during the year.
(d) Payments by other authorities – the supply of goods and services by other authorities.

The balances held at the end of the year were as follows:

1982–83	Current Assets/Liabilities	1983–84	Change
£000s		£000s	£000s
1,859	Stocks	1,922	+63
245	Debtors	1,110	+865
1,069	Cash	27	−1,042
3,850	Creditors	3,817	+33
	NET MOVEMENT IN BALANCES		−81

Thus £81,000 of the Authority's balances was used during the year to finance expenditure.

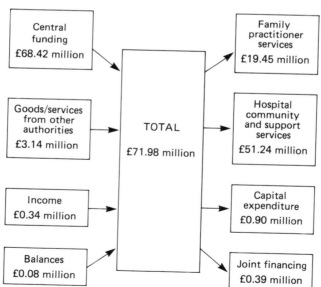

Fig. 8.4 Summary of net revenue expenditure 1983–84. Reproduced from Coventry Health Authority *Financial Report and Accounts 1983–84*, p. 32.

Coventry Health Authority spent £50,966,000 during 1983–84 (excluding Joint Finance and the Family Practitioner service).

What did this money provide?

	£000s	%
Hospital services:		
Direct care of patients	22,848	45
Running the hospitals	14,383	28
Drugs and therapy	3,562	7
X-rays and tests	3,419	7
	44,212	87
Community health service	5,092	10
District administration and other	1,662	3
	50,966	100

How was this money spent?

	£000s	%
Employees:		
Medical and Dental	6,218	12
Nurses	17,432	34
Ancillary	5,458	11
Professional & Technical	4,020	8
Admin. & Clerical	3,912	8
Others	1,528	3
	38,568	76
Drugs and Equipment	5,473	11
Other	6,925	13
	50,966	100

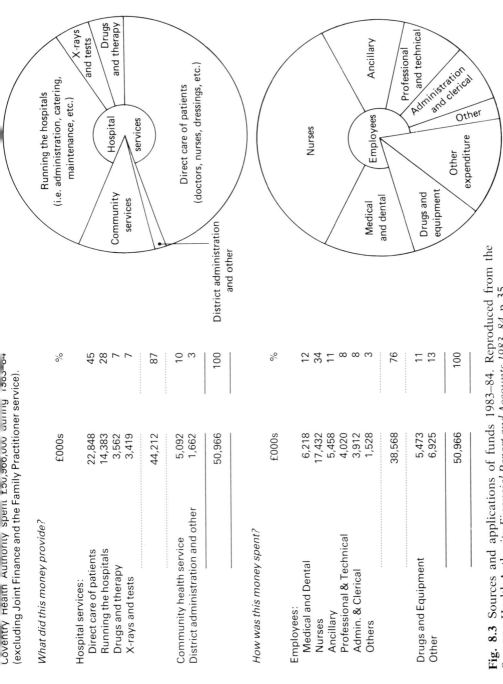

Fig. 8.3 Sources and applications of funds 1983–84. Reproduced from the Coventry Health Authority *Financial Report and Accounts 1983–84*, p. 35.

tive charts and graphs. Extracts from the annual report for 1983–84 of the Coventry Health Authority are reproduced in Figs. 8.3 and 8.4.

Accounting standards and NHS reporting

All professional accountants have a natural interest in how far the Statements of Standard Accounting Practice (SSAPs) adopted by the accountancy profession are relevant to financial disclosure in their own industry or sector. Clearly there is some instinctive feeling that all organizations ought to be able to conform to a common set of accounting measurement and reporting standards, and yet it is clear that many organizational and operational characteristics are very different between trading (and especially profit-seeking) organizations and those organizations whose whole *raison d'être* is the provision of public services, as in the NHS where an unspent surplus at the end of the year would be interpreted as failure to provide maximum service, rather than as evidence of economic efficiency. This problem was examined, as it affects the NHS, by the Association of Health Service Treasurers (Final Report, 1982). Their conclusions were as follows: SSAP 2 (Accounting Policies) 'is of fundamental importance'; certain other standards 'may be relevant' (i.e. SSAP 5 (VAT), SSAP 9 (Stocks and Work in Progress), SSAP 10 (Source and Application of Funds), and SSAP 18 (Accounting for Contingencies)); and other standards 'may have limited application' (i.e. SSAP 6 (Extra-ordinary and Prior-Year Adjustments), SSAP 13 (R&D), and SSAP 17 (Post Balance-Sheet Events)). The remaining SSAPs were considered to be 'not applicable' to the NHS, at least in present circumstances (e.g. where capital assets are neither capitalized nor depreciated). The foregoing is not of great importance to the extent that the existing forms of statutory reporting take no account of standard accounting practices. But this could change within a few years, and anyway, to the extent that DHAs seek to prepare voluntary local reports for the information of Authority members and the local community, treasurers will probably increasingly seek to conform to the standards generally accepted by their peers employed in other industries and other branches of the public services.

Capital

The NHS obtains its capital as a 'free good' from RAWP capital funding. That is, the NHS does not have to pay any interest on its capital funds, let alone repay the principal. This lack of financial discipline on capital arguably makes the NHS lax in extracting the best value for money from capital funding, especially in past years when governments seemed keen to encourage extra capital spending as a means of stimulating the construction industry and economic demand in the economy more generally. This is not to deny that the NHS's hospital stock has not been in need of renewal, much of it being of Victorian origin. Rather, the problem in which the DHSS centrally must take its share of the blame has been that rigorous review of the cost-effectiveness of designs, and the cost of quality of construction, was not maintained. Leslie Chapman made much of this in his book (1979), even if he may have overstated the scale of financial waste. In recent years the DHSS pressed health authorities to be more economical in the use of capital, and guidelines on evaluating capital options have been issued. Economists such as Drummond (1980) also have advised the NHS on better methods of capital appraisal.

During recent years of reduced growth in the (real-terms) funding of the NHS there has been rising interest in (a) releasing any financial resources unproductively tied up in fixed assets surplus to operational needs, (b) measuring the costs of capital consumption and relating these to the accountability of districts, units and even individual budget holders, and (c) introducing greater flexibility and rational choice into decisions at the margin on the spending of capital versus revenue funds.

In 1982 an Enquiry was established to review NHS arrangements for identifying underused and surplus property, and to make recommendations for improvements. This resulted in the Ceri Davies Report (1983). The report concluded that there was significant surplus land and underutilized space within buildings in the NHS, and that motivation needed to be provided for districts to dispose of this. Districts should normally retain the proceeds of sale as encouragement.

Accounting for the use of capital

Turning to the costs of capital consumption and accountability for these, the definitive debate has been published in the Association of Health Service Treasurers' (AHST's) Report from its Capital and Asset Accounting Working Party (1984). Part of this Report dealt with problems of optimizing the use of capital funding in the NHS as summarized below. The other part of the Report was concerned with the risk that wrong judgements on efficiency and on accountability might be taken in the NHS if the costs of capital consumption (i.e. the wearing out of capital resources (see Perrin (1984)) were not included in accounting information and performance indicators. After discussing the principles involved, and noting also the work which would be involved in establishing accurate 'registers' of fixed assets, the AHST Report made a number of recommendations. Full asset registers should be established to contain at least a minimum standard set of data on each asset.

Annual NHS revenue accounts should include a charge for use of capital, and the disaggregation of this should be shown in the budgets and reports supplied to budget holders within the NHS. This would involve the preparation of proper balance sheets, and implicitly it would also involve the adoption of full accrual accounting augmenting the current income and expenditure accounting system. Pilot trials should be carried out in individual health districts to compare the options of (a) 'asset depreciation charges as used by the private sector', (b) 'a system where RHAs would lease all major items of equipment, land and buildings to DHAs', or (c) 'a leasing system for land and buildings, and depreciation charges for equipment'. In this context 'leasing' implies the determination of a reasonable yet market-sensitive annual charge for the use of particular assets during the year in question. It should be remembered that lease charges comprise (in one total figure), (a) recovery of the original (historical) capital outlay over the life of the asset, (b) interest at market rates (including the effects of expected inflation) on the unrecovered portions of the capital outlay, and (c) some profit margin and premium or discount depending upon market conditions. Following successful trials, new standard capital asset accounting methods might be adopted in all health districts.

The Report from the AHST (1984), in search of greater flexibility and rational – or optimal – choice in the use of resources, suggested that in future RHAs should receive a single funding allocation from the DHSS, determined after taking account of both the RAWP revenue and capital allocation formulae. It could then be practicable for Regions more flexibly to take account of the existing levels of capital provision and consumption, as indicated by lease and/or depreciation cost calculations, so as to introduce a stronger discipline into the use of capital by health districts. For example, the use of greater amounts of capital would be reflected in increased capital use charges, which would result in reduced revenue funding – thus concentrating the minds of NHS decision-makers on obtaining the most service-effective balance of use of available funding between capital and revenue applications.

Capital appraisal

Capital appraisal, or investment appraisal, is assigned the title of 'option appraisal' in the NHS. Mainstream capital appraisal derives from for-profit, trading investment situations where estimated future cash flows are discounted to test for positive 'net present values' (and possibly with probability assessments of risk and uncertainty included). But, new 'income generation' projects aside (discussed further later), the NHS does not trade for a profit. Most of its investments generate service and a continuing demand for revenue funds to support this, rather than net cash flow. However, some of its investments are 'cost saving', as in the case of energy conservation outlays for insulation, improved boilers, change of boiler fuels, etc. In such cases the expected financial savings, if realistically estimated, can be used as the net cash flows for discounting as in the conventional business finance model.

However, the major capital expenditure of the NHS is for the construction and modernization of hospitals, clinics and community care facilities. Modern premises may be more energy efficient, or easier to clean or maintain than old buildings, but typically they are larger or at least have additional and costly equipment in order to meet the standards of modern medicine. Therefore they do not generally result in any operational net-cash-flow savings. Of course, alternative building designs can be compared for their relative cash flow demands in use, but this will not lead to a meaningful net present value giving guidance to an optimal decision. Where appraisal by discounting is feasible, the test discount rate used in the NHS is typically 5% applied to future cash flows estimated in constant prices on a similar basis to that generally recommended by government throughout the non-trading public sector.

Where the decision criteria are not narrowly financial, as in the choice between types of fuels and boilers, then recommended practice in option appraisal calls for the use of economic cost-effectiveness studies of the options, i.e. the alternative choices available for the use of capital and other resources. Subjective costs and benefits difficult to value in monetary terms should also be sought out and assessed. To take a simplistic example, the choice in locating a hospital on a site overlooking a park versus overlooking a steelworks should not be made solely on the grounds of the comparative cost of land and of the site works for foundations. Indeed many factors need to be taken into account, including road and public transport access and the suitability of a location to attract the size of labour force required. In effect, option appraisal at its best becomes a form of quite complex cost-benefit analysis.

Trading and rationalization

Traditional sharp demarcations between the public and private sectors, and between service versus trading activities, are becoming increasingly blurred. Government has exerted increasing pressure on the NHS to earn part of its money through trading activities, which we consider below under the subheading of 'income generation'. There was earlier pressure on the NHS to consider if some of its activities were inefficient and could be obtained more cheaply from the private sector through privatization or contracting out. This second aspect will be discussed under 'rationalization'.

Income generation

Family practitioner services for many years have been required to make charges for prescriptions, spectacles, dentistry, etc. (except that children, the elderly and some welfare groups are exempt), partly to raise funds and partly to discourage excessive demands on services. But in the hospital services very little income has been raised directly by charges for services or through commercial activities. Small amounts have been raised through charges to some motoring accident patients and to patients not resident in the UK. Small sums are raised from charges for 'amenity' beds in private rooms, and often larger sums from treating 'private' patients in NHS premises. Recently, however, health authorities have come under pressure to generate increased cash income by a variety of initiatives. These include letting space on hospital premises for shops such as chemists, sports equipment, keep-fit gymnasia and other enterprises, or even joint development with the private sector of these and other relevant initiatives. At the seemingly more trivial level, this initiative extends even to seeking advertising sponsorship for hospital literature from likely sources such as taxi firms, nursing homes and funeral directors.

   Hospitals in prosperous parts of the country where there is extensive demand for private health care – which is normally personally supervised by the NHS's own consultant doctors who have chosen part-time contracts with the NHS – are increasingly seeking to expand their volume of private treatment, including investment to upgrade facilities or even build new wings or units for the higher amenity standards expected in private health care. Health authorities have been given some flexibility in pricing their services to private patients, and of course the main objective is to earn a profit for cross-subsidy to NHS services. These and other initiatives requiring capital investment interrelate with plans to release capital through the disposal of surplus land and buildings. And all this involves the development in the NHS of new skills in financial planning, contract negotiation, etc. For setting profitable prices and rents a more accurate analysis and understanding of NHS costs is needed, including a clearer understanding of the concepts of opportunity cost, marginal cost and contribution analysis.

   Health authorities historically were conceived to provide comprehensive and largely self-sufficient services for their local populations, although there have always been substantial cross-boundary flows of patients because of convenience, the preferences of patients and their family doctors (GPs), and the need to obtain specialist skills not available locally. These cross-boundary flows have been financed by adjustments to DHA revenue and RAWP funding targets, two years in arrears. This delayed recognition of service to non-residents provides very weak motivation to DHAs to seek out any spare capacity and market this to GPs and other health districts which may have waiting lists and resource bottlenecks in the same areas of service. In other words, the total health care output of the NHS may be suboptimized because of lack of financial incentives for the detection and selling of spare capacity.

Growing awareness of the above problems has led to widening debate under the label of the 'internal market'. How far should DHAs go in marketing or selling services to other DHAs (and such services can include everything from laundry to diagnostic laboratory services in addition to the direct care of patients), bearing in mind that contract deals with other health authorities may absorb capacity to the point where the needs – or certainly preferences – of local patients and GPs may not always be capable of being met promptly? Radicals have widened the debate yet further by suggesting that trading should extend beyond the internal market of the NHS to include private hospitals and private support services (e.g. laboratories). This wider approach has come to be labelled the 'provider market'.

By analogy with the private sector, the NHS may be considered as a gigantic holding company with hundreds of operating subsidiaries. Internal trading is important within such an enterprise, but the best use of resources has to be balanced with the opportunities in the external market. There are marketing and other management dimensions to solving this problem, but from a financial point of view it becomes a problem in 'transfer pricing', the art of setting internal prices at a level to motivate managers to maximize profits or, in the context of the NHS, to maximize the output of health care from the available (financial) resources. There is not space here for a detailed debate, but readers may wish to refer to the classic work of Solomons (1965) or to Emmanuel and Otley (1985). At the risk of over-simplification, the essence is that internal market prices should be set in the short run at marginal (variable) cost, plus whatever contribution margin optimizes the motivation of both the 'buyer' and the 'seller' in maximizing the use of spare resources. The long-run situation is more complex, because of eventual need for further capital investment (not yet rationally managed and accounted for in the NHS), and if NHS services are to be marketed additionally to the private sector, then clearly pricing decisions on this must be taken on a fully commercial basis.

Rationalization

The government some years ago began its programme of 'privatization'. The assumption behind this appears to be that private sector, for-profit ownership and management will utilize resources more efficiently and productively than the public sector can achieve. This may well be correct where there is a definable product, clear consumer information and choice, and a genuine free market. In the case of health care, however, these essential conditions do not hold true, and patients in need are in a poor bargaining position with health-care providers. Moreover, some three-quarters of all health care expenditure is on behalf of the elderly, children and the handicapped. The British system of funding health care primarily by central government allocations from general taxation to the NHS has resulted in almost the lowest cost health services in the industrialized world, at under 6% of GDP compared to figures of 7 to 9% typically, and up to 11% (in the USA), in comparable industrialized countries. However, although UK health status indicators compare reasonably equally with those of most of the countries spending more on health care, it is true that we have waiting lists for non-urgent medical treatments, and a need for higher standards in community care, preventive medicine and health screening. At the time of writing this book, a Prime Ministerial Review of the NHS is examining possibilities for funding reform – and certainly managerial reform – of the NHS. It seems unlikely that the Review will recommend that the NHS as a whole should be privatized, but there could well be proposals that some support services and fringe activities be privatized, and that greater progress should be made into the use of internal markets and provider markets.

Privatization normally involves selling an organization as a going concern, including fixed assets, a marketable product or service, and a clear profit potential. Defined thus, privatization has not been applied to the NHS or its support services – as yet at least. However, some support services, notably such as laundry, cleaning and catering, do not involve major skills specific to the NHS (although there is concern for the hygiene aspects of hospital laundry and linen, the role of cleaners as unofficial assistants to nurses, and the dietetic aspect of hospital catering). These services are in the main provided physically on NHS premises and so it is difficult to privatize them literally. However, it is possible to 'contract-out' the 'labour and materials' components of these services, with the contractors using NHS premises and equipment, sometimes augmented by additional equipment or new technology. DHAs have been required to put out to tender their laundry, cleaning and support services, and most have already done so. Existing staff in these services have been allowed to compete in the tendering process, and by sometimes substantial cuts in the numbers employed, they have often succeeded in winning the contracts. There have been many complaints of reduced standards, especially in cleaning, but the evidence suggests that major savings have been achieved, probably greater than £100 million. The question now is whether or not the concept of contracting out by tender should be extended to other activities more specific to health care, for example ambulance services or pathology laboratory services.

When services are contracted out by tender, it is not a simple matter of a health authority member opening envelopes and automatically accepting the lowest bid. Detailed specification of the facilities available, the work to be done and the quality standards expected all have to be carried out before the tendering process begins. The cost of the existing in-house service needs more comprehensive costing than is normally available from functional costing and budgeting as a framework of reference to assess bids, and the creditworthiness and likely survivability of bidders has to be evaluated. There is always the risk of a bidder putting in a low tender just to get 'a foot in the door' but then arguing all sorts of reasons, such as imprecise work specification, why contract remuneration needs to be increased. To cope with all this, similarly as for internal markets and income generation initiatives, NHS accountants need to learn additional skills which effectively involve them in a range of expertise comparable to private trading enterprises.

Budgeting and financial control

Planning for new developments and services and for the improvement or rationalization of existing services and facilities is a continuous, ongoing function at every level of the NHS, from the national Management Board down to local unit management. This applies to the use of both capital funding and revenue funding. It requires an iterative dialogue between the levels of the NHS, in which each lower organizational level is constantly trying to persuade the level above it that it has needs and plans for coping with those needs which should justify increased funding, or funding at an earlier date than might occur without firm proposals and argument.

    While most RHA allocations to DHAs are related to the RAWP and SIFT formulae for funding mentioned earlier, it appears that 'at the margin' evidence of sound planning and good management can earn greater or earlier funding for DHAs. Within each DHA the allocation of available funding among the management units is not governed by formula but instead is very much a process of budget negotiation – that is, a process of bargaining, argument, competition and seeking support for plans and needs from the officers and members of the DHA. Indeed this is what budgeting is all about – a two-way process of bargaining for resources in return for agreed targets in service delivery (outputs), quality standards (outcomes) or efficiency or economy in the use of resources.

Budgeting in the NHS

Previously we have considered how the share of total public sector resources allocated to the NHS by government is successively subdivided by RAWP formulae or other criteria, first to regions, and then again to districts. Aside from regional earmarking for medical education (SIFT), regional specialties and services, and the regional programme for major capital projects, the balance of the allocation to each district health authority has always been in two lump sums, one for revenue and the other for capital. The revenue allocations give no instruction on how expenditure should be broken down between the various categories of cost – for labour, supplies and services, equipment etc. This process is for local determination, through the annual budgetary cycle in each authority. Budgets for minor capital are tied closely to particular approved projects, coordinated at district level, and these are not controlled financially in the NHS in any way especially distinct from other organizations. But the budgeting of revenue funds is distinctive, and so the paragraphs below relate only to revenue unless otherwise stated.

Functional budgeting

The normal form of budgeting and budgetary control in the NHS is based on what is termed 'functional budgeting'. The term derives from the 'functional' form of organization adopted by the NHS at the time of the 1974 reorganization, which laid great stress on the organization and management of the service by functions, i.e. disciplines of professional specialization. Prior to 1974, budgets and accounts had been mainly on a subjective basis for an entire hospital or other organizational unit. After 1974 the subjective data had to be recast across a matrix to relate to the authority and accountability of individual senior managers of functions for the resources they authorized to be used across the whole of each health district, e.g. the salaries, training costs and certain other expenses of nurses in a district for the accountability of the district nursing officer. Each senior functional officer could in turn delegate specified parts of his or her overall budget to particular managers within the function, while of course still retaining overall responsibility for the budgetary performance of that function as a whole. The strengths and weaknesses of the functional budgeting system were explored in some depth in Research Paper No. 2 for the Royal Commission on the NHS (1978): that research examined the position in 1977–78 and since then there have been improvements in the use of functional budgets and in their integration with operational planning.

Unit and general management budgeting

The 1982 reorganization of the NHS abolished area health authorities, raised district health authorities in status, and required that within DHAs there should be designated 'units' of management in order to bring management authority and accountability to a lower organizational level nearer to where operational work is carried out. Typically the new units were based on major acute hospitals (DGHs), on groups of smaller local or long-stay hospitals, on mental handicap or mental illness services, and on other community health care services. The existing functional budgets then had to be subdivided and reallocated between the new units within each district. This appeared to create some degree of potential conflict between functional officers at district level and functional officers in the units with regards to the determination and control of budgets for particular resources (e.g. the appointment and location of nursing staff).

Then came the Griffiths Inquiry Report (1983), whose major recommendation was that the functional/professional consensus/team management approach in the NHS was inefficient and should be replaced by chief executives (to be known as 'general managers') at every level, from the national Management Board through RHAs and DHAs down to the new units of management. At the local level this altered the main debate concerning budgetary allocations and control from a 'horizontal' dialogue between district and unit heads of individual functions (i.e. professions or services), to a 'vertical' dialogue between the new general managers in the districts and their units. Of course the new general managers received advice from their respective functional department heads, but the nature of the budget bargaining process was changed to a more 'businesslike' arrangement in which overall workload targets and performance were central.

Prior to 1974 the standard system of budgeting was based on a 'line item' or 'subjective' classification of the types of goods and services (including staff pay) acquired for an entire district or other major organizational component. The 1982 reorganization retained the above budgetary system, simply subdividing the subjective budgets among smaller organizational units. Even the post-1983 appointments of general managers did not alter the budgets, even if it did often alter role relationships and the channels of communication and decision over the setting of budgets and review of budgetary performance. Thus in 1988/9 the standard budget system in the NHS continued to be on a line item/subjective basis, although subdivided by units and increasingly controlled on an integrated basis by unit general management. Here 'integrated basis' means that, through the coordination provided by the general manager, a conscious attempt is made to optimize the size of the various budget headings to match the real (i.e. physical) resource needs of the separate budget headings and functional management departments in order to deliver a balanced programme of care to meet agreed health service objectives for each unit. (Note: readers may refer to Chapter 3 for more detailed definitions of budgetary terminology used in this chapter.)

Budgets as determined above are essentially 'input budgets', as they are primarily linked to claims of need for resources and are not directly linked to targeted or achieved workload outputs or quality of outcomes (i.e. effectiveness). This approach to budgeting in the NHS (and other public services) has given concern to many accountants, economists and other critical commentators.

Specialty costing

The service outputs of the NHS (and especially of NHS acute hospitals) can be studied and costed at different levels of disaggregation. At the broadest level we can cost and budget for the work and output of individual specialties (such as general surgery or obstetrics). Some specialties are subdivided between 'firms' (i.e. teams) of consultant doctors working together. Or cost analysis can be taken down to the level of the individual consultant doctor, the ultimate decision-maker determining who is admitted for treatment, the mode of treatment, and how available resources shall be used or consumed in providing treatment. But of course specialties, firms and individual consultants are only front-line providers or channels of outputs. The actual outputs are the patients treated and discharged. But the cost and budget consequences of the work of individual consultants, firms or specialties can be taken as relevant surrogates for the treatment of reasonably similar groupings or aggregates of service outputs.

The (Körner) Steering Group on Health Services Information was established about 1980 under joint DHSS and NHS sponsorship to make recommendations on how to improve information for management control in the NHS. This covered information on activity and workload, manpower and its utilization, and finance. In the Sixth Report (1984), the Körner Steering Group recommended that the NHS should adopt 'specialty costing' as part of its financial management information system, both for local management and planning use, and for reporting and performance review at RHA and national levels.

Accurate specialty costing requires the tracing of all direct costs incurred by the consultant members of a specialty, as well as all indirect costs incurred by or attributable to the specialty and the patients it has treated. While direct costs can be traced and validated fairly easily, many indirect costs (e.g. the expense of X-rays, laboratory tests, therapy staff assistance and even the appropriate proportion of nursing pay costs) are much harder to trace, record and validate or audit with a high degree of accuracy.

In the beginning there was the Magee system of specialty costing, intended mainly for broad-brush performance assessment and for use in service planning. The Magee system was inexpensive because it used cost estimation in place of continuous cost recording, and because it relied on the sampling of workload and activity where continuing and accurate record keeping did not exist. For example, an accurate sample of the volume and type of X-rays used might be taken for a single week, and the resulting proportions of use between different specialities would then be generalized as typical over a period of several weeks or months, and would be used as the basis for (a crude) apportionment of X-ray costs between the specialties over that extended period.

Such methodology could lead to errors of perhaps up to 10% or more in calculating the true total costs of individual specialties. This margin of error is probably acceptable in review and forward planning studies for which the Magee system was originally designed, but it is certainly not acceptable as the basis for a budgeting system where budget holders would be expected to be held to account for even quite small excess spending. Unless accountants can guarantee (and prove) something approaching 100% (or at least 98 or 99%) accuracy in the costs charged against budget holders, it becomes difficult to ensure that budget reports are taken seriously and that budgetary discipline is effective. These problems are discussed in much greater detail in *Resource Management in the NHS* (Perrin, 1988).

Clinicians in planning and budgeting

A distinctive feature of financial control in the NHS is the limited role played by its 'production managers'. These are the clinical consultants, and although a few of them double as department managers (e.g. for diagnostic and medical services), the majority of them who treat patients directly and who determine the workload or throughput of the hospitals, do not yet hold budgets for the expenditure they cause. This situation has arisen from the historical background of the development of the role and status of consultants, relative to the hospital management structure. It is defended on the doctrine of clinical autonomy whereby the consultant is personally responsible for the care of all of his patients, so that he argues that he must have the right to call out whatever **available** treatment (i.e. resources) he feels needful for those patients. This doctrine is not in dispute at the level of care for the **individual** patient, but as the growth of the NHS has slowed down and additionally has become constrained at the margin on a cash-limit basis of firm control against any expenditure beyond original authorizations, a growing number of clinicians have come to realize that in order to obtain the best outcome for all patients it is indeed necessary to pay heed to the costs of resources, the comparative costs and benefits of alternative modes of patient management, and the trade-offs of benefit at the margin from using scarce resources in different combinations.

Probably the most interesting initiative to involve clinicians has been the set of projects initiated by CASPE (Clinical Accountability, Service Planning and Evaluation) (see Wickings, 1983). With varying detail, these projects are testing ways in which to involve clinicians – and sometimes nurses and other resource-providers as well – in consultation on choices for the best uses of scarce resources which can be varied in amount by careful planning, but are restricted in their total cost by the cash-limit system. This will often involve making clinicians budget holders, although this is not an essential requirement, and a variety of responsibility-sharing arrangements is possible. Where clinicians do become budget holders, it is essential to segregate the variable costs of services which they can control from the fixed and indirect costs that remain under the decision-making and control of function (and unit) budget holders.

Clinical management budgets

In February 1983 the Secretary of State for Social Services commissioned an NHS Management Inquiry under the chairmanship of Mr Roy Griffiths. The Inquiry reported in October of that year (the Griffiths Report, 1983). The Report dealt particularly with the need for the NHS to develop the 'general management' style and structure of management (i.e. the designation of 'general managers' at every level who would integrate across functions and expedite decision-making when the traditional search for consensus or unanimity might otherwise delay action).

But also there were two main recommendations in the Report which were specifically financial. One was that all health authorities should be required to develop formal 'cost improvement' programmes and that progress on these should be monitored through the annual performance review process. The second was that NHS clinicians, as the natural managers of health care delivery, should be made financially accountable for the resources consumed in treating their patients. This should extend to clinical budgets which include not just the costs clinicians personally control, but also the indirect costs they can strongly influence (e.g. the volume of testing activity in laboratories) and even their proportion of the overheads of the health district.

Progress in introducing clinical budgeting was slow, however, as was implicit in the DHSS's circular HN(85)3, released early in 1985. By 1986 the priority and emphasis for the development of new NHS financial information evolved into the wider 'resource management' approach (see below). Nevertheless, many health authorities are still working on the data collection systems and methods of cost analysis and allocation necessary for effective clinical budgeting.

An example of the kind of monthly budgetary-control report which can be used in clinical management budgeting is reproduced as Table 8.2. Current-month and cumulative year-to-date expenditure is shown, together with budgeted amounts and variances. The report, which is simulated and does not itemize as many categories of cost as may in practice come to be used regularly in clinical budgets, begins with two sections detailing costs directly controlled by the head of the surgical team. The next section lists budgetary costs influenced by the team (i.e. costs of resources administered by nurses and other department heads, but which are dependent on the admission and treatment policies of clinical consultants). These include both the variable costs of wards and clinics, i.e. the consumables, and also the service department overheads which are fixed costs in the short run but may be altered by policy decisions on the form and volume of treatment over the longer run. The final two sections show the share of general overheads (over which the consultant has no direct influence) apportioned, plus a set of memorandum statistics which comprise selected indicators of both the surgical team's workload or throughput, and its volume consumption of key resources controllable by the team's decisions.

Resource management

'Resource management' is the name given to a new generation of projects to involve doctors and nurses in using financial and other management information to help achieve more efficient and effective use of resources (Perrin, 1988). This initiative was announced in the DHSS's HN(86)34 (1986), which in effect admitted that attempts to interest clinicians in management budgeting to date had not been very successful. This was probably partly because Griffiths's clinical management budgeting had come to be seen as primarily a cost control tool mainly of benefit to financial and general management, and partly because of the serious delays in getting resource use information systems computerized, so as to be prompt and accurate in their reporting of data doctors could see to be meaningful to their improving the management of their own workloads.

The Griffiths management budgeting approach was largely a top-down system in practice, creating resentment among health care professions not accustomed to close managerial monitoring or discipline. The new approach is bottom-up, involving finding out what information doctors and nurses think would be helpful, and then developing data capture and information analysis systems to meet these interests. Evaluation reports on the first six resource management trial projects should become available during 1989. These trial projects have included work on clinical budgeting, on nursing cost and management information systems, and on case-mix costing, i.e. the costing of the treatment of individual patients, or of patients classified by similar diagnostic conditions and likely treatment costs (e.g. patient diagnosis related groups (DRGs) – see Perrin (1988)). Whatever the results of the present trials, it seems almost certain that cost and budgetary control analysis in the NHS will become increasingly detailed and rigorous, as on the one hand pressure on the efficient use of funds becomes greater, and on the other hand the cost of data processing of resource use and cost data becomes relatively cheaper.

Table 8.2 Budget variance report for surgical team

	Current month			Expense codes		Year to date		
	Budget	Actual	Variance			Budget	Actual	Variance
				Staff costs controlled by team				
	10,998	10,697	–301	800	Medical staff costs	54,990	53,166	–1,024
				Other exp controlled by team				
	12,499	12,014	–485	809	Prescribed drugs	62,495	58,712	–3,783
	290	248	–42	811	Histopathology – consumables	1,450	1,193	–257
	7,697	9,016	1,319	820	Radiology – consumables	40,837	44,808	3,971
	7,283	7,892	609	821	Operating theatre consumables	36,415	38,878	2,463
	38,767	39,867	1,100		Total costs controlled by team	197,187	196,757	570
				Costs influenced by team				
	4,166	5,152	986	840	Ward – consumables	20,830	22,584	1,754
	83	149	66	841	Outpatient – consumables	415	495	80
	11,572	10,983	–589	845	Ward – overheads	57,860	58,592	732
	41	193	152	846	Outpatient – overheads	205	452	247
	1,565	1,782	217	849	Pharmacy – overheads	7,825	8,571	746
	833	814	–19	851	Histopathology – overheads	4,165	4,046	–119
	8,208	7,932	–276	861	Operating theatre – overheads	41,040	40,643	–397
	4,107	4,182	75	868	ECG – overheads	20,535	21,916	1,381
	15,485	15,654	169	880	Physiotherapy-hydrotherapy	77,425	75,296	–2,129
	46,060	46,841	781		Total costs influenced by team	230,300	232,595	2,295

Code	Item						
	General services overheads						
890	Unit administration	2,499	2,261	−238	12,495	11,236	−1,259
891	Catering	973	1,028	55	4,865	5,386	521
892	Domestic	1,219	817	−402	6,095	3,932	−2,163
894	Linen/laundry	832	946	114	4,160	4,701	541
896	Estate management	7,499	6,753	−746	37,495	35,388	−2,107
	Total general serv. overheads	13,022	11,805	−1,217	65,110	60,643	−4,467
	Total costs for team	97,849	98,513	664	491,597	489,995	−1,602
	Memorandum statistics						
900	Inpatients – days	857	878	21	4,285	4,382	97
903	Outpatients – attendances	148	193	45	740	849	109
914	Histopathology – tests	499	296	−203	2,495	2,650	155
937	Radiology – tests	473	682	209	2,801	3,690	889
940	Operating theatre – hours	599	634	35	2,995	3,286	291

Preliminary draft for a report, with simulated cost figures, reproduced from the CASPE Project at Lewisham and N. Southwark Health Authority, by permission.

Performance review

'Performance review' is a process of monitoring and evaluating recent progress to objectives, targets, priorities, budgets, etc., typically for the joint purpose of enhancing managerial discipline and pressure for good performance, and of setting new, future objectives and targets, etc. For discipline to be effective, the objectives, targets, priorities and budgets must be realistic, and they must be realizable through good management short of unforeseeable and uncontrollable events, such as epidemics, catastrophes or the failure of governments to meet staff pay increases in full. Effective reviews must be based upon accurate and reliable – and relevant – information.

It was argued by the recent Körner working parties on NHS information for management control that effective assessment of performance depended not just on using financial information in isolation, but rather on the capacity to relate financial information to comparable information on the use of manpower and other physical resources, and on the workload of patient care and treatment provided by the financial and manpower resources. Traditionally three main performance indicators were used: cost per day (per hospital patient), cost per case and average length of stay – the implication being that all three of these indicators should be minimized through good management. Here the degree of success in minimization would be assessed by comparison to previous years (after adjusting for inflation), and by comparison to similar specialties, hospitals or community health services in other health districts. Of course such simplistic performance comparisons are fraught with risk of error or misinterpretation. A particular problem in performance comparisons between hospitals is that their case mixes may vary considerably with regard to the type of condition or type of treatment (i.e. 'specialty'), or with regard to how seriously ill the patients are and how intensive the nursing and medical attention needs to be. More serious and complex cases tend to get referred onwards from local hospitals to bigger regional centres for particular specialties, or even to the regional centres of excellence, normally in teaching hospitals linked to universities.

The first response to the above problem and the search for more reliable performance criteria is to analyse costs and resource use by 'specialty' (general surgery, obstetrics, etc.) instead of just at the level of the average for the entire hospital. The routine analysis and reporting of specialty costs as required by the Körner information reforms should help, but will still not adequately differentiate case-mix costliness. However, a patient classification system originally of American origin and capable of classifying patients into some 468 categories will soon be generally available and will give greater insight into the variations and inherent costliness of different case mixes. This system is known as diagnosis related groups (DRGs). In future it may be used additionally as the basis for hospital budgeting based on planned clinical workloads.

The production of performance indicators is a technical challenge and of interest to accountants, but it is a time-consuming exercise and not worth its considerable cost unless the resultant information is relevant to, and used by, managers and other decision-makers (including hospital consultant doctors in the case of the NHS). This brings us back to the concept of performance review, which in essence is the process of requiring each level of management to monitor the performance of its subordinates at least once a year, to stimulate better performance and set new targets. Some 400 performance indicators are now reported and checked at district, regional and national level for the NHS. There is a greater time delay than ideal in the NHS in processing the great mass of statistical and financial data involved, but the completed performance information is then made available on tape for computer terminal interrogation and performance comparisons to be made at the local level. The most robust of this information, and out-of-line indicators selected on the 'exception principle', can then be discussed as relevant at each level of the performance review.

At the top of the pyramid of reviews there is an annual review between the Secretary of State or Health Minister and the top management of each RHA. The latter in turn hold similar reviews with the top management of DHAs, who of course hold reviews with their unit general managers, and so on. At the higher-level performance reviews attention will focus relatively more on progress towards national policies and priorities, i.e. progress towards change and innovation, while at lower levels attention will focus relatively more on efficiency and effectiveness in the use of resources in carrying out current programmes and in meeting current financial and manpower budgets. *Comparing Health Authorities* (DHSS, 1988) gives examples and advice for using performance indicators in inter-authority comparisons. However, such comparisons can be misleading and need further detailed analysis because of likely differences in workload, case-mix, age and efficiency of premises and equipment, etc. Sometimes trend analysis of key performance indicators within a single health authority over a period of years can provide more useful efficiency control information than will interauthority comparisons.

Postscript: prime minister's review

The White Paper, *Working for Patients*, (1989) must be added to the Further Reading for this chapter. This is the outcome of a year-long

242 The National Health Service

policy review of the future of the NHS led personally by the Prime Minister. The White Paper was delayed and was published only after the main part of this chapter had been sent for typesetting. Even so, the whole chapter could have been revised. However, the main financial reforms in the White Paper will not begin to operate widely before 1991 and may not become universal before 1995, if then; so it was decided to summarize the key points from the White Paper in this separate postscript, presenting a view of how important aspects of NHS financial practice are intended to change in the years ahead.

The changes expected in 1989 and 1990 will be mainly organizational but will also include preparatory work on improved computer and financial information systems needed for the major financial reforms of 1991 and later. The NHS Structure in England will be altered by replacing the Health Services Supervisory Board with a new NHS Policy Board (See Figure 8.1 to plot the changes). The NHS Management Board will be reconstituted as a Management Executive. The accountability of Family Practitioner Committees will be transferred to the Regional Health Authorities, and their management and accounting functions will be strengthened. The Resource Management approach to improving cost and workload information and involving doctors and nurses in the use of this information will be extended to a greatly expanded number of hospitals. The Audit Commission will take over from the former DHSS Audit units the main responsibility for financial and value-for-money auditing in the NHS. Regions will begin paying directly for work they do for each other, in place of the present time-lagged RAWP adjustments to RAWP targets in respect of cross-boundary flows.

The main financial changes will come into operation from 1991. Probably the most dramatic change will be the conversion of many acute hospitals now run as 'units' of management into self-governing NHS Hospital Trusts (See figure 8.2). Hospitals with this new status will have greater autonomy than previously, but they will have to generate much of their revenue by attracting NHS (and private) patients, either as individuals or by agreeing contracts with health authorities (as holders of NHS funding) or with GPs or private health care providers or insurers. Such hospitals will buy and sell specialist skills and spare capacity, and it appears there will be implicit financial incentive to increase the volume and productivity of health care. This innovation involves many of the issues mentioned earlier in this chapter under the heading of Income Generation, and certainly most hospitals will have to improve their management accounting greatly and quickly in order to have adequate information for good cost control and good pricing/contract decisions by as early as 1991.

Budgeting is to be developed further for GPs also. By 1991, there are to be 'indicative drug budgets' for all GPs: for 'indicative' read 'target and notional'. It appears that these budgets will set out the spending that ought to be sufficient for a GP with a given workload. It is not a fixed budget system and GPs may overspend to meet the needs of patients. But significant overspendings will be investigated, to see if some doctors may be prescribing excessive quantities of drugs, or drugs which are more expensive than required. In a further initiative, GP practices large enough to afford the necessary financial and administrative support are to be allowed to have so-called 'practice budgets' covering defined areas of the care of their patients. The GPs are intended to search for cost-efficient care for their patients from the new hospital trusts, other NHS hospitals or private suppliers; for a defined range of (largely non-emergency) treatments. If GPs give satisfactory service to their patients but manage to underspend their budgets, the incentive is that the GPs should be allowed to spend savings on improving the staffing, facilities and services provided by their own health centres or surgeries. Initially, the practice budgets will only cover some 10% or less of total NHS spending: and while the concept may be sound as an incentive to good value for money management, the problems of administration, contracting, invoicing, and especially of determining what is allowable at the boundaries of the scheme (which may require extensive auditing, and appeals) could make this innovation unworkable. But at least a great deal of extra work will be created for accountants and auditors.

Thus, by 1991 some GPs will be buying-in some services against planned budgets, and the new NHS Hospital Trusts will be engaged in both buying and selling services as largely autonomous profit centres. In addition, District Health Authorities will begin paying directly for work they do for each other, which could include back-up services but in particular will include charging for the care of patients resident in other Districts. The extra administration and the need for sound and defensible costing information will become urgent and costly. The government recognizes this problem and has allowed in the future funding plans of the NHS for major additional investment in computing and information systems. However, shortages of skilled computing and financial staff could turn out to be a cause of delay even if there is no lack of funding. Introducing local pay bargaining into the NHS, most notably into the Hospital Trusts, could attract additional skilled staff into the NHS, but perhaps only at the cost of broadening the range of levels of resources and performance between different hospitals, and between different districts.

Chapter 8 refers to the present system for the revenue funding of health authorities whereby the RAWP formula is used to determine the theoretical health care costs of the local population. This is termed the target funding, and the current actual funding, which may be higher or lower than the target for historical reasons, is moved gradually towards the target, in small annual changes. But the White Paper states that, after a transitional period, health authorities should receive access to all the cash represented by their local populations weighted for health status. Some health districts will gain revenue beyond current spending and will be able to expand: other districts will find their revenue is below current spending and will either have to cut staffing and services, or, as will be encouraged, will need to market actively and sell part of their capacity to other health districts, Hospital Trusts, GPs with Service Budgets, or private care providers. This is part of the encouragement of the Internal Market approach, or competition in health care provision, as discussed in Chapter 8 in Income Generation.

Chapter 8 cites the problem of rational control of capital in the NHS because up until now this has been allocated as a free good, with no repayment required, no interest charged, and no depreciation accounting. The White Paper indicates that this will be changed in future, at least as regards the introduction of depreciation accounting and the charging of interest on the value of capital employed. Although the final details of this will take some time to work out, the practical effect will be that health districts that spend a great deal on capital will have less to spend on revenue. This is a link with the government's insistence that land and buildings should be effectively managed as a resource, with surplus assets disposed of profitably. Powers of capital borrowing, at least for Hospital Trusts, and powers to enter into joint capital developments with the private sector, are to be introduced with the other capital reforms, probably by 1991.

Summary

Budgetary control is obviously the prime vehicle by which NHS treasurers exercise financial control. Budgets and all other accounting systems in the health authorities, except accounting for capital expenditure, are based on income and expenditure accounting. That is, accruals are brought into account for debtors, creditors and stocks, but not for capital consumption, whereas the government's primary financial control concern is with actual cash payments, receipts and balances under the cash-limit control system. Generally this does not cause too much of a problem. For example, the invoiced expenditure can be charged properly to the internal accounts and budgets, for accuracy of measurement and for controlling budget holders, while the cash payments owing to suppliers can be paid early or late within the authorized period as best meets balancing-out to cash limits. It is possible for over- and underspending to be balanced out between districts within a region, or even between regions, so long as the total authorized spending of the NHS as a whole is not exceeded. It is recognized, after all, that there is unmet need for the services of the NHS, and that there is no inherent virtue in the service failing to spend the full moneys voted by Parliament.

Within each health authority financial control of budgets is supported

by other conventional forms of internal control over purchasing, contracts and cash disbursements, etc. But formal systems of commitment
accounting are not widely used. NHS authorities are not allowed to invest
any savings or surplus funds (except trust funds), or any end-of-year
balances. Rather these must be netted-in with the cash balance at bank,
and this is never supposed to exceed a modest working balance. The latter
is regulated by control of the timing of drawing further funds from
government against the authorized cash limits (see CIPFA, 1980, and
updates). These regulations reflect the fact that NHS finance is an
integral part of Exchequer financing.

Clinician or specialty budgets are still only developmental. So the main
focus of internal financial control is on expenditure against management
budgets at unit level. This involves keeping the expenditure accounts up
to date, and reporting on progress at least monthly. The best form of
control is self-control – in this case the control exercised by budget
holders over their own budget balances and expenditure commitments. A
guideline rule in good budgetary reporting is that performance reports
on the preceding period should be supplied to budget holders before the
midpoint of the succeeding period, so that budget holders will feel able
and motivated to correct their performance in time to improve the next
reports they receive on progress to budget.

The latest approach to improved financial control and efficiency in the
NHS is 'resource management', which in concept involves matching cost
and other resource consumption information alongside workload and
activity information which doctors and nurses find relevant to understanding and monitoring their treatment of patients. Other managers can
use this information also, to improve both current control and forward
planning. Eventually this may lead to standard systems of clinical
management budgeting and patient costing. More detailed and accurate
cost information will be needed in the NHS if health authorities are
expected to earn part of their revenue through pricing and selling services
through the 'internal market' in place of the traditional almost total
reliance on funding from central allocations under the RAWP system.

Further reading

NHS accounting and finance is covered in *Health Service Finance* by
Jones and Prowle (1987), while NHS management accounting is treated
in greater depth in *Resource Management in the NHS* (Perrin, 1988).
Updated technical information on NHS accounting and finance is
available from Volume 30 of CIPFA's *Financial Information Service*.
Journalistic coverage of developments in NHS accounting and finance is
best obtained from the weekly *Public Finance and Accountancy*, and there

is some coverage in the weekly *Health Service Journal*. There are occasional articles on the NHS in the academic quarterlies, *Financial Accountability and Management* and *Public Money and Management*. The White Paper, *Working for Patients*, (1989) is the outcome of a year-long policy review of the future of the NHS led personally by the Prime Minister.

Chapter 9

External audit

AUDIT OF CENTRAL GOVERNMENT

This chapter discusses the external audit of public sector bodies, its nature and its objectives. Comparisons will be made with the audit of companies and other organizations in the private sector. There will be discussion of recent developments in public sector audit and of the differing views which have emerged about its proper scope and organization. There will be no attempt to give instruction in detailed audit techniques: for that a specialized professional training is necessary.

Introduction

It has already been shown that the public sector in the UK comprises a variety of organizations, but the main divisions of the sector into central government, local authorities and nationalized industries and other public corporations will be followed in examining the role of audit. Before examining the three main areas, it is necessary to be clear about the essential nature of an external audit. What is it? What is it for?

The clues to the answers to these questions lie in the words 'external' and 'independent'. In the UK public sector, an external audit is intended first to provide an assurance as to the reliability of the published accounts of the audited body. Second, it is intended to provide a further assurance as to the regularity of the underlying transactions. Third, in the central and local government sectors but not the nationalized industries it aims to provide an assessment of the efficiency and effectiveness with which the body performs its functions. The auditor provides these assurances and assessments from the standpoint of someone outside the body in question and independent of it. His examinations and reports are expected to be honest, impartial, dispassionate, indeed fearless, as well, it is to be hoped, as expert and thorough. The independence of the external auditor is crucial if his reports are to have credibility and authority. How such independence may be secured is discussed below.

This brief definition of external audit leads immediately to two further questions. First, to whom are these assurances about financial or other matters, provided by this independent character, to be addressed? Second, what is the relationship between external and internal auditors? An answer to the second question can conveniently wait. The answer to the first depends on the constitutional position of the audited body: to whom is it answerable for its actions? A government department is answerable through its minister and accounting officer (see below) directly to Parliament. A nationalized industry is answerable to the responsible minister and through him to Parliament on its general performance, but not on its day-to-day operations. A local authority is constitutionally independent of Parliament but can do only what Parliament empowers it to do. While Parliament acts on behalf of national electors and taxpayers and is distinct from the Executive – i.e. the central government – local authorities act on behalf of local electors and ratepayers in both a representative and an executive capacity. It follows that the external auditor of a government department reports to Parliament, the auditor of a nationalized industry to the Secretary of State, and the auditor of local authorities to the authority itself. In doing so, however, they always have in mind the interests of the general public, particularly their interests as the providers of the funds to pay for public services, and all these audit reports are normally publicly available.

The public audit services of most advanced countries set out to provide, in very broad terms, a financial audit of accounts and an efficiency or value for money audit of activities. The first of these centres on the adequacy of the systems for controlling the receipt and payment of public funds, the second on the way the resources purchased with those funds – manpower, capital equipment, buildings, supplies and so on – are allocated and utilized.

The term audit is sometimes applied to a different type of external check; for example, a 'social audit', advocated by some people, would attempt to establish how far public institutions, and indeed large private corporations, had contributed to social, community or similar goals. We are not concerned here with these wider remits as such, though social considerations often play a part in public expenditure decisions and must be recognized and allowed for by the auditor. The critical examination of financial and resource management is a convenient general description of much of the auditor's activity.

Audit of central government: the statutory basis

The law which for many years governed the external audit of central government, and still provides the basic authority for some of it, was the Exchequer and Audit Departments Act of 1866, as modified, in significant but not fundamental respects, by the 1921 Act. The 1866 Act brought together, under the newly created office of the Comptroller and Auditor General, the duties formerly discharged separately by the Comptroller

General of the Exchequer, whose origins went back for several centuries, and Commissioners of Audit. It was part of the nineteenth-century reforms intended to give Parliament an effective and unified control over the use of public revenues. At that time the largest spenders of those revenues were the Army and the Navy, and what was then called the Office of Works and Public Building. The Act provided for the appointment, by the Crown, of the Comptroller and Auditor General (whose full title is Comptroller General of the Receipt and Issue of Her Majesty's Exchequer and Auditor General of Public Accounts), but it did not give a separate statutory existence to his department, the Exchequer and Audit Department. It provided instead (as amended in 1921) that the C&AG, as he is always called for short, might appoint staff who would assist him in carrying out his statutory responsibilities for the examination, certification and reporting on government departments' accounts. The C&AG thus took personal responsibility for all the work of his officers, and until the 1970s signed personally the audit certificate and report on virtually every account which the department audited. This contrasts with the arrangements in private auditing firms, where each partner manages the audit of his own clients' accounts, or in local government where each district or commercial auditor is responsible by law for auditing and reporting on particular local authorities' accounts.

The C&AG has usually been appointed from outside his Department, with a wide experience of public expenditure and finance provided by service as a top departmental official, and has not himself been a professional auditor or accountant. Appointment of someone with the latter kind of background would be possible, but since public audit is by no means confined to the financial audit of accounts and demands a close knowledge of the operations of Parliament and of the departments of state, it is clearly desirable that the person in charge should be familiar with public finance and with the problems of managing large departments and securing the best use of very large sums of public money.

The independence of the C&AG, and thus of all his staff, is secured by his appointment by the Queen, on the advice of the Prime Minister, by the payment of his salary directly from the Consolidated Fund, not from annual Votes, and by his freedom from dismissal except on a motion passed by both Houses of Parliament. He does not answer to any minister of the Government, and indeed, although he works on behalf of Parliament, makes most of his reports to Parliament, and is now under the National Audit Act 1983 (see below) an officer of the House of Commons, and as such cannot be instructed by the House, or by any of its Committees, to undertake particular investigations. Thus within the broad statutory framework governing his audit he decides himself how to lay out the resources of his staff, how to conduct his audit work, and whether to report.

The audit of government departments can be divided into two sectors: the financial, more strictly the certification, audit, and the value for money audit. The basis for the certification audit was laid down in the 1866 Act, which established the arrangements by which the executive – the government – should account for the public revenues they raised and the public funds they spent. Much of the Act dealt with accounting procedures and responsibilities, but its main provisions, which still apply, can be simply summarized. Departments were required to prepare annually 'appropriation accounts' showing how the sums voted by Parliament for specific purposes and services had been spent. The C&AG had to examine and certify these accounts and report thereon to Parliament. If the Treasury failed to present to Parliament by the due date any report by the C&AG, then the C&AG himself was empowered to do so. This power has never had to be invoked.

Moving forward over 50 years, the Exchequer and Audit Departments Act of 1921 modified and updated the 1866 Act in three respects. First the C&AG was allowed to dispense with the 100% audit of transactions which appeared to be required by the original Act, though it must be highly doubtful whether for many years before 1921 anything of this order had been achieved, or even attempted. Instead he was given discretion to have regard to the departments' own examination in deciding the extent of his check of transactions. Though not specifically mentioned in the Act, the concept of a 'test audit' was thus established. The way in which test audits should be carried out, to give a reasonable degree of assurance about the particular accounting systems to which they are applied, is an important aspect of audit techniques. It has led into the systems-based audit and the use of statistical sampling where large numbers of transactions are involved, and its application is having to be rethought with the rapid extension of computerized accounting systems and auditing software.

Second, the 1921 Act provided for the preparation and audit in suitable cases of trading, manufacturing or production accounts as well as the cash-based appropriation accounts. Trading accounts are prepared on a similar basis to private sector commercial accounts, with balance sheets and sources and application of funds statements, and are fully accrued.

The third innovation in 1921 was to require the C&AG to examine the revenue departments' accounts (Inland Revenue, Customs and Excise) as well as those of the spending departments. But there is an important difference. The C&AG is expected to satisfy himself, and to assure Parliament and the public, about the regularity of the appropriation accounts. In his audit of the Revenue Departments, however, he is required to satisfy himself only that the departments have established satisfactory procedures for the assessment and collection of all revenue due. He is not required to certify that all revenue which should have been collected has been, still less that individual taxpayers have been correctly assessed for tax. That would indeed have been an impossible task. This approach appears to be an early formulation of a 'systems-based audit', antedating by several decades the general adoption of that technique in both commercial and public audit work.

No further change in the law governing the C&AG's work occurred for another 60 years. But it was progressively developed on a non-statutory basis, particularly in the value for money field, with the active encouragement of Parliament through the Public Accounts Committee (see below) and the acquiescence of government departments. In the late 1970s and early 1980s an upsurge of Parliamentary interest in the public audit system coinciding with a new approach by the C&AG to his role and the responsibilities of his department led to a wide ranging debate and to the National Audit Act of 1983. The main strands in that debate are discussed below, but it is convenient to conclude this section with a summary of the main provisions of the 1983 Act.

The Act provided that:

(a) The C&AG should continue to be appointed by Her Majesty on a motion for an address by the House of Commons made by the Prime Minister, whose advice now, however, had to be tendered in agreement with the Chairman of the Committee of Public Accounts, recognizing the close interest of Parliament in the person, as well as the office.

(b) The C&AG should be an officer of the House of Commons; but – subject of course to his statutory duties – he should have 'complete discretion in the discharge of his functions' including in particular whether and how to carry out a '3E' type examination under the Act (see (e) and (f) below). In taking such decisions, however, he was required to 'take into account any proposals made by the Committee of Public Accounts'. So was resolved the argument whether the C&AG should be subject to the directions of the PAC or, as some members of Parliament would have liked, also of other select committee.

(c) A Public Accounts Commission should be set up, to include the Leader of the House and the Chairman of the PAC, with the functions of:
   (i) examining and presenting to the House of Commons the financial estimates for the National Audit Office, modified or not, for which purpose the Commission was to have regard to any advice given by the PAC and the Treasury;
  (ii) appointing the Accounting Officer for the National Audit Office;
 (iii) appointing an auditor for the National Audit Office, who would have power to carry out economy, efficiency and effectiveness examinations of its use of resources.

(d) A National Audit Office should be set up, headed by the C&AG and consisting of such staff appointed by him as he considered necessary 'for assisting him in the discharge of his functions'; their remuneration and other conditions of service also to be decided by him, thus ending the Treasury's powers in these respects.

(e)   The C&AG should have a discretionary power to carry out examinations of the economy, efficiency and effectiveness with which government departments and other bodies subject to his audit or inspection used their resources, without, however, being entitled to question the merits of their policy **objectives**, and to report to the House the results of such examinations; (Author's emphasis.)

(f)   The C&AG should have power to carry out 3 Es examinations in any body (except the nationalized industries and certain other public authorities) whose members were appointed by the Crown and which he had reasonable cause to believe was funded as to more than half its income from public funds: thus was resolved the argument as to whether the C&AG should have the right 'to follow public money wherever it goes'.

The Act also repealed a provision of the 1866 Act relating to the appropriation accounts, to allow for some flexibility in the year of account, to speed up certification and presentation; and it removed or amended certain powers by which the Treasury could require the C&AG to carry out particular investigations.

The objectives of the financial audit

The financial audit of government departments is intended to give an assurance that in all material respects:

(a)   Their accounts properly present the transactions to which they relate;

(b)   They have spent the money voted to them only for the purposes intended by Parliament, as described in the Estimates and Supplementary Estimates presented at the beginning of each financial year and subsequently; and

(c)   That the expenditure conforms to the authority governing it, i.e. has met the requirements of 'regularity'.

In even plainer words, this means that the money provided by Parliament has been spent as intended, that no unlawful, improper or irregular payments have been made, and that the figures are satisfactory.

These simple-sounding objectives conceal some complex problems for the C&AG and his staff. Although the basic form of the appropriation accounts is simple – cash spent in the year compared with cash voted – the figures in the final accounts run into billions of pounds for all the major departments, and they represent and summarize not only very large numbers of transactions, but very complex purchasing, construction, contracting and staffing operations. The building of hospitals, the design and development of advanced military equipment, the installation of large computer systems, the payment of many millions of social security benefits each week, are just a few of these highly diverse activities. It is therefore a major technical audit task to check that the accounting and financial control systems underlying the figures in the account are reliable and efficient. This work is necessarily done on a selective basis and increasingly utilizes techniques, such as statistical sampling and the evaluation and testing of systems, similar to those applied by commercial auditors in the audit of large private sector concerns.

To check that government spending conforms with the specific terms of statutes, for example that financial assistance given by the Department of Industry to private firms is in accordance with the broad conditions laid down in the Industry Act or other governing legislation, does not in practice raise many difficult problems, or usually take much time. But the audit of regularity extends a good way beyond this. Detailed rules and regulations are often drawn up, under the authority of the governing Acts themselves, to set out the exact conditions and criteria which have to be met if people or companies are to be entitled to various types of state payments. The largest, but by no means the only, services of this kind are social security, and agricultural and industrial assistance schemes. Some social security benefits are payable only if the applicant has made sufficient national insurance contributions. To be entitled to unemployment benefit, a person has to be 'genuinely seeking work'. To qualify for a hill farming subsidy, a farmer may have to maintain his sheep for sufficient periods above certain altitudes. To qualify for an industrial grant, a company may have to build a factory within particular areas and to equip it for specified industrial purposes. These rules and regulations can be voluminous, complex and open in some cases to arguments about interpretation. They may take the form of 'subordinate legislation', for example a statutory instrument which has to be laid before, and in some cases approved by, Parliament. They may simply be departmental rules, sometimes approved by the Treasury, sometimes not, which the responsible Minister is entitled to lay down by administrative action.

Very large sums of public money are disbursed under systems of this kind. As a matter of just and efficient administration people should get what they are entitled to, and not more. It is the duty of the National Audit Office, as part of their regularity audit, to check that departments are applying such rules correctly. They will do so selectively, and with regard, as in all their work, for the relative importance, or materiality, of the various areas of expenditure. They may find that some rules are prone to cause errors because they are overcomplicated or unclear. They may find that officials have made payments which, through an honest but excessive exercise of their initiative, bend the rules unduly. They may even come to the view that a scheme, let us say for paying farmers to drain or fence certain types of land, is so complex that it takes too much manpower to administer and might with advantage be replaced by a simpler one.

With the exception of the last, all these illustrations relate to the concept of regularity of expenditure. Similar examples can be found in other government programmes, for example the rules governing the distribution of funds to promote the arts, or sport, or research. Such functions as these are often entrusted to special bodies or councils, subject to rules and guidance by their parent departments: the Arts Council under the Department of Education and Science, the Medical Research Council under the Department of Health, and so on. In such cases as these the rules to which they have to work will be relatively simple, unlike those governing social security schemes, which run into many volumes. But they are further aspects of the way in which regularity, in matters of government spending, is defined.

It is to these features of the accounts – accuracy of the figures, legality and regularity of the transactions – that the C&AG's certificate to Parliament exclusively relates. It is sometimes called the 'attest' function of an audit. It gives independent assurance, within approved standards, that the audited body has properly presented its financial transactions in its accounts and has conformed to the rules governing them. In principle this kind of audit can be, and is, applied to a wide range of bodies, from international organizations, such as the Food and Agriculture Organization or the World Health Organization of the United Nations, to the local cricket club, as well as to government departments.

The essential point with which to close this part of the discussion is that the financial or certification audit, constitutionally important as it is, has limited objectives in the assessment of operational efficiency. It is true that the analysis of government activities and expenditure which is a necessary part of a well conducted financial audit may well lead into wider studies. It is also the case that an evaluation of financial control and information systems is likely to be of value not only for certification purposes but to judge a department's progress in the development of effective internal management systems. But other operational audit techniques, conveniently subsumed in the term 'value for money audit', need to be developed. Before discussing them, it is first necessary to make a brief digression into the field of commercial accounting and audit.

Commercial and government accounting

Government spends money and uses large resources of manpower to provide a wide variety of services to the community: defence, health, support for industry and agriculture, social security, and many others. For the most part these services are not paid for directly by those who benefit from them. Some charges, such as those for medical prescriptions, or for use of the Severn bridge or Dartford tunnel, are made; but the former covers only a small part of the cost and most of the services are not provided with a commercial motive – to make a profit.

It is true that a relatively small part of the activities of government departments or closely related bodies is commercial in its nature and aims. The Royal Mint, as well as manufacturing the coin of the realm, which is 'sold' to the Treasury under rather special arrangements, also manufactures and sells coins and medals for overseas customers and is expected to cover its costs and charge market prices for this business. Her Majesty's Stationery Office publishes and sells many official documents and reports, if not at a profit at any rate with the intention of recovering the cost. The national museums run shops for their prints, replicas and so on where they aim to break even or do better. The special accounts for these activities are themselves commercial in style; they present their results in essentially the same way as an industrial or trading company, and they are audited accordingly. But in the scale of government activities as a whole, this kind of activity is relatively small.

Commercial accounts are intended to show the results of trading operations over the year, and the financial state of the business – more specifically its net book value – at the end of each year. To do so, both income and expenditure have to be assessed as accurately as possible, which is a more complex task than simply logging-up cash payments and receipts. Income has to take account of sums due in respect of various activities and attributable to the year in question; expenditure has to include amounts representing the proportion of the firm's assets, stocks and work in progress used up in producing the year's income; provisions against future loss or liabilities have to be assessed – and so on. When to these calculations it is necessary to add an assessment of the effect of inflation on the firm's profit and asset valuations, through the application of current cost accounting, the production and audit of the accounts of any sizeable commercial concern is a considerable exercise, involving acts of judgement as well as of record and classification.

This brief sketch of commercial accounting is intended only as background to two points. First, as mentioned above, there are some government activities which can and should be presented and accounted for in this way. They include not only the production and sale of a range of goods, from coins and medals to prints of medieval manuscripts, but also, for example, the provision of offices and supplies to departments, where it is thought desirable to work out the 'full cost' on some appropriate type of commercial accounting, to assist control and to promote the right decisions. Pressure is also growing for some form of accounts which recognize the consumption of capital where this is an important feature of the use of resources, for example in NHS hospitals.

The second point is a wider and crucial one. The making of profit or loss, and the increase or decrease each year in the value of a business, are critical tests of its success or failure. They measure the extent to which it achieves its essential objectives. There may be others. A firm which contributes to social progress or cultural achievement, which makes its staff happy in their work, or sponsors a tennis tournament, may earn applause for doing so. Its far-sighted directors may well judge that there are also likely to be financial benefits. But if it consistently fails in the primary task of profit making, it is unlikely to survive, short of government rescue, for long.

Value for money audit

None of this applies, clearly, to government departments providing or promoting the large communal services of defence, education, health, law and order, and so on. Their efficiency, their performance, their success has to be judged by quite different tests, and by quite different methods. This is the field in which the public audit services seek to apply the concepts now broadly known as value for money or efficiency auditing. They do not displace the audit of accuracy in accounting or of propriety and regularity of transactions described earlier. They complement and extend it, and require different techniques. Good financial auditors have also produced useful value for money reports on a wide range of financial management matters. Such work can also be satisfactorily done by people without professional accountancy or audit training if they have the right aptitudes and approach.

The prime responsibility for achieving value for money or efficiency is the management's and not the public auditor's. Senior civil servants, and ultimately their ministers, are responsible and are held accountable for all their actions in running and managing their departments. But the C&AG and his staff play their same independent role in assessing and where necessary criticizing the performance of the bodies they audit in these respects as they do in what may be described as the more formal financial audit field. They thus promote two distinct objectives: accountability of the executive government to Parliament and, it is hoped, its efficiency and effectiveness.

The terms 'value for money' and 'efficiency audit' are not terms of art, still less precise definitions. Value for money audit was commonly used in the UK as a convenient description of the evolving interests and work of E&AD over many decades, with its origin sometimes pinpointed at the year 1888 when there was an interesting confrontation between the C&AG and the Army Council over a little matter of contracts for Army ribbon, from which the former emerged the winner. The argument was whether the C&AG was within his rights in extending his examination of Army expenditure beyond the accepted matters of conformity with Parliamentary authorization into the area of economy in contracts. The C&AG owed his success largely to the support of the Public Accounts Committee of the House of Commons, established in 1861, whose present role is described below. Over the succeeding century the C&AG has developed the application of value for money audit into many aspects of the financial management of government departments, with a marked acceleration in scale and coverage from the early 1950s, as the great post-war surge in government activity and the corresponding expenditure programmes gathered weight.

Traditionally this work focused on 'the elimination of waste and extravagance'. Within recent years the wider role of national audit offices has been more closely analysed and defined in a way which now has widespread international recognition. The General Accounting Office of the USA is usually credited with formulating, and publicizing, the three-fold division into economy, efficiency and effectiveness audit.

In this context economy is taken to mean the achievement of a given result with the least expenditure of money, manpower or other resources, while efficiency imports the idea of converting resources into a desired product in the most advantageous ratio. But this is sometimes a rather subtle distinction, and the more important divide is between the pursuit and audit of economy and efficiency on the one hand and of effectiveness on the other, because the latter brings into account the goals or objectives which the activity in question is intended to meet.

The examination of effectiveness in government and other public sector programmes and policies raises issues which are often intractable and sometimes controversial. The development or purchase of nuclear weapons is intended to contribute to the goal of national security. The extension of comprehensive education is intended to promote educational and social aims. The introduction of the family income supplement was hoped to secure a minimum standard of living for the families of low-paid workers in employment. Subsidies for defined forms of industrial investment aimed to encourage the development of particular parts of the country, and reduce unemployment. The transformation of the old employment exchanges into job centres and their siting in the high street has a similar aim. These cases and a great many more raise the questions:

(a)   Should the auditor be involved in effectiveness at all?
(b)   If so, does this not bring him to question policy decisions?
(c)   Has he the necessary skills?

Parliament decided, in the National Audit Act and the Local Government Finance Act 1982, that the audit of both central and local government should cover effectiveness. In this respect, so far at least as central government operations are concerned, the United Kingdom has lined up with the legislatures of the United States, the Netherlands and Sweden among others, while the Australians, for example, have decided otherwise.

The question of the involvement of the external auditor in policy questions is a sensitive one. It is for those running an organization, and answerable for its results, to take and defend policy decisions, for example to develop a new civil aircraft, to build a new comprehensive school, or to broadcast news in English to various parts of the world. But the auditor may feel it necessary and justifiable:

(a) To question whether the goals which the policy decisions are meant to serve have been established;
(b) To examine whether managements have themselves established adequate procedures and criteria to assess the effectiveness of their policies;
(c) To quantify the costs of the decisions taken;
(d) To report on whether the goals have in fact been achieved;
(e) To suggest alternative ways in which the goals might have been more effectively met.

This is a formidable list of possibilities. Few national auditors regard the whole lot as within their remit; probably only the General Accounting Office of the USA covers (e). The Australian and Canadian Auditors General are required to stop at (c) and do not go on to (d) or (e). The C&AG would regard all except (e) as in principle within his remit. But he would be circumspect and realistic in deciding which particular government projects or programmes to examine in this way. He would have in mind the degree of authority and cogency his report was likely to have, and the impact it was likely to make. He would not be in business to study policy options, nor to write academic studies. His object, in this part of his value for money work, would be to contribute to more effective decision-taking, and more efficient execution of policies, by reference to past and current experience, problems and mistakes.

Although it is useful to analyse value for money auditing as above, it is as well not to conceptualize too far. In the UK, at any rate, value for money audit has come to describe a wide variety of enquiries into central government operations, including the development and production of military equipment, the building of hospitals, factories and offices, the application of agricultural and industrial assistance, the design and installation of computer systems, charging policies for government services, use and disposal of land and control of civil service manpower. The C&AG's reports have concentrated on financial management in the broadest sense, including the management of contracts. They have also raised matters of organization, and the control of civil service manpower. They have not, however, extended into the field of operational research or work study. Some people find difficulty in accepting that the 'value' in value for money can be judged by an auditor. As in so much intellectual discourse it depends on what you mean by value. In the practice of public audit it is often necessary to stop short of an assessment of ultimate value, and be content with 'intermediate objectives'. But the questions 'what is to be achieved, by when, and at what cost?' are now supposed to be applied to all expenditure programmes, and recent NAO reports on the FMI and on financial reporting to Parliament assessed progress in these areas. To judge and to report whether performance has measured up to plans, budgets and intentions is certainly one main object of value for money audit.

Traditionally, most E&AD value for money reports had concentrated on individual examples of waste, contractual failings, inadequate planning, or other aspects of financial mismanagement. Such examinations were, however, by no means small in scale: the building of the Thames barrier, the refit of a warship, the construction of motorways or hospitals, and many other governmental operations cost many millions of pounds and require expert planning, contracting and financial control. Scope for shortcomings in one or more of the 3 Es was not lacking, either in major projects of this type or in smaller scale activities, ranging from university land holdings to the provision of meteorological information. Value for money audit was therefore nothing new to the C&AG and the E&AD, whose archives are full of such reports dating back many years.

Nevertheless it became clear in the later 1970s that further development of this work was necessary, and this has been achieved. In particular:

(a) A much greater degree of 'top-down' planning and supervision was required to ensure that resources were efficiently used and priorities established. Formerly, most value for money reports had emanated from the audit divisions, often though not exclusively as an offshoot of their financial audit work. This approach fostered and rewarded individual initiative, but could not ensure that the most significant areas were covered. A strategic planning system, looking five years ahead, now operates. Senior management is involved in the choice and conduct of all major studies.

(b) Wider studies of departmental operations, including their systems for financial control and the provision and use of management information, needed to be made. From the early 1980s studies looked at programmes, schemes, major activities and whole organizations in a much broader way than formerly. Examples include the C&AG's reports on the development of nuclear power, the monitoring and control of nationalized industries, the housing benefit scheme, the control of NHS nursing manpower, and the financial control and accountability of the metropolitan police.

(c) Some subjects important for government efficiency and of interest to Parliament could only be effectively studied by investigating the practice of several government departments. Examples in recent years have been the organization and use of internal audit, the Rayner scrutiny programmes, financial reporting to Parliament, the financial management initiative, and computer security in government departments.

(d) The E&AD needed to extend their links with the departments and bodies they audited, to spread awareness of their own evolving aims, ideas and methods and to make their decisions on what to investigate and how to do so better informed. By long standing tradition, E&AD's relationship with departments had been markedly at arm's length, with the overrriding aim of safeguarding the C&AG's independence. This has now changed and the NAO discuss with departments likely choices for studies. There are also regular contacts between the NAO and departmental finance officers;

(e) New methods of value for money investigation, sometimes using skills additional to those of financial audit and applied by specially constituted teams, needed to be tried and assessed. These are now part of NAO's standard approach; academics and management consultants take part in VFM investigations.

To effect changes in these directions, to ensure high standards of financial audit, and to deal satisfactorily with staff recruitment, professional training, relations with other public audit bodies at home and abroad and with the private sector, the senior management of E&AD/NAO has been expanded and strengthened, a central capability developed, and the methods of work of the whole office reviewed. Explicit auditing standards, covering both the financial and value-for-money work, have been adopted and published.

The new look to value for money work which emerged from these developments is well summarized in Table 9.1, an extract from the booklet published by the National Audit Office in 1983 explaining the C&AG's role and the responsibilities of the Office.

It is worth considering how value for money audit relates to the Rayner studies mentioned in Chapter 4, to assignments undertaken by management consultants, and to the efficiency studies of nationalized industries commissioned by the government from the Monopolies and Mergers Commission or private accounting/consultancy firms. There are some similarities:

(a) All such examinations proceed by rigorous assembly and analysis of evidence, both from documents and discussion;

(b) Every attempt is made to reach agreement with the body under examination on the factual adequacy and accuracy of material in the final report;

(c) Provisional conclusions are tested by the reactions of the body under examination and account taken of objections or counter arguments;

(d) The objective is a fair, balanced report, making whatever criticisms and recommendations for improvement are thought to be justified, on the sole responsibility of the examining body.

But there are significant differences, both constitutional and methodological:

(a) The external auditor takes his own unfettered decisions as to what he will examine, when he will do so and whether he will make a public or other report. Consultancies are by invitation of the client, who

Table 9.1 Main stages of a typical major audit investigation

Survey of main areas of expenditure and risk	1
Selection of area, programme or project for examination	2
Preliminary study to determine scope, objectives, time-scale and staffing of main exercise, and to prepare plans and work allocations	3
Main exercise carried out by auditor or audit team. Progess and results monitored as study proceeds	4
Results reviewed by senior staff; decisions taken on necessary action	5
Correspondence and discussion with audited body, leading up to draft report (if necessary)	6
Report approved by C&AG; sent to Accounting Officer for confirmation of fairness and accuracy	7
Considered by Committee of Public Accounts with evidence from audited bodies	8
Committee report published and presented to Parliament	9
Treasury Minute published in response to criticisms, comments and recommendations made; confirms remedial action taken or proposed	10
Consideration of Treasury Minute by Committee of Public Accounts, with further follow-up and report as necessary	11

The target time-scale for completion of stages 4–7 would normally not exceed 6–9 months, so as to maintain topicality and impact. Later stages might then occupy a further 39 months from the date of the Committee hearing, depending on the scale of the further examination and the nature of the Government's response to the matters raised.

Source: National Audit Office (1983), by permission.

decides – no doubt in discussion with the consultant – the scope of the enquiry and how it is to be conducted. The report is an internal one. Monopolies and Mergers Commission enquiries, or those undertaken by consultants on the invitation of the central government, are external to the body under examination and are normally published but are not self-initiated.

(b) Major MMC or consultancy efficiency studies have been wideranging investigations into the operations of public bodies, leading to numerous conclusions and recommendations, sometimes disputed. An internal consultancy report is usually more narrowly defined and is to some extent judged by the acceptability of its recommendations to the client, who will have spent money on the study in an endeavour to improve efficiency and profitability. The C&AG's investigations into the efficiency of departments' use of resources are designed for further examination by Parliament under the arrangements described below. Local authority auditors and the Audit Commission have broadly followed the same approach, though they stress the comparative performance of local authorities and they have nothing comparable to the external influence of the Public Accounts Committee to strengthen their impact;

(c) The Rayner studies are carried out internally by particular departments, using selected members of their own staff who examine in considerable detail a specific aspect of administration or policy, questioning both its objectives and its methods. They are supported by the small central efficiency unit and enjoy strong ministerial backing.

Special audit features

There are two important parts of the central government sector where special audit features apply, namely the National Health Service and the universities.

The National Health Service

The National Health Service (NHS) is under the full control of the Secretary of State for Health and his department, the Department of Health (DH). Audit of the NHS is shared between the C&AG and the department. The accounts of the individual health authorities are audited by the 'statutory auditors'.* They are in the main civil servants of the DH, assigned to this special duty and trained for it; they make their reports to the Secretary of State. The C&AG is responsible for examining and certifying the summarized health authority accounts, which bring together the operations of all the individual authorities. But his staff have full access to the books and records of all the health authorities, as well as those of the DH and the corresponding Scottish and Welsh Departments. He is therefore in a position to examine and report on all aspects of the financial control and management of the NHS and its constituent authorities. Reports on health service matters have featured largely in the C&AG's annual reports to Parliament. They have dealt recently for example with community care developments, the use of operating theatres, and the management of the family practitioner service.

It was suggested during the 1980–81 review of the C&AG's role (see below) that it would be desirable to bring the statutory auditors into the E&AD under his direction, so that there would be a fully integrated audit service for the NHS. The PAC recommended in favour, but the government preferred not to disturb the existing arrangements. In several cases, however, the audit of health authorities has been placed by the DH with private accounting firms as part of the government's policy of increasing their participation in the audit of public services.*

* In 1989, the government asked the Audit Commission to undertake the audit of health authorities.

The universities

Most of the funds provided to the universities, for both capital and current expenditure, come from the Exchequer. They are distributed by the Secretary of State for Education and Science to individual universities on the advice of the University Grants Commission, to be superseded by the Universities Funding Council. The accounts of the universities themselves are audited by commercial auditors and until 1967 the C&AG had no access to their records or responsibility to report on their affairs. This reflected the view, since proved unfounded, that to involve him would be prejudicial to the universities' autonomy and a possible threat to academic freedom. After sustained pressure from the PAC the government agreed in 1967 to allow the C&AG to inspect the universities' books and to report as he saw fit on their financial management. Since then the C&AG has made many such reports, and it has become generally accepted that the provision of large sums of public money justifies this extra measure of public accountability.

It should be noted that an 'inspection audit' of this kind provides the National Audit Office with the necessary information for examining and if necessary reporting on value for money matters affecting an organization, even though the financial audit is carried out by other auditors. The universities are the most important example of an inspection audit but there are many others in the central government area. As already noted, the 1983 Act authorizes the C&AG to conduct them in certain bodies receiving at least half their income from public funds.

Internal and external audit

Most large organizations, in both the public and private sectors, have their own internal audit arrangements. The essential difference between internal and external audit is that the former is part of the management, is organized and directed and reports as senior management decides, whereas the latter is completely independent and, subject to the law, decides these matters for itself. Internal audit is intended to contribute to the probity and efficiency of the enterprise from within; external audit shares this objective, operating from outside, but also serves the further objective of external accountability. The scope of the work of internal audit staff may therefore be wide or narrow, varying from straightforward matters of internal financial control to a remit virtually as wide as that of the C&AG himself. The staff are nowadays likely to be led by, and to contain a growing proportion of, professionally qualified people. Some concern has been expressed in recent years about the quality of the approach and work of internal audit in both public and private bodies, and both central and local government are taking steps to raise its standards and improve its effectiveness. This is a matter of considerable interest to the external auditor; despite the significant constitutional difference in the two roles it is generally accepted that the measure of independence given to the internal auditor within the public authority or firm should justify the external auditor in relying on his work where he is satisfied that it meets the necessary professional standards. Subject to this essential condition an agreed division of labour between internal and external audit is accepted as a sensible and economic arrangement.

Reporting to parliament: the role of the Public Accounts Committee

As external auditor does not address his reports to the body he audits, except in the case of local authorities. In the case of a company, the auditor reports to the shareholders, not to the directors. In the case of government departments, the C&AG reports to Parliament, not to ministers. He and his staff may, and often do, bring to the notice of government departments various matters which appear to him to need action but do not merit a public report. But that is part of the normal constructive relationship which ought to exist between the two organizations.

By long tradition the reports of the C&AG are considered by the Committee of Public Accounts (PAC) of the House of Commons. The Committee's terms of reference empower them to examine any of the accounts which are laid before Parliament. It should be noted that this gives the Committee a considerably wider remit than that of the C&AG. For example, all the annual reports and accounts of the nationalized industries and other public corporations are laid before Parliament, and could therefore be examined by the PAC, even though the C&AG is not the auditor of most of them. In practice, an understanding was reached that the PAC would leave the examination of the nationalized industries to the former Select Committee on Nationalized Industries – not so far (1988) replaced by any one comparable select committee.

The PAC does not nowadays spend much time on matters of financial irregularity or constitutional impropriety. There are not many of them, and most which do occur are not of sufficient seriousness to warrant intervention by the committee. Serious fraud cases, fortunately rare in central government administration, certainly engage their attention, as might a failure by a department to secure Parliamentary authority for expenditure. But most of the committee's work is based on the C&AG's value-for-money reports on financial management, and in deciding which matters merit a report the C&AG has much in mind the likely interest of the subject to the committee and the prospect of useful recommendations for improvement arising from their enquiries.

NAO staff have full access, not only to the accounts of departments, but to all papers and documents relevant to the departments' financial administration that may reasonably be required for the purposes of a value-for-money audit. They can thus form their own independent judgement of the merits or shortcomings of departmental action; they are not dependent on government officials to produce their version of events. In the preparation of draft reports care is taken to establish a solid basis of fact upon which the C&AG can take his decision whether to report or not. If he does decide to report he gives the departmental accounting officer concerned an opportunity to comment on the report whose accuracy as to fact is thereafter seldom challenged.

The method of the PAC's own examination is also of special significance. Again, by long tradition, when they decide to take evidence on matters raised in the C&AG's reports they summon the accounting officer, who is not a finance officer, however senior, but the permanent secretary or other official in charge of the whole department. He may be and usually is supported by senior colleagues, but he is the official witness. The duty of answering to the PAC for the regular and economical administration of his department is a duty which is taken very seriously. Though arduous and sometimes gruelling, the Committee's examination of these senior witnesses sets out to be fair and constructive. The Committee makes its own report to the House on the basis of its examination of the accounting officer and any other witnesses outside his department it may decide to call. It includes criticisms if thought justified, and any necessary recommendations for change or improvements. It may even, on rare occasions, commend good performance.

The next step is for the department to consider the Committee's report and to prepare a reply. It is unusual for the Committee's recommendations to be rejected, but by no means unheard of. The replies of all departments on whose activities the PAC has reported are agreed with the Treasury, and submitted as a Treasury minute to the House of Commons. This is in effect the response of the government to the PAC. A debate is arranged on the PAC's reports, and in the succeeding session of Parliament it is normal for the accounting officers to be examined further on any points in the Treasury minute on which the PAC remains unsatisfied.

This is an effective and well tried system of accountability. The C&AG works closely with the PAC, though without being subject to their directions, and they with him. The Treasury is always represented at PAC hearings, and though they themselves are sometimes in the dock as well as the witness box their officials also seek to cooperate as far as possible with the Committee. The effect of the system is not confined to the particular matters on which the C&AG reports. The probability that any serious failure of financial control or inefficiency in administration will lead to a report by the C&AG and to a PAC investigation exercises a sharpening effect throughout departmental hierarchies.

Proposals for change

The current system of public audit described above has emerged in the last few years as a result of very rapid change. So far as the E&AD/NAO was concerned the initiative for this came largely from within, but there was also an upsurge of Parliamentary interest in the public audit, and no less than three select committees of Parliament enquired into it and made recommendations for change: the former Expenditure Committee, the Procedure Committee, and the PAC itself. The PAC's review of the role of the C&AG in the 1980–81 session of Parliament was the first of its kind since the C&AG and his department had been established well over a century ago. It was itself preceded by the government's decision, stimulated by the increased Parliamentary interest in matters of financial control and accountability, and perhaps by the C&AG's own views, to review the C&AG's role.

In 1980 the government issued a consultative Green Paper. It summarized the C&AG's existing role, supported his development of a systems-based financial and regularity audit, encouraged him to extend his value for money work while stopping short of involvement in the merits of particular policy objectives, but it provisionally opposed any significant extension of the range of his activities to cover other parts of the public sector, as had been suggested by the C&AG himself and generally supported by the other select committees.

Criticism of the existing audit system had concentrated on these points:

(a) Compared with other advanced national audit offices, E&AD did too much financial and regularity audit and not enough efficiency and effectiveness audit;

(b) The C&AG and the PAC examined past transactions instead of considering current policy options;

(c) The C&AG and his staff should be officers of Parliament, subject to directions from the House of Commons;

(d) The range of the C&AG's rights of access needed to be extended so that he could examine the use of public funds by all bodies receiving them, and should include access to books and records of the nationalized industries and other public corporations;

(e) The C&AG needed to take over responsibility for the local authority audit service in order to improve accountability to Parliament in respect of the very large central government subventions to local authorities through the rate support and other grants.

These criticisms and suggestions are fully explored in the government's Green Paper (Cmnd. 7845, March 1980), the PAC's first special report in session 1980–81 on the role of the C&AG (HC 115–1), and the government's response to that report giving their conclusions (Cmnd. 8323). A considerable volume of evidence, both written and oral, was given to the

PAC by several interested bodies and persons, and published by the PAC in their report. A guide to these reports and evidence is included in the bibliography for this chapter. They provide, for the first time in over 100 years, a source of authoritative material and argument on the subject of the National Audit Office. A summary of the main issues follows.

Complaint (a) that the C&AG's work was largely restricted to financial and regularity audit was misconceived. He, the government and the PAC continued to put much importance on the need for a sound financial and regularity audit supporting his certification of government accounts; but the criticism appeared to ignore the large volume and wide scope of his reports directed to value for money matters, extending over several past decades.

There is not much more substance to the 'stable door' criticism (b).It is of the essence of an audit that it investigates what has happened or is happening, and seeks to draw useful conclusions and recommendations for change from past experience, and no doubt in many cases past mistakes. In this sense it is concerned with the working out of existing decisions or policies, particularly their financial and economic consequences. It is not primarily concerned with suggesting alternatives, though in some cases this may be a clear implication of audit findings. In short, from an audit of past and present practice one hopes to secure future improvement.

The proposal that the C&AG and his staff should be House of Commons staff, subject to Parliamentary direction, was rejected. Its constitutional attraction was apparent, since the C&AG reports to Parliament and works in many ways 'on their behalf'. It was opposed by the C&AG and the professional accountancy institutions, and was turned down by the government. The main argument was that the C&AG should have full independence, within his statutory remit, to decide on his own enquiries and dispose his resources as he thought best. The C&AG stressed in his evidence that in so doing the wishes and suggestions of the PAC would be given full weight, and this has now been reflected in the 1983 Act.

The view that the national auditor should have powers to follow public money – or as the Procedure Committee more narrowly defined it, 'money provided by Parliament' – wherever it went, also has constitutional appeal. Money voted by Parliament finds its way through many different types of grant and assistance to individuals and companies. It had to be asked how practicable and acceptable it would have been to expect the audit staff to have rights of access to all their books and records. The issue has been resolved in the 1983 Act as described above.

The arguments for and against giving the C&AG access to the books and records of some or all of the nationalized industries and public corporations so that he could report on their operations are fully discussed in the evidence submitted to the PAC in the course of their review. The essential arguments in favour were:

(a) The industries' assets are acquired from public funds or on Exchequer credit and many of them have a monopolistic position conferred by Parliament;
(b) Examinations and reports by the C&AG would fill an important gap in the accountability of the industries;
(c) They would be a check on and stimulate their efficiency.

The arguments against were:

(a) The industries already operate under statutory provisions, report to Parliament and the public through their annual reports and accounts, and readily respond to requests to give written or oral evidence to select committees of Parliament;
(b) The responsible ministers have certain statutory powers of control, most significantly in relation to investment programmes, and have in practice influenced other policies, particularly on prices and major plant closures. Ministers have to answer for these actions to Parliament;
(c) The government had indicated that it proposed to extend the use of enquiries by the Monopolies and Mergers Commission to provide an external check on efficiency, so that a further incursion by the C&AG was unnecessary. (This was subsequently carried out in the Competition Act 1980);
(d) The need to justify decisions to the C&AG's staff would inhibit speed and enterprise in decision-taking, responding to external audit enquiries would be expensive in staff time and money, and there would be difficulties about the confidentiality of some information, particularly where commercial partners were involved.

The sponsor departments added:

(e) That if the C&AG were to be given access to the records of the industries with a view to reporting on value-for-money matters, the responsible departments would also need to seek more information to establish satisfactorily their own positions.

The C&AG argued that (a) and (b) did not adequately meet the point about a gap in accountability. There was in his view no effective substitute, from this point of view, for free access by his staff and his right to report to Parliament, independently of both ministers and the industries, as he saw fit. As regards (c) the Monopolies and Mergers Commission had no such independent role; they would operate in this field only when so instructed by the government. On (d) the E&AD had long experience of handling confidential matters; and a body subject to his audit should continue to take whatever decisions they thought right – they did not have to be justified to him.

The PAC reported in favour of giving the C&AG this extended remit. The government disagreed. In the debate on the National Audit Bill the advocates of change failed to carry the day, so that the nationalized industries and the local authorities remained outside the C&AG's purview.

It may in consequence be suggested that the 1983 Act was of limited significance. So far as the scope of the C&AG's audit within the public sector is concerned, this is true. But the Act gave statutory recognition to important changes in the approach and standing of the C&AG and his office. His complete independence of any constraint, actual or potential, by the executive government was assured by the substitution of direct Parliamentary controls on his budget for those of the Treasury. His establishment as an officer of Parliament, and the provision giving Parliament, through the chairman of the PAC, a statutory voice in his appointment neatly recognized his close relationship with Parliament without subordinating to MPs his judgement in discharging his statutory duties and the use of his resources. His long standing commitment to value-for-money audit as a major part of his activities was endorsed and the 3 Es given statutory status. Moreover, as explained below, he had already, in the Local Government Finance Act 1982, been given a role in the examination of relationships between central and local government, and certain rights in relation to the Audit Commission for Local Authorities to assist him to discharge it. The change of name, from Exchequer and Audit Department, with its undertones of Treasury connection, to National Audit Office was more than symbolic of the ending of a long historical phase. It expressed a new outlook and a new approach.

AUDIT OF LOCAL AUTHORITIES

England and Wales

For 140 years, the external audit of local authorities was undertaken primarily by the District Audit Service, succeeded in 1983 by the Audit Commission for Local Authorities in England and Wales.

The district audit system dated from the Poor Law Amendment Act of 1844, which created the office of district auditor to examine the accounts of the local bodies that administered poor law relief. During the succeeding half century, the duties of district auditors were gradually extended to cover the accounts of highway, public health and education bodies, as local administration itself was expanded under Acts of Parliament into these wider fields. By the end of the century, the accounts of most of the local authorities in England and Wales were audited by district auditors.

District auditors were independent statutory officers who took in-dependent personal authority for the audit of the accounts of all the local authorities in their district. In addition to the normal duties of auditors, they had quasi judicial powers to deal with illegality and losses caused by fraud and other wilful misconduct. On these matters, they were answerable to the courts. But while district auditors and their staff were formally civil servants, by reason of their statutory office and long tradition they were not subject to control or direction by the minister in the execution of their duties. Staff numbers apart, which was a subject of contention, they were treated as an independent professional service.

In addition to the district auditors themselves, the service also included the important post of Chief Inspector of Audit, with a small central staff reporting directly to him. Since district auditors had full personal and professional responsibility for their audit work, the Chief Inspector had no power to direct them. But his responsibility to ensure that proper standards were being maintained gave him considerable influence as the *de facto* head of the service.

Prior to 1974, the accounts of most local authorities were compulsorily subject to audit by the district auditor. But for boroughs and county boroughs, this was the position for only some of their accounts. For the remainder, they could choose either the district auditor or a professional accounting firm. From 1 April 1974, when provincial local government reorganization took effect, all the new local authorities were given the right to choose their auditors; they could have either the district auditor or an 'approved auditor', i.e. a firm whose appointment had to be approved by the Secretary of State. In practice, most authorities, about 90%, chose the district auditor at that time. There were some differences in powers between district auditors and firms. In particular, the illegality and wilful misconduct powers were reserved to district audit. But otherwise the emphasis was on achieving common standards, working to the same code of audit practice, and reimbursement through the same scale of audit fees charged to the local authorities.

In the later 1970s, central government, in particular the Treasury, were taking an increased interest in the audit and accountability of local authorities as one aspect of central/local government financial relations and the drive for greater efficiency and cost consciousness in public bodies. In 1976, the Layfield Committee on Local Government Finance (Report, Cmnd. 6453) recommended the appointment of 'an independent official with a similar status to that of the Comptroller and Auditor General' to head an expanded and strengthened local audit service, whose functions would include:

(a) The assignment of auditors to each authority, who would no longer have any choice in the matter;
(b) The making of regular reports on 'issues of general interest or public concern', which should be made available to the public.

The Committee also recommended the establishment of a 'higher institution' to which the head of audit's reports would be submitted:

either a Parliamentary committee with terms of reference similar to those of the Public Accounts Committee, or a body with representation drawn largely from local government. While this particular concept was challenged as constitutionally faulty, the Committee's analysis of the need to strengthen local authority audit was sound. But the proposals were not immediately followed up. Instead, the Secretary of State for the Environment set up an Advisory Committee on Local Government Audit (in England and Wales), headed by an independent chairman and including other independent members as well as experienced councillors and the C&AG. The committee, which was advised by the Chief Inspector, was intended to give greater weight to the work of the local government audit service and to propose ways in which it could be usefully developed.

At the same time, the C&AG had himself been considering the local authority audit arrangements in relation to his own responsibilities and future role. He put forward a proposal to merge the E&AD and the local government audit service, arguing that:

(a) The nature and objectives of the work of the two services were basically similar;

(b) Local government provides important services, such as education, housing and personal social services, under statutory arrangements and guidance from central government, and for which the taxpayer provides over half the funds;

(c) Parliament therefore has a major interest in the arrangements whereby central government departments influence and, to some extent, control these expenditures;

(d) Bringing together the two audit services under one head would be the best way of achieving an integrated examination of the provision and control of services, respecting the right of individual local authorities to remain free of accountability to Parliament.

In opposition to those views, the local authority associations and other local authority interests argued that the proposal would lead to an unjustified and unconstitutional incursion of central government and Parliament into the affairs of local authorities, who were solely responsible to their own electors.

After some two years of debate, the government decided 'that the interests of all parties concerned, including local electorates, will best be served by the establishment of an Audit Commission for Local Authorities in England and Wales' (Cmnd. 8323, paragraph 16). They attached particular importance to the value for money content of local authority audit, and agreed that it was desirable for cooperation on technical matters to be developed between the District Audit Service and the Exchequer and Audit Department (now the National Audit Office).

The establishment of the new Audit Commission was provided for in the Local Government Finance Act 1982. Its provisions cover the following main points:

(a) Members of the Commission are appointed by the Secretary of State, who has power to give the Commission directions, but not directions relating to particular audits;

(b) The Commissioners appoint their own staff subject only to approval by the Secretary of State of the appointment of the Commission's chief officer, the Controller of Audit;

(c) The Commissioners appoint auditors to local authorities, either from their own staff or from professionally qualified firms;

(d) The Commission prescribes scales of fees for audits;

(e) The Commission is required to produce an audit code of practice, embodying what appears to them to be the best professional practice with respect to standards, procedures and techniques. This code requires Parliamentary approval every five years;

(f) Auditors have comparable responsibilities as formerly with regard to financial and regularity audit and as to illegality or wilful misconduct, and in addition must give an opinion on the accounts;

(g) Auditors are required to satisfy themselves that proper arrangements are being made by the audited body 'for securing economy, efficiency and effectiveness in its use of resources';

(h) Auditors are required to consider whether there is any matter which, in the public interest, should be reported to the body concerned so that it may be considered by the body, or brought to the attention of the public;

(i) 'Any person interested' may inspect the accounts and related documents, and a local government elector may question the auditor or object in respect of matters of illegality, wilful misconduct, or failure to secure value for money.

In addition, the Commission was given important new duties to carry out studies of local government activities and to publish reports on how local authorities might secure improved economy, efficiency and effectiveness in the provision of services. A further duty requires the Commission to carry out other studies (Section 27 studies) into the effects on local government of the actions of central government, through legislation or ministerial directions. These studies at the interface of central and local government are an obvious area for cooperation with the NAO. Copies of these Section 27 reports are required to be sent to the C&AG, who in turn is required to report to the House of Commons on any matter arising out of the Commission's studies which he considers ought to be drawn to the attention of that House. For this purpose, the C&AG may require the Commission to provide him with any information obtained in the preparation of the report, other than information in respect of any particular authority.

The main aims of these important statutory changes in audit arrangements for local authorities were to increase the weight and effectiveness of the audit, particularly in the pursuit of value for money, to establish its independence of the government more clearly, and to involve private auditing firms in the work to a substantially greater extent. The power of the Secretary of State to give the Commission directives may be thought to conflict with its independence. It is justified by the government on the grounds that Parliament, which provides substantial funds to local authorities and regulates their activities, would expect the government to have such a power in reserve. In practice, no directions have been issued in the first five years of the Commission.

The Commission started operations in April 1983. Its first Chairman was an experienced businessman and among its other 15 members were senior local councillors and former officers and independent businessmen and academics; that balance of membership has been maintained. Its staff was recruited from the District Audit Service, other public bodies and the private sector. The first Controller and his successor were both experienced management consultants and had worked in the public sector.

This new body, launched at a time of exceptional tension between central government and local authorities in constitutional, political and financial relationships, faced three main tasks:

(a) To establish itself as competent, fair and forceful, and independent of both central and local government;
(b) To create an effective and unified approach to wide-ranging audit operations in a large number of disparate authorities;
(c) To establish cooperation between its own operational staff and the substantially increased numbers of commercial accountants who had entered an unfamiliar field.

This was a formidable programme. Immediately, the Commission had to appoint auditors for the 456 major authorities. In the first year, 70% of the audits were awarded to the directly employed District Audit Service and 30% to major commercial firms, a proportionate distribution which left the private sector somewhat short of the share which the government had envisaged but which was a matter for the Commission's judgement. The Commission has announced that any changes in the proportionate allocation of audits should be based on performance.

The Commission also set out to establish both a professional and philosophical framework within which its audits would be directed and supervised. Elements in this framework were country-wide comparative analyses of local authority functions, staffing patterns and expenditure programmes, suggested principles of organization, accountability and motivation of staff, and comprehensive guides for the conduct of both the regularity audit and value for money studies.

In producing and disseminating this substantial collection of material, the Commission was at pains to stress its intentions to help local authorities to help themselves, to improve their use of resources and to disprove the view that it had been established as an instrument of central government to help curb and cut local expenditure. It was not their role to determine local government policy, nor to set spending levels or service priorities. But it could consider the consequences of policies being pursued by authorities and comment on their financial and other effects.

The Code of Local Government Audit Practice, prepared following consultation with the local authority associations and the professional accountancy bodies and approved by Parliament, sets out in some detail how the audit is to be conducted. Within these guidelines, the auditor is expected to do his job independently of both the Commission and the local authority. The Code covers both the regularity audit and the value-for-money work or 3Es audit. It remains a primary objective to check that public money is spent only as authorized by law, to expose improper or fraudulent practices and to ensure that the financial statements give an accurate and complete picture of an authority's expenditure, revenue and financial position. In these respects, the auditor is required to apply best professional practice in terms of standards, procedures and techniques.

The importance of sound financial accounting systems for efficiency, clarity and public accountability should not be underrated. Linked, as they should be, with the production of financial management information for councillors and staff, they provide an essential basis for policy decisions, monitoring of service operations and day-to-day control. But emphasis has increasingly been laid on the adequacy of council management structures, the machinery for taking and implementing policy decisions, and the effective use by local authorities of the very large sums of public money and skilled manpower for which they are responsible – in other words, on value for money in its widest definition.

For many years, a value-for-money audit had been applied to the affairs of local authorities, though its extent had been limited by the available staff resources. The Commission has vigorously developed this work through central studies using teams drawn from consultancy experts and the particular specialism under investigation as well as auditors. Many areas of local government activity have been examined; and reports have been published on further and secondary education, care of the elderly and mentally handicapped, housing, highways, property management, vehicle fleet management and maintenance, refuse collection, energy conservation, purchasing, cash flow management, rent arrears, and other topics. In addition, the Commission has published reports of Section 27 studies into the grant distribution system, capital controls and community care.

In developing this work, the Commission has linked the study processes with the auditor's value-for-money responsibilities. As well as the reports, the studies generate audit guides which, after training, the auditors use in examining the various activities at individual local authorities. This linkage has proved to be highly effective. Auditors are enabled to identify issues for local consideration and these are taken up with the individual local authorities. The Commission has reported that at March 1988 authorities have implemented recommendations giving better value for money to the extent of over £200 million a year.

The Commission has also sought to assist authorities and auditors by the development of statistical profiles of each authority. These analyse the comparative statistics in ways which highlight differences and so identify areas for detailed examination. Further work has been done on the identification of issues and yardsticks for use in the performance review functions for each local authority service. Recognizing the importance of overall management, work has been carried out in this area too, and guides and training provided to auditors to assist them in discharging their remit of satisfying themselves that authorities have made proper arrangements for securing value for money in use of resources.

The broad ambit of the local government audit service is thus nowadays similar to that of the National Audit Office, though the structure of local authority accounts and the system of reporting show important differences from those applicable to central government. Five points require specific mention.

(a) The right of members of the public, as local government electors, to inspect, question and object to the accounts and to inspect the auditor's report. Any objection is heard by the auditor and if he upholds it, he may take action as in (b) and (c) below. There are no such rights in respect of the accounts of central government;

(b) If it appears to the auditor that any item of account is contrary to law, he may apply to the court for a declaration accordingly, except where the item is sanctioned by the Secretary of State. If the court makes that declaration, it may order any person, councillor or official, who is responsible for incurring or authorizing the unlawful expenditure, to repay it in whole or in part. Where the amount exceeds £2,000 and the person responsible is a councillor, there is provision for the court to disqualify him from local government office.

(c) Where money has not been brought to account or loss has been incurred through wilful misconduct, the auditor must certify the amount as being due from that person and, subject to right of appeal to the courts by the person(s) affected by the auditor's certificate, the amount then becomes recoverable. Disqualification from membership again ensues in the case of a wilful misconduct certificate where the amount involved is over £2,000 and the person involved is a member;

(d) A local elector may make an objection on any matter about which he considers the auditor should make a report in the public interest. In these cases, the final decision is taken by the auditor, as he is the only arbiter of whether or not such a report should be made;

(e) Local government auditors have recently been given powers of early intervention where a local authority has taken a decision which would involve unlawful expenditure or a course of conduct which would lead to unlawful loss. The Local Government Act 1988 enables the auditor to issue a prohibition order which, subject to a right of appeal to the courts, precludes an authority from implementing such a decision. The Act also empowers the auditor to apply to the courts for judicial review of an authority's decision. The purpose of these additional powers is to enable auditors to take early action on issues which could be substantial, either in amount or principle, rather than have them dealt with after the event by action as in (b) or (c) above.

The Audit Commission has set out to combine strong 'top-down' direction and assistance for its auditors with a recognition of their full independence in forming their opinions and framing their reports. It has adopted a much more public style than the District Audit Service, which like the former Exchequer and Audit Department operated in a low key with the minimum of publicity. It has sought to involve the local authorities in its broad objectives and has largely overcome the initial suspicion of local authorities about its creation and, particularly, about value-for-money studies. It is a safe prediction that an extended 3Es audit of publicly accountable non-commercial bodies is here to stay.

Scotland

Prior to the Local Government (Scotland) Act 1973, which reorganized the pattern of Scottish local government, Scottish local councils and associated public bodies were audited individually by private accounting firms, appointed by the Secretary of State. The 1973 Act provided for the creation of an independent Commission for Local Authority Accounts in Scotland, consisting of not more than 12 or less than 9 members, appointed by the Secretary of State for Scotland after consultation with local authority associations and other appropriate organizations.

The Commission's main duties are:

(a) To secure the audit of the local authority accounts by appointing 'such officers and agents as they may determine to carry out the audits';
(b) To consider all audit reports and to investigate all matters raised therein;
(c) To make recommendations accordingly to the Secretary of State;
(d) To advise the Secretary of State on any matter relating to the

accounting of local authorities which he may refer to them for advice;

(e) To appoint a Controller of Audit.

Recently, again in the Local Government Act 1988, the Commission and the auditors have been given statutory value-for-money responsibilities. These are similar to the responsibilities of the Audit Commission for England and Wales except that there is no provision for studies at the interface of central and local government.

The Controller of Audit, who is responsible for coordinating, guiding and supervising the conduct of the audit, has statutory status and specific functions. He is **required** to make to the Commission such reports as they may require with respect to local authority accounts. He **may** make a report to the Commission on any matters arising out of the accounts so that they may be considered by the local authority or brought to the attention of the public. And he is **required** to report to the Commission on various types of illegal or improper accounting, or loss caused by negligence or misconduct.

The other main feature of the Scottish local audit arrangements was the appointment by the Commission, on the advice of the Controller, of their own permanent audit staff who now share with private accounting firms responsibility for the individual audits, in the proportion of about 60% private to 40% permanent staff. In this respect, therefore, the arrangements for local authority audit in Scotland are now similar to those in England and Wales, although they have developed by different routes. But the Controller of Audit has a more independent position in Scotland, standing, as it were, between the individual auditors and the Commission rather than acting simply as the Commission's chief executive. The difference finds expression in the form of the Scottish Commission's annual report, which is divided into a report by the Commission and a report by the Controller. All individual audit reports, whether they take the form of formal qualification, a report to members or a report to officers, have to be copied to the Controller who himself then decides whether to report to the Commission.

Summary

This chapter has explained the nature, purposes and methods of the external audit of the various parts of the public sector. It has described the constitution and responsibilities of the Comptroller and Auditor General and the National Audit Office, the Audit Commission and the Scottish Accounts Commission, and the way in which the first, but not the other two, work closely with the Public Accounts Committee of Parliament. It has stressed the important part which is played by '3 Es' audit – economy, efficiency and effectiveness – in the public sector in addition to the financial audit, thus differentiating the public from the private sector in this respect.

Further reading

There are few books on the audit of either central or local government. There is, however, an extensive range of reports by the C&AG and the Public Accounts Committee, covering many subjects and illustrating the way the National Audit Office discharges its remit. The NAO (Buckingham Palace Road, London, SW1W 9SP) would recommend particular reports, to illustrate general or specific interests.

During 1980–81 an extensive and authoritative discussion on the role of the C&AG and related topics, covering central government, local authorities and nationalized industries, took place. This began with the issue of a government Green Paper, *The Role of the Comptroller and Auditor General* (Cmnd. 7845) in March 1980 and led to a major report by the PAC in February 1981, *First Special Report from the Committee of Public Accounts, Session 1980–81*. The government's response to this report was published in July 1981 (Cmnd. 8323).

On local government audit the Local Government Finance Act 1982 and the Audit Commission Code of Practice (HMSO) give the statutory framework. The Audit Commission issues an *Annual Report and Accounts* (HMSO) and like the NAO has produced a wide range of reports on specific subjects. A detailed list is available from the Commission (1 Vincent Square, London SW1P 2PN).

Chapter 10

An overview

This book is neither a primer on bookkeeping for the public sector nor a detailed treatise containing all the statutory and other professional requirements expected of financial officers in any particular branch of the public sector. The former is dealt with in other books with a different kind of purpose, the latter is beyond the capability of any single book. The aim here is to stimulate a greater interchange of ideas and skills, not only among current practitioners in the public sector but also among the students who will be their heirs.

The non-commercial part of the public sector used to be an island – indeed a group of separate islands – of distinctive financial and accounting practice. To some extent that has been changing. But there remains a need for the development of more effective dialogue between the public and private sectors in this field. Both sectors have much to learn from each other. Increasing job mobility for financial managers, for example into the NHS from local authorities, nationalized industries or the private sector and vice versa, is helping this process.

This final chapter steps aside from the discussion of financial practice in the individual branches of the public sector discussed earlier, and seeks to deal with some matters of general relevance.

Financial control

Many of the issues in the field of financial control are common to all types of organization, public or private, profit-seeking or charitable, those producing, transporting or retailing goods, providing personal services or promoting sport or the arts. Such issues include the matching of expenditure and revenue over an appropriate time span, deciding on objectives and priorities, establishing information and control systems, and monitoring results.

In the remaining nationalized industries the techniques of control are essentially the same as those applied in private industry, though sometimes interventions by the government have introduced non-commercial factors and complicated the process. Output is conditioned by demand in the contemporary market and pricing situation. In contrast, in parts of the non-commercial public sector, demand for services, if not unlimited, is not for the most part constrained by people having to pay for what they use or consume. The professionals in charge, and the ministers ultimately answerable to Parliament and the public, are naturally prone to believe that the resources allocated to them by the mechanisms described earlier are in varying degree inadequate to meet 'needs', or even to discharge the broad statutory objectives governing their activities. In a commercial organization a manager may be given a specific workload to complete and be expected to do so at minimum cost. This can also apply in the provision of the more routine of public services, but in other cases the idea of providing anything less than the best possible level of services is unattractive. It is presumed that cost minimization conflicts with this goal. But it is more difficult to monitor and control the best possible level of services for a given expenditure than it is to monitor and control the minimization of cost for the completion of an assigned volume of tasks. The use of performance indicators and other techniques to promote the best use of available resources, though greatly extended in recent years and applied with increasing sensitivity, has yet to attain full acceptance. Some public services, particularly in the NHS and local authority sectors, have traditionally been dominated by the professional rather than the managerial ethos – a problem also responsible for some notable failures in the business world – with the presumption that only some form of peer review, if that, can provide an appropriate evaluation of performance.

These attitudes were fostered during a long period of sustained growth in the public services in the post-war period. With pressure on public spending it is now widely accepted that efficiency must be improved to maintain existing services, and to provide resources to develop new services of high priority. Thus the problem for the budgetary control process is not only that of containing expenditure within prescribed limits, but of finding activities of low benefit relative to cost on which savings can be made and diverted to activities with high benefit relative to cost. All this involves difficult judgements, and finance staffs on their own clearly cannot achieve it. Rather their task is to help create a climate of opinion favouring efficiency and the continuing attempt to maximize the benefit achieved from a given input of resources. They must also supply relevant and timely information on costs and resource uses to assist the identification of opportunities for efficiency improvements and for savings. Finally, it may be necessary to build incentives into the system, so that managers who take action to improve efficiency or make savings can obtain recognition or indeed the opportunity to use some part of the savings they have achieved on other activities under their control. This may require a change of attitude all round, with finance staff pressing for close personal interaction with other managers and professions to help maximize their contribution to the organization.

In central government operations the problem is less that of welding professional and financial managers into a cohesive team than of giving those in charge sufficient delegated authority, within a 'framework of policy', to match their personal responsibilities for the efficient delivery of services. This requires a greater flexibility in their use of staff and other resources, and in matters of grading and organization, than is traditionally associated with Civil Service methods. The budgetary system must be adapted accordingly.

Measures of performance

Measuring the resources put into a non-profit making public sector organization is easier than measuring how effectively those resources are used. Attention has been increasingly given across the whole of the public sector to the provision of non-financial performance indicators to assess how well an organization has performed, and whether the trends are going the right way. For nationalized industries, these measures have been additional to the financial control framework since 1978. For local authorities and health authorities, a mass of indicators is available to enable comparisons to be made across the country. In central government, performance indicators now feature in all the main published documents. Persistent examination of the objectives of public service programmes and more refined analysis of what they produce is showing that an assessment of effectiveness is not exclusively dependent on the availability of markets.

Performance indicators are undoubtedly a useful addition to the methodology of control. But they need to be used with caution. The outcome of an examination of their validity is no longer, as Mr Enoch Powell, then Minister of Health, concluded in a Parliamentary debate many years ago 'a lemon'; but they must be closely analysed in relation to the operations they are intended to illuminate, and their use as comparators for individual authorities, or through time, must allow for the effects of extraneous factors which may influence performance. For example, numbers of patients treated per day is not necessarily a good indication of the quality of health care, or a reduction in the number of social workers per head of population an indication of improved productivity. If an increase in productivity can only be achieved at the cost of a reduction in quality, the trade-off between the conflicting objectives must be established and agreed. Professionals and administrators should be jointly involved in devising and using the indicators, to make them credible and to promote their acceptability within the service.

Accounting principles and practices

The private sector has relatively homogeneous objectives and a common statutory framework of accountability. Thus there can be generally accepted accounting principles which cover most aspects of individual organizations' accounts, however great their variety. But in the four main branches of the public sector – central government, the NHS, local government and the public corporations – there is great diversity of operational objectives, organizational structure and financial management. This is necessarily reflected in their accounting and reporting systems. Uniformity, either within the public sector or between the public and private sectors, is not therefore to be expected. No accounting principle or system has any inherent validity. It derives its value from its contribution to the efficient performance and presentation of the activities to which it relates. That is not to question the need for the distillation of accounting principles of wide application in business or elsewhere and for them to be actively promulgated by the professional bodies or other authorities. Nor is it suggested that the public sector need pay no attention to them, still less that its own systems are incapable of improvement.

The nature of the various accounting systems in the public sector has been explained in preceding chapters. Some salient points which have emerged in recent discussions are worth noting.

The nationalized industries, and other public corporations which operate in the market, can be quickly disposed of in this context. With important qualifications deriving from public policy and their statutory positions their accounting and reporting systems are fully commercial in nature, they are all audited by private accounting firms and they willingly subscribe to professional standards and guidelines. The same applies (apart from audit) to government operations with a substantial commercial element constituted as trading funds, or if not formally so constituted, of a similar character.

No such conformity or set of standards applies to the other components of the public sector. Central government has not adopted the accounting principles and practices prescribed by the accountancy profession, at least in its external reporting. Its formal financial accounts have been developed over 100 years and more, primarily to give parliamentary and public assurance that public money has been allocated and spent as intended, and with probity. The cash basis of appropriation accounts serves these purposes well, though it has been argued earlier that it also has wider justification. Whether these arguments are accepted or not, there are two respects in which central government accounting practice, by general agreement, has needed marked improvement:

(a) Greater clarity in the structure of the appropriation and related accounts;
(b) Much more extensive development and use of management information systems.

Considerable movement is now apparent in respect of (a) above. The structure of both the Supply Estimates, which are necessarily long and detailed, and the more concise Appropriation Accounts is increasingly based upon the specific functions for which departments are responsible, and it is being progressively assimilated with other forms of public expenditure and financial reporting, particularly the Public Expenditure White Paper, now itself in course of evolutionary reincarnation. But more remains to be done. For more informative reports and assessments of achievement, the purely financial reports, in whatever format, need extensive supplementation as already described.

The point at (b) above is primarily directed to internal departmental planning and control. It is accepted that the formal annual accounts should, as far as practicable, link with departmental organization and responsibilities. But civil servants as line managers cannot work successfully without a properly devised system of management accounting and control which provides information on which decisions can be taken, in far more detail and much more promptly, than on the basis of the annual accounts. The financial management initiative (FMI) is in part directed towards this requirement, and here there is considerable scope for the contribution of professional accountants. The most effective accounting and control arrangements for internal use may combine elements from both commercial and non-commercial systems. A cash system can be converted, if it serves a useful purpose to do so, to a partial accrual system, to give a more accurate idea of 'true' costs or expenditure during a given period and an estimate of future liabilities, without necessarily bringing in depreciation of capital assets, e.g. office buildings. The way in which separate activities are differentiated for budgetary purposes, or overhead and other costs are attributed to individual services under the control of one undersecretary, are examples of the kind of analysis where the skills and experience of professional accountants are likely to make an impact. There are many more possible developments in the field of management information, at whatever level of information technology the problems are being addressed. It is in these areas, whose significance has only in recent years been adequately recognized, that Whitehall has previously failed to apply sufficient professional accounting expertise. In the broader field of public expenditure control, in its macroeconomic and financial context, financial administrators with wide experience of government operations and finance should be well equipped to take decisions and provide ministers with the necessary advice. The wide ranging reforms of the Exchequer and Audit Department/National Audit Office over the last 10 years or so, affecting all aspects of the structure and work of that specialized professional body, were initiated and carried through by C&AGs with that background, and the process is continuing.

External reporting

Improving the basis of accounting is one element in improving public sector external financial reporting, but not the only one. Within the public sector there have been criticisms both of the form and content of external reports and also of the systems by which they are generated and used. This topic runs deep into the whole question of accountability in the public sector.

Accountability is of course the basis on which public sector external reports are produced. Yet there are a number of uncertainties and ambiguities after the need for accountability has been established. For example, external reports are certainly used as public relations documents throughout the public sector. This is entirely understandable bearing in mind that public sector bodies are bound to be involved in lobbying for resources and for policies, and that an external financial report is a useful vehicle for such activity. But there must then be an implicit conflict between the idea that a document is designed to give an account of stewardship of public funds and the idea that it is a vehicle for political pressure. This does not mean that there is cheating on the figures themselves, but it is likely that the dual roles will give rise to a conflict about the way the facts are presented and interpreted. Such a conflict is not peculiar to the public sector.

Public sector external reports are also often used for reference purposes, as a means of communicating to staff and, in the case of central government, some of the documents are even used as the basis of internal control. But there is a problem throughout the public sector in deciding who exactly the potential readers are and what they require. The constitutional position of elected bodies is usually clear enough, but the fact is that many elected members of such bodies, including many members of Parliament, are not financially trained. A further conflict therefore often arises in external reporting about the level at which external reports should be pitched. On the one hand there are some elected representatives who are highly trained financially and expert in the field. On the other there are those (usually the majority) who are interested laymen and women without financial knowledge. The problem of addressing both audiences is solved in some cases by providing more than one document, in others by providing information aimed at different types of reader in the same document. But often both sets of readers are left unsatisfied because the same document is aimed at the wrong level for each audience. A further difficulty in resolving this problem is that there is usually no easy way of finding what users want and how their information needs can best be met.

Taking various parts of the public sector in turn, there are those who have said that local government suffers from a surfeit of accountability. Certainly the multiplicity of documents provides a benchmark against which other parts of the public sector can be compared. First there are the **Financial Accounts**, which are more often now prepared in line with generally accepted accounting principles and standards. Then there is the mandatory, increasingly comprehensible and in some cases first-class **Annual Report**, which includes performance indicators. Then there is the **Ratepayers' Leaflet**, published before the financial year, which gives key aspects of the budget. During the course of the year, reports on the progress of local authority spending are typically presented in open committee. Finally, before the audit is completed, 'interested persons' may inspect the detailed accounts and put questions to the auditor.

The National Health Service is organizationally similar in one main respect to local authorities in that it has a large number of diverse units, each with a specific controlling body (the health authority) which has a measure of discretion as to how its allocated resources for capital and current expenditure are to be applied. There are also major differences. The NHS is operationally unified and responsible to the Secretary of State, and unlike local authorities it has no significant autonomous source of finance. But there are sufficient similarities to ask whether there is a practical reason (other than administrative effort) why each health authority should not be required to publish comprehensible financial accounts and an Annual Report of the kind that a growing number of authorities already produce voluntarily.

The position of central government ought to be much simpler, since Parliament is the main 'customer' for the financial information, with the Press, pressure groups and other interested parties interpreting the information for the general public. Yet although the sheer volume of information is impressive, the users have made it clear that they do not feel well served and the reports need to be much clearer to achieve the objectives of financial reporting. This could be provided in a readable and interesting way, with no loss of accuracy but a great gain in comprehensibility and therefore public appeal.

Finally the position of the nationalized industries is probably the simplest of all the public sector bodies. This is because both the industries and the government have been keen for many years to try and ensure that the industries are as close as possible to private sector practice. Their annual reports are generally of high quality by the standards of either the public or the private sectors and in most cases much more informative. Yet they too suffer from the ambiguities discussed at the beginning of this section.

Audit

The professional skills and techniques of the auditor of financial statements and accounts are broadly similar and transferable between the public and private sectors, and between profit-making and non-profit organizations. Many non-commercial public sector bodies, including the universities, an increasing proportion of local authorities and several health authorities are now audited by private sector firms. But there are also important differences. For profit-making organizations the dominant objectives of the audit must be to validate the fairness of the profit figure, and the truth and fairness of the valuations in the balance sheet. This assists owners and lenders, as well as their professional advisers, to assess the value, prospects and risk of their debt or investment. But the non-trading parts of the public sector do not use their assets to produce goods or services for sale, and do not therefore generate profits from their activities. Instead, typically, they expend all their allocated funds on providing services. It is a reasonable concern of Parliament and the public that public expenditure should be made only for duly authorized purposes and should conform to high standards of probity. It follows that public audit must pay careful attention to those requirements.

Beyond this, however, there is growing parliamentary and public concern to make the best use of resources which are scarce in relation to needs by improving efficiency or productivity. In recent years this has provided increased emphasis on the value for money dimension of public sector auditing. Private sector audits do not include this value for money dimension since a simpler criterion of success in meeting commercial objectives is readily available and the statutory framework within which private sector audit is conducted has, accordingly, more limited responsibilities. Private sector auditing firms normally concentrate their evaluations of efficiency in their management consultancy departments, which operate not as auditors but at the invitation of clients. But where the firms are appointed as auditors to public authorities, they are having to extend their activities into the value for money field as an integral part of the audit operation.

Summary

In general, nationalized industries and most other public sector trading organizations follow 'best commercial practice' accounting, financial control and audit procedures – focused on the accurate estimation of profit or loss. But in the non-trading public services quite different accounting systems have developed, perhaps most notably in local government, and usually with particular concern for accountability for cash income and expenditure. Research and debate continues regarding how far local government and other public services such as the NHS should move to adopting full accrual accounting, inclusive of depreciation accounting, on a basis of external reporting and disclosure more comparable to the private sector.

Given the absence of the profit motive and measure for non-trading public services, audit has developed strong emphasis on methods of measuring and reporting performance in 'value for money terms'. This has necessitated closer study of the multiple service objectives of most non-trading organizations, and a great many performance measures have been developed for managerial review and future target-setting, as well as for reference in audit and for Parliamentary scrutiny.

Much of the work of non-trading public services has to be tailored to the particular needs of individual clients, patients, students, etc., so that the output or 'product' is non-standard and it has been difficult to introduce standard costing or other conventional management accounting information systems. However, there is progress in developing these, and in linking them to wider performance measures and reviews, and to better systems of budgetary allocation and control. Given cash-limited resource allocations for many public services, good management planning and control by budget is especially important.

Effective financial control in the public sector can be achieved only by accountants working closely with other professions, general managers, planners, economists, senior hospital doctors, etc. Thus wide understanding and good communication skills are needed. Perhaps unlike the private sector, specialization or demarcation boundaries between finance/financial accounting and management accounting/financial control are minimal, and effective chief financial officers in the public sector will typically have obtained training and experience in both of these key professional areas, and often in internal audit and management information/computer systems as well.

Study questions

Chapter 1

1.1   Historically, public sector accounting and external reporting have developed many practices and conventions which are quite different from the private sector. Why do you think this has happened, and what arguments can be used to explain or defend such differences?

1.2   Even within the public sector there is great diversity in financial accounting and reporting practice, although there is increasing pressure for uniformity of practice. What arguments may be advanced for and against uniformity?

1.3   One argument for diversity between public and private sector financial accounting and reporting is that the 'user groups' for their published financial information are different. Explain this claim and give arguments for and against its validity.

1.4   Figure 1.1 subdivides public expenditure in four different ways. Why is this important as an alternative to a conventional private sector business analysis directly comparing total costs and expenses against income?

1.5   What material trends or changes in patterns of public expenditure can you identify from Table 1.1? Can you suggest likely explanations for the major changes in *relative* expenditure between departments?

1.6   Obtain a copy of the annual financial report and accounts for one or more public bodies and study these and make a list of any differences in respect of layout, disclosure, reference to SSAPs, accounting practices, type and detail of information included, etc., as compared to the typical or standard financial accounting model for private companies (as set out in good financial accounting textbooks). N.B.: accounts of nationalized industries, local authorities, health authorities, and some other public corporations such as the BBC (i.e. look for the *BBC Handbook*), may be found in your college library, or try the local public library, or failing these sources your own local authority or health authority may be willing to give you copies of their reports.

1.7   In the public sector, compared to the private sector, there is much more frequent reference to the concept of 'accountability' for financial performance and use of resources. Define 'accountability' in the context of accounting and finance, and suggest possible reasons for its apparently greater importance in the public sector.

Chapter 2

2.1 'Public sector financial reports are really just public relations documents.' Discuss.
2.2 Evaluate the financial report of your own local authority.
2.3 'Public sector financial reports are neither better nor worse than those prepared for the private sector.' Discuss.
2.4 Explain why accounting standards (e.g. SSAPs) cannot necessarily be applied to public sector organizations.
2.5 Explain how you might find out about users and potential users of the financial report of a public sector organization.
2.6 Describe the role of the Accounting Standards Committee and discuss its relevance to public sector accounting (CIPFA PE2, 1980).
2.7 Explain to what degree you think public sector financial reports provide good measurement and disclosure of public sector performance and accountability.
2.8 Can you suggest reasons why some public sector organizations still do not use full accrual accounting, in the manner required under 'best commercial practice' accounting in the private sector and indeed in many public corporations?

Chapter 3

3.1 'Unlike with financial accounting and external reporting, management accounting in the public sector is not distinctively different from the private sector.' Discuss.
3.2 What is the difference between economy, efficiency and effectiveness; and how might our awareness of these three different types of concern and measurement affect the design of cost and management information systems in the public sector?
3.3 What is Zero-base Budgeting and why do you think it has not become widely adopted?
3.4 VFM, or value for money, has become a major influence on public sector management, and on public sector audit. Discuss the management accounting problems in measuring and reporting VFM, given the wider concern for 'effectiveness and quality of outcomes'.
3.5 Describe and evaluate the cost and management accounting information systems in one institution or branch of the public sector with which you are familiar.
3.6 What differences are there between capital asset financing and accounting between the public and private sectors, and why and to what extent do you think the continuation of these differences may be justifiable?
3.7 Explain how and why project capital appraisal or option appraisal is likely to differ in non-trading public services as compared to private or public trading enterprises.

3.8   Do you think the concepts of fixed cost and variable/marginal cost, and of contribution analysis, are as relevant in the public sector as in the private sector? Why, or why not?

3.9   Discuss the reasons why it may be more appropriate to apply a cost benefit approach to certain types of public sector investment, rather than use a straightforward investment appraisal (CIPFA, PE2, 1985).

Chapter 4

4.1   Examine the problems that the absence of a profit motive poses for management control of an organization in the public sector (Chartered Association of Certified Accountants, 1986).

4.2   Can Parliament really control public expenditure?

4.3   The Appropriation Accounts of government departments show cash spent on various heads and subheads compared with cash voted by Parliament. What additional types of accounts would you expect a department to maintain (a) for its own use; (b) for public information?

4.4   What do you understand by a management accounting system in central government?

4.5   The government uses the Public Expenditure Survey Committee process in planning and controlling public expenditure. Discuss the usefulness and importance of this process to the government (CIPFA, *Policy Making in the Public Sector*, November 1980).

4.6   Outline the Public Expenditure Survey System. In what ways does it influence or control the policies of public sector organizations? (CIPFA, November, 1979).

4.7   Why has value for money become so important for monitoring central government activities? Why is it difficult to measure in some cases?

4.8   'Financial information provides the basis for decision-making.' Discuss this statement in relation to central government financial reporting.

4.9   What is the significance of the Financial Management Initiative?

4.10   What are the major differences between controlling public expenditure and controlling spending in private sector organizations?

4.11   Explain the relationship between Parliamentary control of expenditure and control of cash limits.

Chapter 5

5.1   Assess the local government finance reforms of the late 1980s in the context of the Layfield Committee's criteria for a coherent financial system.

5.2   Discuss whether reducing the amount of local authority revenue income funded from local sources is likely to promote the search for efficiency and effectiveness.

5.3   What would be suitable characteristics for new sources of local government income?

5.4   Discuss, from an economic point of view, the advantages and disadvantages of replacing domestic rates with a poll tax (CIPFA, *Public Sector Accounting*, 1985).

5.5   Identify the major economic implications of the introduction of a national non-domestic rate.

5.6   'Local authorities should promote the standards of service they regard as appropriate despite central government policy towards public expenditure.' Discuss.

5.7   Describe the system of local authority capital controls introduced from 1st April 1990, and review their advantages and disadvantages to both local and central government.

5.8   'If central government has developed rigorous controls over councils' revenue spend, and the revenue effects of capital expenditure are fully provided for, it is illogical to continue with separate controls over capital expenditure.' Discuss.

Chapter 6

6.1   Discuss the importance of a two/three year financial and operational plan in policy making in a public sector organization of your choice (CIPFA, *Policy making in the Public Sector*, November 1985).

6.2   Critically examine the contention that party politics is now assuming too great a role in the decision making processes of local authorities (CIPFA, *Policy Making in the Public Sector*, November 1984).

6.3   Discuss the impact on finance departments of compulsory competitive tendering for a wide range of council services:
(a) In the short term;
(b) In the long term.

6.4   Would it be desirable if local authority accounts were made to conform fully with Companies Act accounts?

6.5   Describe the proposed system of local authority capital accounting put forward by CIPFA 1988/89. Discuss how far this will overcome the problems of the system it is proposed to replace.

6.6   Examine the problems that the absence of a profit motive poses for management control of an organization in the public sector (ACCA, Level 2 Public Sector Accounting, June 1986).

6.7   'Decentralized resource management has been over-sold as a technique for promoting value for money in local government.' Discuss.

6.8   Comment on the assertion that the wider dissemination of inter-authority comparisons will improve a local authority's accountability to the public (CIPFA, *Policy Making*, 1980).

Chapter 7

7.1   How would policy making in a public corporation be changed if equity capital were introduced? (CIPFA, *Policy Making in the Public Sector*).

7.2   Under the 1978 White Paper, nationalized industries like gas and electricity were asked to aim for a required return on their investment programme. Examine the rationale. (CIPFA, *Public Finance*)

7.3   Explain the strong opposition of nationalized industries to the use of EFLs as the most important element in financial control by government.

7.4   'It is unrealistic to have multiple targets for nationalised industries of the kind set out in the 1978 White Paper. They are difficult to calculate, impossible to reconcile and not understood by managers.' Discuss.

7.5   Outline the objectives of nationalized industries and discuss the methods available for determining whether or not the objectives are being achieved (ACCA Pilot question for Public Sector Accounting).

7.6   'Cash flow is the key to nationalized industries' performance since the calculation of profit and loss is too subjective.' Discuss.

7.7   'Historic cost figures are misleading but current cost figures are wrong.' Discuss this statement in relation to one particular nationalized industry or nationalized industries as a whole.

7.8   Discuss the case for setting accounting standards for nationalized industries in a different way to those for the private sector.

7.9   'The accounts of nationalized industries are just like those of private sector organizations except that the Government is the sole shareholder.' Discuss.

Chapter 8

8.1   Explain how the financial resources of the National Health Service (NHS) are funded centrally and then allocated to regional, district and operational levels of the NHS. Discuss the likely strengths and weaknesses of this system of funding and resource allocation.

8.2   Discuss the advantages and disadvantages of joint financing arrangements between local authorities and health authorities (CIPFA, *Policy Making in the Public Sector*, November, 1980).

8.3   'The government is currently encouraging the 'privatization' of as many public sector services as possible. Discuss the policy-making implications of privatization . . .' in respect of the management of the NHS (CIPFA, *Policy Making in the Public Sector*, November, 1981).

8.4   Consider the implications for financial management of the NHS that until now, and indeed until new financial regulations are implemented, capital has been provided as a 'free good', with no depreciation charges, no asset registers, and no payments of interest or principal required.

8.5   Health authorities have to maintain accurate cash receipts and payment accounts in order to comply with the 'cash limits' system of government funding. However, typically they appear to prefer to maintain their main financial and management accounts on an 'income and expenditure' basis, often reconciling the two accounting approaches through a 'source and application of funds' analysis. Can you explain and justify this behaviour?

8.6 'Explain the main points of SSAP2, Disclosure of Accounting Policies; in particular the four fundamental accounting concepts. Discuss its application . . .' to the NHS (CIPFA, *Public Sector Accounting*, November, 1981).

8.7 'Outline and discuss the function of performance indicators in the policy process of . . .' managing the NHS (CIPFA, *Policy Making in the Public Sector*, December, 1983).

8.8 The Griffiths Inquiry of 1983 and more recent government initiatives in Resource Management have sought to involve doctors, nurses and other health-care professional staff more actively in the use of costing, budgeting and other performance-related monitoring and control systems. What are the difficulties, and the potential benefits, in seeking to involve such professional staff in the financial information and control process?

Chapter 9

9.1   Describe briefly the role of the Comptroller and Auditor General as the external auditor of central government. What are his relations with Parliament?

9.2   What are the main similarities and differences between external audit in the public and private sector? What special experience would you expect private accounting firms to bring to the audit of public bodies?

9.3   What do you understand by value for money audit? Explain, with examples, what is meant by the examination of economy, efficiency and effectiveness in public sector operations.

9.4   What are the arguments for and against an external value for money audit of nationalized industries and other public corporations of a commercial type? Do these arguments apply equally to such government trading fund bodies as the Stationery Office and the Royal Mint?

9.5   In what way do local authorities differ from central government departments? How far do these differences support the view that external audit of local authorities should not come under the C&AG?

9.6   The creation of the Audit Commission under the Local Government Finance Act 1982 raised many doubts and criticisms. It was suggested that the Commission would be a highly paid organization lacking independence but having the power to interfere in the management of a local authority's affairs. It was also suggested that the Commission would

simply increase audit fees and expand the role of private audit and consultancy firms in the public sector.
(a) By reference to the Commission's audit code of practice and the policies it has adopted discuss whether these criticisms are fair;
(b) How far has the Commission achieved the objectives for which it was established (CIPFA; Professional Examination 2, 1985)?
9.7 If you were appointed Controller of Audit Commission for Local Authorities in England and Wales, what would your plan of action be?
9.8 Suggest and evaluate the possible advantages and disadvantages of the transfer of responsibility for operational external auditing of health authorities in the NHS from the Department of Health (formerly DHSS) audit staff to the Audit Commission.

Chapter 10

Note: In preparing answers to these questions it could prove helpful to refer back to earlier chapters and the publications included in their recommended reading and source citations (See Bibliography).

10.1 Are there any reasons of substance for concern at the present degree of difference in the practices of accounting and external reporting followed in the non-commercial public sector as compared to the commercial sector? Illustrate your arguments.
10.2 Explain, with reasons, why you think each Accounting Standard (i.e. SSAP) is, or is not, relevant to one branch of the Public Sector with which you are familiar.
10.3 Explore the relevance of the capital maintenance concept, and of depreciation accounting, to non-commercial public bodies such as universities, the NHS or the armed forces.
10.4 At a time when the private sector appears to be minimizing the importance of inflation accounting (e.g. CCA) in published accounts, the government appears to be encouraging public bodies taking up depreciation accounting to base this on current replacement values. How do you explain or justify this apparent paradox?
10.5 Local government accounting appears to be more distinctively different from the private sector model of 'best commercial practice' than in most other public bodies. How is this explained and justified?
10.6 What differences would you expect to find in the budget-setting and budgetary-control practices of a public sector trading enterprise as compared to a non-trading public service? Why may such differences exist, and how far and why may they be justifiable in future?
10.7 'Accountability is unthinkable without good accounting.' Discuss.
10.8 Value-for-money auditing appears to receive a much higher allocation of time and status in the public sector than in the private sector. Can this be explained and justified?

10.9 For a branch of the public sector with which you are familiar, specify, explain and justify any additions to the current roles and activities of finance staff that you think would improve the quality of management and/or accountability in the organization concerned.

Bibliography

AICPA (1973) *Objectives of financial statements (The Trueblood Report)* American Institute of Certified Public Accountants, USA.

Anthony, R. N. (1978) *Financial Accounting in Nonbusiness Organizations*, Financial Standards Accounting Board, USA.

Anthony, R. N. and Young, D. W. (1984) *Management Control in Nonprofit Organizations* 3rd edn, R. D. Irwin, Homewood, Illinois.

Association of Health Service Treasurers (AHST) (1982) *Standard Accounting Practices for the National Health Service*, Final Report, CIPFA, London.

Association of Health Service Treasurers (AHST) (1984) *Report of the Capital and Asset Accounting Working Party*, CIPFA, London.

ASC (1976) *The Corporate Report*, Accounting Standards Committee, UK.

Audit Commission *Report and Accounts*, Annual, HMSO, London.

Audit Commission Studies, Reports and Occasional Papers, HMSO. (Detailed publications list available from the Audit Commission).

Audit Commission (1984) *The Impact on Local Authorities' Economy, Efficiency and Effectiveness of the Block Grant Distribution System*, HMSO, London.

Audit Commission (1988) *Code of Practice*, HMSO, London.

Audit Commission (1988) *The Competitive Council Audit Commission*, London.

Australian Accounting Research Foundation (1985) *Financial reporting in the public sector – a framework for analysis and identification of issues*, Accounting Theory Monograph No5.

Bains Report (1972) *The New Local Authorities: Management and Structure*, HMSO, London.

Barlow, J. (1981) The Rationale for the Control of Local Government Expenditure for the Purposes of Macro-economic Management, *Local Government Studies*, May/June 1981, 3–13.

Barnett, J. (1982) *Inside the Treasury*, Andre Deutsch, London.

Beard, G. C. (1985) *Government Finance and Accounts*.

Beesley, M., Likierman, A. and Bloomfield, S. *Controlling public enterprise in Europe*, Economic Council of Canada, Discussion Paper No 302.

Bennett, R. J. (1981) The Local Income Tax in Britain: A Critique of Recent Arguments against its Use. *Public Administration*, Autumn 1981, 295–312.

Bevan, G., Copeman, H., Perrin, J., and Rosser, R. (1980) *Health Care Priorities and Management*, Croom Helm, London.

Brown, C. V. and Jackson, P. (1986) *Public Sector Economics*, 3rd ed, Martin Robertson.

Bruce-Gardyne, J. (1986) *Ministers and Mandarins*, Sidgewick and Jackson, London.

Butt, H. and Palmer, B. (1985) *Value for Money in the Public Sector*, Blackwell, Oxford.

Byatt Report (1986) *Accounting for Economic Costs and Changing Prices* (a Report to HM Treasury by an Advisory Group, in 2 vols), HMSO, London.

Byrne, P. (1981) *Local Government in Britain*, Penguin Books, Harmondsworth.

Carsberg, B. and Lumby, S. (1983) Current cost accounting in the water industry. *Public Finance and Accountancy*, September.

Chapman, L. (1979) *Your Disobedient Servant*, Penguin, Harmondsworth.

CIPFA (1975) Local Authority Accounting Exposure Draft 1, *Accountancy Principles*.

CIPFA (1980) *Health*, Vol. 30 of the CIPFA Financial Information Service (with frequent looseleaf updates), CIPFA, London.

CIPFA (1980) Institute Statement: Applicability of Accountancy Standards to Local Government. *Public Finance and Accountancy*, September 1980, 19–21.

CIPFA (1982) *Guidance Notes on Accounting for the Costs of Management and Administration in Local Government*.

CIPFA (1983) *Capital Accounting*.

CIPFA (1985) *Standard Classification Service Guidance Booklets*.

CIPFA (1987a) *Accounting for Support Services*.

CIPFA (1987b) *Code of Practice on Local Authority Accounts*.

CIPFA (1988a) *Compulsory Competition: Meeting the Challenge Part VI*, Provisional Code of Practice for Direct Service Organisations.

CIPFA (1988b) *Code of Practice on Local Authority Accounts, Guidance Notes for Practitioners*.

Collins, B. and Wharton, B. (1984) Investigating Public Industries: how has the Monopolies & Mergers Commission performed? *Public Money*, Vol 4, No2, September.

Commission for Local Authority Accounts in Scotland, *Annual Reports*.

Committee on the Management of Local Government (1967) *Report* (Maud Management Report), HMSO, London.

Culyer, A. J. (1973) *The Economics of Social Policy*, Martin Robertson, Oxford.

Curwen, P. (1986) *Public enterprises*, Wheatsheaf Books, Brighton.

Danziger, J. M. (1978) *Making Budgets*, Sage Publications.

Davies, C. (1983) *Underused and Surplus Property in the National Health Service*, DHSS, London.

Davies, J. R. and McInnes, W. M. (1982) The efficiency and accountability of UK nationalised industries, *Accounting and Business Research*, Winter.

Davies, J. R. and McInnes, W. K. (1982) The valuation of fixed assets in the financial accounts of UK nationalised industries and the implications for monitoring performance: a comment. *Journal of Business Finance and Accounting*, Summer.

Department of Health (1989) *Working for Patients*, White Paper on the Health Service for the 1990s, HMSO, London.

Departmental Committee on Accounts (1907) *Report*.

DHSS (1976) *Sharing Resources for Health in England*, Report of the Resource Allocation Working Party (the RAWP Report), HMSO, London.

DHSS (1980) *Report of the Advisory Group on Resource Allocation* (AGRA).

DHSS (1981) *Care in the Community*, HMSO, London.

DHSS (1985) *Health Services Managment Budgeting* (HN(85)3).

DHSS (1986) *Resource Management (Management Budgeting) in Health Authorities* (HN(86)34).

DHSS (1988) *Health Service Costing Returns*, 1986–87.

DHSS in collaboration with Coopers & Lybrand (1988) *Comparing Health Authorities*, DHSS, London.

DOE (1977) *Local Government Finance*, Green Paper.

DOE (1981a) *Annual Reports and Financial Statements*.

DOE (1981b) *Capital Programmes*, Circular 14/81.

DOE (1986) *Paying for Local Government* Cmnd. 9714, HMSO, London.

DOE (1988a) *Consultation Paper on Capital Expenditure Controls*.

DOE (1988b) *Local Government Financial Statistics*, 1985–86.

DOE (1988c) *Capital Expenditure and Finance*, Consultation Document.

Drebin, A. R., Chan, J. L. Ferguson, L. C. (1981) *Objectives of Accounting and Financial Reporting for Governmental Units: A research study*, National Council on Governmental Accounting, USA.

Drummond, M. F. (1980) *Principles of Economic Appraisal in Health Care*, Oxford University Press, Oxford.

Drury, C. (1988) *Managment and Cost Accounting* Van Nostrand Reinhold (International), London.

Emmanuel, C. and Otley, D. (1985) *Accounting for Management Control*, Van Nostrand Reinhold (International), London.

Englefield, D. (1985) *Whitehall and Westminster*, Longman, London.

Expenditure Committee (1977–8) *Financial Accountability to Parliament*, 14th Report Session, HC 661.

FASB (1980) *Objectives of financial reporting by nonbusiness organisations*, Financial Accounting Standards Board, USA.

Glynn, J. J. (1985) *Value for Money Auditing in the Public Sector*, Prentice/Hall International in association with ICAEW, London.

Glynn, J. J. (1987) *Public Sector Financial Control and Accounting*, Blackwell, Oxford.

Great Britain, White Paper (1989) *Working for Patients*, CM 555, HMSO, London.

Grieve-Smith, J. (1984) *Strategic planning in the nationalised industries*, Macmillan, London.

Griffiths, R. (1983) *NHS Management Inquiry Report* (i.e. the 'Griffiths Report'), DHSS, London.

Hale, R. (1988) The Poll Tax: How accountable is it? In *Public Finance and Accountancy*, 22nd July 1988, pp. 12–14.

Hatch, J. and Redwood, J. (1981) *Value for Money Audits*, Centre for Policy Studies.

Hatry, H. P., Clarren, S. N., Van Houten, T., Woodward, J. P. and Don Vito, P. A. (1979) *Efficiency Measurement for Local Government Services*, Urban Institute, Washington, DC.

Heald, D. and Rose, R. (1987) *The Public Expenditure Process: Learning by Doing*, Public Finance Foundation.

Heald, D. and Steel, D. (1981) Nationalised industries: the search for control. *Public Money*, Vol 1, No 1, June.

Healthcare Financial Management Association (1987) *Health Service Trends: the CIPFA database*, in 2 vols., Chartered Inst. of Public Finance & Accountancy, London.

Heclo, H. and Wildavsky, A. (1981) *The Private Government of Public Money* 2nd edn, Macmillan Press, London.

Hepworth, N. and Vass, P. (1984) Accounting standards in the public sector. In *Issues in Public Sector Accounting* (eds A. Hopwood and C. Tomkins), Phillip Allan, Deddington.

Hofstede, G. H. (1968) *The Game of Budget Control*, Tavistock Institute, London.

Hofstede, G. (1981) Management Control of Public and Not-for-profit Activities. *Accounting, Organizations & Society* 6(3), pp. 193–211.

Holland, W. W. *et al.* (1980) *The RAWP Project*, Social Medicine and Health Services Research Unit, St. Thomas's Hospital and Medical School, London.

Holtham, C. W. and Stewart, D. D. (1981) *Value for Money: A Framework for Action* INLOGOV, Birmingham.
Holtham, C. (1984) Financial Planning and Control. In *Issues in Public Sector Accounting* (Eds A. Hopwood and C. Tomkins).
Holtham, C. W. and Stewart, D. D. (1986) *Decentralized Resource Management* Local Government Training Board, Luton.
Hone, M. (1988) Support Service Accounting and Compulsory Competition *Public Finance and Accountancy*, 11th March, 1988, pp. 14–15.
Hopwood, A. and Tomkins, C. (eds) *Issues in Public Sector Accounting*, Philip Allan, Deddington.
IMTA (1963) *The Standardisation of Accounts: General Principles*.
IMTA Output Measurement Working Party (1974) Output Measurement *Public Finance and Accountancy*, October 1974, 339–42.
INLOGOV (1981) *Codes of practice on the publication of information*, Institute of Local Government Studies, University of Birmingham.
Jones, R. and Pendlebury, M. (1988) *Public Sector Accounting* 2nd edn, Pitman, London.
Jones, T. and Prowle, M. (1987) *Health Service Finance: an Introduction* 3rd edn, Certified Accountants Educational Trust, London.
Kay, J. A. (1976) Accountants, too, could be happy in a golden age: the accountant's rate of profit and the internal rate of return. *Oxford Economic Papers*, 28.
Kilgour, L. and Lapsley, I. (1988) *Financial reporting by Local Authorities in Scotland*, Institute of Chartered Accountants in Scotland.
Körner, E., chair for various Körner Reports (See entry under NHS/DHSS Steering Group).
Layfield Committee (1976) *Local Government Finance: Report of the Committee of Enquiry*, Cmnd. 6453, HMSO, London.
Lee, T. A. and Stark, A. W. (1984) A cash flow disclosure of government supported enterprises' results. *Journal of Business Finance and Accounting*, Spring.
Likierman, J. A. (1981) Cash Limits and External Financing Limits. *Civil Service College Handbook No 22*, HMSO, London.
Likierman, J. A. (1983) Evidence on accusation of manipulating profitability: adjustments for inflation by the nationalised industries 1976–81. *Accounting and Business Research*, Winter.
Likierman, J. A. (1983) Setting accounting standards for nationalised industries. *Public Finance and Accountancy*, November.
Likierman, A. (1988) *Public Expenditure*, Penguin, Harmondsworth.
Likierman, A. and Vass, P. (1984) *Structure and form of government expenditure reports – proposals for reform*. Certified Accountants Educational Trust.
Local Authority Associations (1981) *The Rate Support Grant (England) 1981–2*, ACC, AMA, ADC, LBA and GLC.
Local Government Act (1972).
Local Government (Scotland) Act (1973).
Local Government Finance Act (1982).
Local Government Act (1988).
Local Government Training Board (1984) *Why Local Government?* LGTB, Luton.
Lumby, S. (1988) *Investment Appraisal & Financing Decisions* 3rd edn, Van Nostrand Reinhold (International) London.
MacArthur, J. B. (1980) Valuation of fixed assets in the financial accounts of UK nationalised industries and the implications for monitoring performance *Journal of Business Finance and Accounting*, Spring.
MacArthur, J. B. (1982) Valuation of fixed assets in the financial accounts of UK

nationalised industries and the implications for monitoring performance: a reply. *Journal of Business Finance and Accounting*, Summer.

Macve, R. (1981) *A conceptual framework for financial accounting and reporting. The possibilities for an agreed structure*, Institute of Chartered Accountants in England and Wales.

National Association of Health Authorities (NAHA) (1988) *Funding the NHS: which way forward?* NAHA, Birmingham.

National Audit Office (1986) *Financial Reporting to Parliament*, HC 576, HMSO, London.

National Audit Office (1987) *Financial reporting to Parliament*.

NHS/DHSS Steering Group on Health Services Information (Chair, Mrs. E. Körner) (1984) Sixth Report (on the collection and use of financial information), HMSO, London.

Norton, A. and Wedgwood-Oppenheim, F. (1981) The Concept of Corporate Planning in English Local Government – Learning from its History, *Local Government Studies*, September/October 1981, 55–72.

Parkes, J. A. (1988) *Capital Accounting – the way forward*, CIPFA, London.

Parris, H. (1985) *Public enterprise in Western Europe*, Acton Society Trust.

Perks, R. W. and Glendinning, R. (1981) Performance indicators applied to the nationalised industries, *Management Accounting*, October and Little progress seen in published performance indicators, *Management Accounting*, December.

Perrin, J. (1978) see entry under Royal Commission on the NHS research paper.

Perrin, J. (1984) Accounting for Public Sector Assets. In *Issues in Public Sector Accounting*, (eds A. Hopwood and C. Tomkins), Philip Allan, Deddington.

Perrin, J. (1988) *Resource Mangement in the NHS*, Van Nostrand Reinhold (International) London, in association with Health Service Management Centre, Birmingham.

Pliatzky, L. (1982) *Getting and Spending*, Basil Blackwell, Oxford.

Pliatzky, L. (1985) *Paying and Choosing*, Basil Blackwell, Oxford.

Procedure (Supply) Committee (1982–3) *1st Report Session* HC 24.

Prosser, A. (1986) *Nationalised industries and public control*, Blackwell, Oxford.

Pryke, R. (1981) *The Nationalised Industries, Policies and Performance since 1968*, Martin Robertson.

Public Accounts Committee (PAC) (1976–7) *Cash Limits*, 3rd Report Session, HC 274.

PAC (1977–8) *Supply Estimates and Cash Limits*, 4th Report Session, HC 288.

PAC (1978–9) *Parliamentary Control of Public Expenditure*, 3rd Report Session, HC 232.

PAC (1979–80) *Parliamentary Control of Public Expenditure*, 13th Report Session, HC 570.

PAC (1979–80) *Carry-over of Cash Limits at the End of the Financial Year*, 27th Report Sessions, HC 766.

PAC (1980–81) *Treasury Carry-over of Cash Limits at the End of the Financial Year*, 14th Report Session, HC 376.

18th Report Session 1981–2 HC 383.

PAC (1986–7) *Financial Reporting to Parliament*, 8th Report Session, HC 98.

Public Finance & Accountancy (1988) *Financial Management Initiative* (ten reprint articles with new foreword by Professor P. Jackson), CIPFA, London.

Puxty, A. G. and Dodds, J. C. (1988) *Financial Management: Method and Meaning* Van Nostrand Reinhold (International), London.

Raine, J. W. (ed) (1981) *In Defence of Local Government*, Institute of Local Government Studies, Birmingham.

Royal Commission on the National Health Service Research Paper No. 2 (1978) *Management of Financial Resources in the National Health Service* (the Perrin Report) HMSO, London.

Royal Commission on the National Health Service (1979) *Report*, Cmnd. 7615, HMSO, London.

Rutherford, B. A. (1983) *Financial Reporting in the Public Sector*, Butterworths, London.

Samuels, J. M. and Wilkes, F. M. (1986) *Management of Company Finance* 4th edn, Van Nostrand Reinhold (International), London.

Sarant, P. C. (1978) *Zero-Base Budgeting in the Public Sector*, Addison – Wesley.

Sharpe, L. J. (1970) Theories and Values of Local Government *Political Studies* 18(2) 153–74, Butterworths, London.

Solomons, D. (1965) *Divisional Performance: Measurement and Control*, R. D. Irwin, Homewood, Illinois.

Stamp, E. (1980) *Corporate reporting: Its future evolution*, Canadian Institute of Chartered Accountants.

Stewart, J. (1983) *Local Government: The Conditions of Local Choice*. George Allen & Unwin.

Stoker, G., Wedgwood-Oppenheim, F. and Davies, M. (1988) *The Challenge of Change in Local Government* INLOGOV, Birmingham.

Tomkins, C. R. (1987) *Achieving Economy Efficiency and Effectiveness in the Public Sector*, Institute of Chartered Accountants of Scotland, Edinburgh.

HM Treasury (1978) *The Nationalised Industries*, Cmnd. 7131, HMSO, London.

HM Treasury (1978) *The Test Discount Rate and the Required Rate of Return on Investment*, Treasury Working Paper No. 9.

HM Treasury (1982) *Investment Appraisal in the Public Sector*, 3rd edn.

HM Treasury (1986) *The Management of Public Spending*.

HM Treasury (1987) *Central Government: Financial and Accounting Framework*, Treasury Working Paper.

HM Treasury (1987) *Output and Performance Measurement in Central Government. Progress in Departments*, Treasury Working Paper.

HM Treasury (1988) *Financial Reporting to Parliament* Cm 375, HMSO, London.

HM Treasury (1988) *A New Public Expenditure Planning Total* Cm 441, HMSO, London.

Treasury and Civil Service Committee (TCSC) (1980–1) *The Form of the Estimates*, 6th Report Session, HC 325.

TCSC (1981–2) *Efficiency and Effectiveness in the Civil Service*, 3rd Report Session, HC 326.

TCSC (1981–2) *Budgetary Reform*, 6th Report Session, HC 137.

TCSC (1984–5) *The Structure and Form of Financial Documents Presented to Parliament*, 2nd Report Session, HC 110.

TCSC (1986–7 *Financial Reporting to Parliament*, 6th Report Session, HC 614.

TCSC (1987–8) *The Government's Public Expenditure Plans 1988–9 to 1990–1*, 2nd Report Session, HC 292.

Van Horne (1986) *Financial Management and Policy*, Prentice Hall, London.

Vernon, R. and Aharonyi, Y. (1981) *State-owned enterprise in the Western economies*, Croom Helm, Beckenham.

White Paper (1989), *Working for Patients*, HMSO, London.

Whitehead, C. (ed) (1988) *Reshaping the nationalised industries*, Policy Journals.

Wickings, I. (1983) *Effective Unit Management*, King Edward's Hospital Fund for London, London.

Widdicombe Report (1986) *The Conduct of Local Authority Business* HMSO, Cmnd. 9797.

Wildavsky, A. (1975) *Budgeting: A Comparative Theory of Budgetary Processes*, Little Brown, Boston.

Wilson, R. M. S. and Chua, W. F. (1988) *Managerial Accounting: method and meaning*, Van Nostrand Reinhold (International), London.

Wright, M. (1984) Auditing the efficiency of the nationalised industries: exit the Comptroller and Auditor General? *Public Administration*, Spring.

Index